C++ Coding Standards

The C++ In-Depth Series

Bjarne Stroustrup, Editor

"I have made this letter longer than usual, because I lack the time to make it short."
—BLAISE PASCAL

The advent of the ISO/ANSI C++ standard marked the beginning of a new era for C++ programmers. The standard offers many new facilities and opportunities, but how can a real-world programmer find the time to discover the key nuggets of wisdom within this mass of information? **The C++ In-Depth Series** minimizes learning time and confusion by giving programmers concise, focused guides to specific topics.

Each book in this series presents a single topic, at a technical level appropriate to that topic. The Series' practical approach is designed to lift professionals to their next level of programming skills. Written by experts in the field, these short, in-depth monographs can be read and referenced without the distraction of unrelated material. The books are cross-referenced within the Series, and also reference *The C++ Programming Language* by Bjarne Stroustrup.

As you develop your skills in C++, it becomes increasingly important to separate essential information from hype and glitz, and to find the in-depth content you need in order to grow. The C++ In-Depth Series provides the tools, concepts, techniques, and new approaches to C++ that will give you a critical edge.

Titles in the Series

Accelerated C++: Practical Programming by Example, Andrew Koenig and Barbara E. Moo

Applied C++: Practical Techniques for Building Better Software, Philip Romanik and Amy Muntz

The Boost Graph Library: User Guide and Reference Manual, Jeremy G. Siek, Lie-Quan Lee, and Andrew Lumsdaine

C++ Coding Standards: 101 Rules, Guidelines, and Best Practices, Herb Sutter and Andrei Alexandrescu

C++ In-Depth Box Set, Bjarne Stroustrup, Andrei Alexandrescu, Andrew Koenig, Barbara E. Moo, Stanley B. Lippman, and Herb Sutter

C++ Network Programming, Volume 1: Mastering Complexity with ACE and Patterns, Douglas C. Schmidt and Stephen D. Huston

C++ Network Programming, Volume 2: Systematic Reuse with ACE and Frameworks, Douglas C. Schmidt and Stephen D. Huston

C++ Template Metaprogramming: Concepts, Tools, and Techniques from Boost and Beyond, David Abrahams and Aleksey Gurtovoy

Essential C++, Stanley B. Lippman

Exceptional C++: 47 Engineering Puzzles, Programming Problems, and Solutions, Herb Sutter

Exceptional C++ Style: 40 New Engineering Puzzles, Programming Problems, and Solutions, Herb Sutter

Modern C++ Design: Generic Programming and Design Patterns Applied, Andrei Alexandrescu

More Exceptional C++: 40 New Engineering Puzzles, Programming Problems, and Solutions, Herb Sutter

For more information, check out the series web site at www.awprofessional.com/series/indepth/

C++ Coding Standards

101 Rules, Guidelines, and Best Practices

Herb Sutter

Andrei Alexandrescu

✦ Addison-Wesley

Boston

The authors and publisher have taken care in the preparation of this book, but make no expressed or implied warranty of any kind and assume no responsibility for errors or omissions. No liability is assumed for incidental or consequential damages in connection with or arising out of the use of the information or programs contained herein.

Publisher: John Wait
Editor in Chief: Don O'Hagan
Acquisitions Editor: Peter Gordon
Editorial Assistant: Kim Boedigheimer
Marketing Manager: Chanda Leary-Coutu
Cover Designer: Chuti Prasertsith
Managing Editor: John Fuller
Project Editor: Lara Wysong
Copy Editor: Kelli Brooks
Manufacturing Buyer: Carol Melville

The publisher offers excellent discounts on this book when ordered in quantity for bulk purchases or special sales, which may include electronic versions and/or custom covers and content particular to your business, training goals, marketing focus, and branding interests. For more information, please contact:

> U. S. Corporate and Government Sales
> (800) 382-3419
> corpsales@pearsontechgroup.com

For sales outside the U. S., please contact:

> International Sales
> international@pearsoned.com

Visit us on the Web: www.awprofessional.com

Library of Congress Cataloging-in-Publication Data:

Sutter, Herb.
C++ coding standards : 101 rules, guidelines, and best practices / Herb Sutter, Andrei Alexandrescu.
    p. cm.
Includes bibliographical references and index.
ISBN 0-321-11358-6 (pbk. : alk. paper)
C++ (Computer program language) I. Alexandrescu, Andrei. II. Title.

QA76.73.C153S85 2004
005.13'3—dc22

                                            2004022605

ISBN 0-321-11358-6
Text printed in the United States on recycled paper at Courier in Stoughton, Massachusetts.
Third printing, February 2005

For the millions of current C++ programmers

Contents

Functions and Operators   **45**

Class Design and Inheritance   **55**

Preface

Get into a rut early: Do the same process the same way. Accumulate idioms.
Standardize. *The only difference(!) between Shakespeare and you was the*
size of his idiom list—not the size of his vocabulary.

— Alan Perlis [emphasis ours]

The best thing about standards is that there are so many to choose from.

— Variously attributed

We want to provide this book as a basis for your team's coding standards for two principal reasons:

- *A coding standard should reflect the community's best tried-and-true experience:* It should contain proven idioms based on experience and solid understanding of the language. In particular, a coding standard should be based firmly on the extensive and rich software development literature, bringing together rules, guidelines, and best practices that would otherwise be left scattered throughout many sources.

- *Nature abhors a vacuum:* If you don't consciously set out reasonable rules, usually someone else will try to push their own set of pet rules instead. A coding standard made that way usually has all of the least desirable properties of a coding standard; for example, many such standards try to enforce a minimalistic C-style use of C++.

Many bad coding standards have been set by people who don't understand the language well, don't understand software development well, or try to legislate too much. A bad coding standard quickly loses credibility and at best even its valid guidelines are liable to be ignored by disenchanted programmers who dislike or disagree with its poorer guidelines. That's "at best"—at worst, a bad standard might actually be enforced.

How to Use This Book

Think. Do follow good guidelines conscientiously; but don't follow them blindly. In this book's Items, note the Exceptions clarifying the less common situations where the guidance may not apply. No set of guidelines, however good (and we think these ones are), should try to be a substitute for thinking.

Each development team is responsible for setting its own standards, and for setting them responsibly. That includes your team. If you are a team lead, involve your team members in setting the team's standards; people are more likely to follow standards they view as their own than they are to follow a bunch of rules they feel are being thrust upon them.

This book is designed to be used as a basis for, and to be included by reference in, your team's coding standards. It is not intended to be the Last Word in coding standards, because your team will have additional guidelines appropriate to your particular group or task, and you should feel free to add those to these Items. But we hope that this book will save you some of the work of (re)developing your own, by documenting and referencing widely-accepted and authoritative practices that apply nearly universally (with Exceptions as noted), and so help increase the quality and consistency of the coding standards you use.

Have your team read these guidelines with their rationales (i.e., the whole book, and selected Items' References to other books and papers as needed), and decide if there are any that your team simply can't live with (e.g., because of some situation unique to your project). Then commit to the rest. Once adopted, the team's coding standards should not be violated except after consulting with the whole team.

Finally, periodically review your guidelines as a team to include practical experience and feedback from real use.

Coding Standards and You

Good coding standards can offer many interrelated advantages:

- *Improved code quality:* Encouraging developers to do the right things in a consistent way directly works to improve software quality and maintainability.
- *Improved development speed:* Developers don't need to always make decisions starting from first principles.
- *Better teamwork:* They help reduce needless debates on inconsequential issues and make it easier for teammates to read and maintain each other's code.
- *Uniformity in the right dimension:* This frees developers to be creative in directions that matter.

Under stress and time pressure, people do what they've been trained to do. They fall back on habit. That's why ER units in hospitals employ experienced, trained personnel; even knowledgeable beginners would panic.

As software developers, we routinely face enormous pressure to deliver tomorrow's software yesterday. Under schedule pressure, we do what we are trained to do and are used to doing. Sloppy programmers who in normal times don't know good practices of software engineering (or aren't used to applying them) will write even sloppier and buggier code when pressure is on. Conversely, programmers who form good habits and practice them regularly will keep themselves organized and deliver quality code, fast.

The coding standards introduced by this book are a collection of guidelines for writing high-quality C++ code. They are the distilled conclusions of a rich collective experience of the C++ community. Much of this body of knowledge has only been available in bits and pieces spread throughout books, or as word-of-mouth wisdom. This book's intent is to collect that knowledge into a collection of rules that is terse, justified, and easy to understand and follow.

Of course, one can write bad code even with the best coding standards. The same is true of any language, process, or methodology. A good set of coding standards fosters good habits and discipline that transcend mere rules. That foundation, once acquired, opens the door to higher levels. There's no shortcut; you have to develop vocabulary and grammar before writing poetry. We just hope to make that easier.

We address this book to C++ programmers of all levels:

If you are an apprentice programmer, we hope you will find the rules and their rationale helpful in understanding what styles and idioms C++ supports most naturally. We provide a concise rationale and discussion for each rule and guideline to encourage you to rely on understanding, not just rote memorization.

For the intermediate or advanced programmer, we have worked hard to provide a detailed list of precise references for each rule. This way, you can do further research into the rule's roots in C++'s type system, grammar, and object model.

At any rate, it is very likely that you work in a team on a complex project. Here is where coding standards really pay off—you can use them to bring the team to a common level and provide a basis for code reviews.

About This Book

We have set out the following design goals for this book:

- *Short is better than long:* Huge coding standards tend to be ignored; short ones get read and used. Long Items tend to be skimmed; short ones get read and used.

- *Each Item must be noncontroversial:* This book exists to document widely agreed-upon standards, not to invent them. If a guideline is not appropriate in all cases, it will be presented that way (e.g., "Consider X..." instead of "Do X...") and we will note commonly accepted exceptions.

- *Each Item must be authoritative:* The guidelines in this book are backed up by references to existing published works. This book is intended to also provide an index into the C++ literature.

- *Each Item must need saying:* We chose not to define new guidelines for things that you'll do anyway, that are already enforced or detected by the compiler, or that are already covered under other Items.

  Example: "Don't return a pointer/reference to an automatic variable" is a good guideline, but we chose not to include it in this book because all of the compilers we tried already emit a warning for this, and so the issue is already covered under the broader Item 1, "Compile cleanly at high warning levels."

  Example: "Use an editor (or compiler, or debugger)" is a good guideline, but of course you'll use those tools anyway without being told; instead, we spend two of our first four Items on "Use an automated build system" and "Use a version control system."

  Example: "Don't abuse **goto**" is a great Item, but in our experience programmers universally know this, and it doesn't need saying any more.

Each Item is laid out as follows:

- *Item title:* The simplest meaningful sound bite we could come up with as a mnemonic for the rule.

- *Summary:* The most essential points, briefly stated.

- *Discussion:* An extended explanation of the guideline. This often includes brief rationale, but remember that the bulk of the rationale is intentionally left in the References.

- *Examples (if applicable):* Examples that demonstrate a rule or make it memorable.

- *Exceptions (if applicable):* Any (and usually rare) cases when a rule doesn't apply. But beware the trap of being too quick to think: "Oh, I'm special; this doesn't apply in my situation"—that rationalization is common, and commonly wrong.

- *References:* See these parts of the C++ literature for the full details and analysis.

In each section, we chose to nominate a "most valuable Item." Often, it's the first Item in a section, because we tried to put important Items up front in each part; but other times an important Item couldn't be put up front, for flow or readability reasons, and we felt the need to call it out for special attention in this way.

Acknowledgments

Many thanks to series editor Bjarne Stroustrup, to editors Peter Gordon and Debbie Lafferty, and to Tyrrell Albaugh, Kim Boedigheimer, John Fuller, Bernard Gaffney, Curt Johnson, Chanda Leary-Coutu, Charles Leddy, Heather Mullane, Chuti Prasertsith, Lara Wysong, and the rest of the Addison-Wesley team for their assistance and persistence during this project. They are a real pleasure to work with.

Inspiration for some of the "sound bites" came from many sources, including the playful style of [Cline99], the classic **import this** of [Peters99], and the legendary and eminently quotable Alan Perlis.

We especially want to thank the people whose technical feedback has helped to make many parts of this book better than they would otherwise have been. Series editor Bjarne Stroustrup's incisive comments from concept all the way through to the final draft were heavily influential and led to many improvements. We want to give special thanks to Dave Abrahams, Marshall Cline, Kevlin Henney, Howard Hinnant, Jim Hyslop, Nicolai Josuttis, Jon Kalb, Max Khesin, Stan Lippman, Scott Meyers, and Daveed Vandevoorde for their active participation in review cycles and detailed comments on several drafts of this material. Other valuable comments and feedback were contributed by Chuck Allison, Samir Bajaj, Marc Barbour, Damian Dechev, Steve Dewhurst, Peter Dimov, Alan Griffiths, Michi Henning, James Kanze, Matt Marcus, Petru Marginean, Robert C. "Uncle Bob" Martin, Jeff Peil, Peter Pirkelbauer, Vladimir Prus, Dan Saks, Luke Wagner, Matthew Wilson, and Leor Zolman.

As usual, the remaining errors, omissions, and shameless puns are ours, not theirs.

Herb Sutter
Andrei Alexandrescu

Seattle, September 2004

Organizational and Policy Issues

If builders built buildings the way programmers wrote programs,
then the first woodpecker that came along would destroy civilization.

—Gerald Weinberg

In the grand tradition of C and C++, we count the zero-based way. The prime directive, Item 0, covers what we feel is the most basic advice about coding standards.

The rest of this introductory section goes on to target a small number of carefully selected basic issues that are mostly not directly about the code itself, but on essential tools and techniques for writing solid code.

Our vote for the most valuable Item in this section goes to Item 0: Don't sweat the small stuff. (Or: Know what not to standardize.)

0.   Don't sweat the small stuff.
(Or: Know what not to standardize.)

Summary

Say only what needs saying: Don't enforce personal tastes or obsolete practices.

Discussion

Issues that are really just personal taste and don't affect correctness or readability don't belong in a coding standard. Any professional programmer can easily read and write code that is formatted a little differently than they're used to.

Do use consistent formatting within each source file or even each project, because it's jarring to jump around among several styles in the same piece of code. But don't try to enforce consistent formatting across multiple projects or across a company.

Here are several common issues where the important thing is not to set a rule but just to be consistent with the style already in use within the file you're maintaining:

- *Don't specify how much to indent, but do indent to show structure:* Use any number of spaces you like to indent, but be consistent within at least each file.
- *Don't enforce a specific line length, but do keep line lengths readable:* Use any length of line you like, but don't be excessive. Studies show that up to ten-word text widths are optimal for eye tracking.
- *Don't overlegislate naming, but do use a consistent naming convention:* There are only two must-dos: a) never use "underhanded names," ones that begin with an underscore or that contain a double underscore; and b) always use **ONLY_UPPERCASE_NAMES** for macros and never think about writing a macro that is a common word or abbreviation (including common template parameters, such as **T** and **U**; writing **#define T** *anything* is extremely disruptive). Otherwise, do use consistent and meaningful names and follow a file's or module's convention. (If you can't decide on your own naming convention, try this one: Name classes, functions, and **enum**s **LikeThis**; name variables **likeThis**; name private member variables **likeThis_**; and name macros **LIKE_THIS**.)
- *Don't prescribe commenting styles (except where tools extract certain styles into documentation), but do write useful comments:* Write code instead of comments where possible (e.g., see Item 16). Don't write comments that repeat the code; they get out of sync. Do write illuminating comments that explain approach and rationale.

Finally, don't try to enforce antiquated rules (see Examples 3 and 4) even if they once appeared in older coding standards.

Examples

Example 1: Brace placement. There is no readability difference among:

```
void using_k_and_r_style() {
  // ...
}

void putting_each_brace_on_its_own_line()
{
  // ...
}

void or_putting_each_brace_on_its_own_line_indented()
  {
  // ...
  }
```

Any professional programmer can easily read *and write* any of these styles without hardship. But do be consistent: Don't just place braces randomly or in a way that obscures scope nesting, and try to follow the style already in use in each file. In this book, our brace placement choices are motivated by maximizing readability within our editorial constraints.

Example 2: Spaces vs. tabs. Some teams legitimately choose to ban tabs (e.g., [BoostLRG]), on the grounds that tabs vary from editor to editor and, when misused, turn indenting into outdenting and nondenting. Other equally respectable teams legitimately allow tabs, adopting disciplines to avoid their potential drawbacks. Just be consistent: If you do allow tabs, ensure it is never at the cost of code clarity and readability as team members maintain each other's code (see Item 6). If you don't allow tabs, allow editors to convert spaces to tabs when reading in a source file so that users can work with tabs while in the editor, but ensure they convert the tabs back to spaces when writing the file back out.

Example 3: Hungarian notation. Notations that incorporate type information in variable names have mixed utility in type-unsafe languages (notably C), are possible but have no benefits (only drawbacks) in object-oriented languages, and are impossible in generic programming. Therefore, no C++ coding standard should require Hungarian notation, though a C++ coding standard might legitimately choose to ban it.

Example 4: Single entry, single exit ("SESE"). Historically, some coding standards have required that each function have exactly one exit, meaning one **return** statement. Such a requirement is obsolete in languages that support exceptions and destructors, where functions typically have numerous implicit exits. Instead, follow standards like Item 5 that directly promote simpler and shorter functions that are inherently easier to understand and to make error-safe.

References

[BoostLRG] • *[Brooks95] §12* • *[Constantine95] §29* • *[Keffer95] p. 1* • *[Kernighan99] §1.1, §1.3, §1.6-7* • *[Lakos96] §1.4.1, §2.7* • *[McConnell93] §9, §19* • *[Stroustrup94] §4.2-3* • *[Stroustrup00] §4.9.3, §6.4, §7.8, §C.1* • *[Sutter00] §6, §20* • *[SuttHysl01]*

1.   Compile cleanly at high warning levels.

Summary

Take warnings to heart: Use your compiler's highest warning level. Require clean (warning-free) builds. Understand all warnings. Eliminate warnings by changing your code, not by reducing the warning level.

Discussion

Your compiler is your friend. If it issues a warning for a certain construct, often there's a potential problem in your code.

Successful builds should be silent (warning-free). If they aren't, you'll quickly get into the habit of skimming the output, and you *will* miss real problems. (See Item 2.)

To get rid of a warning: a) understand it; and then b) rephrase your code to eliminate the warning and make it clearer to both humans and compilers that the code does what you intended.

Do this even when the program seemed to run correctly in the first place. Do this even when you are positive that the warning is benign. Even benign warnings can obscure later warnings pointing to real dangers.

Examples

Example 1: A third-party header file. A library header file that you cannot change could contain a construct that causes (probably benign) warnings. Then wrap the file with your own version that **#include**s the original header and selectively turns off the noisy warnings for that scope only, and then **#include** your wrapper throughout the rest of your project. Example (note that the warning control syntax will vary from compiler to compiler):

```
// File: myproj/my_lambda.h -- wraps Boost's lambda.hpp
//   Always include this file; don't use lambda.hpp directly.
//   NOTE: Our build now automatically checks "grep lambda.hpp <srcfile>".
// Boost.Lambda produces noisy compiler warnings that we know are innocuous.
// When they fix it we'll remove the pragmas below, but this header will still exist.
//
#pragma warning(push)      // disable for this header only
  #pragma warning(disable:4512)
  #pragma warning(disable:4180)
  #include <boost/lambda/lambda.hpp>
#pragma warning(pop)        // restore original warning level
```

Example 2: "Unused function parameter." Check to make sure you really didn't mean to use the function parameter (e.g., it might be a placeholder for future expansion, or a required part of a standardized signature that your code has no use for). If it's not needed, simply delete the name of a function parameter:

```
// ... inside a user-defined allocator that has no use for the hint ...
```

```
// warning: "unused parameter 'localityHint'"
pointer allocate( size_type numObjects, const void *localityHint = 0 ) {
  return static_cast<pointer>( mallocShared( numObjects * sizeof(T) ) );
}
```

```
// new version: eliminates warning
pointer allocate( size_type numObjects, const void * /* localityHint */ = 0 ) {
  return static_cast<pointer>( mallocShared( numObjects * sizeof(T) )  );
}
```

Example 3: "Variable defined but never used." Check to make sure you really didn't mean to reference the variable. (An RAII stack-based object often causes this warning spuriously; see Item 13.) If it's not needed, often you can silence the compiler by inserting an evaluation of the variable itself as an expression (this evaluation won't impact run-time speed):

```
// warning: "variable 'lock' is defined but never used"
void Fun() {
  Lock lock;

  // ...

}
```

```
// new version: probably eliminates warning
void Fun() {
  Lock lock;
  lock;

  // ...

}
```

Example 4: "Variable may be used without being initialized." Initialize the variable (see Item 19).

*Example 5: "Missing **return**."* Sometimes the compiler asks for a **return** statement even though your control flow can never reach the end of the function (e.g., infinite loop, **throw** statements, other **return**s). This can be a good thing, because sometimes you only *think* that control can't run off the end. For example, **switch** statements that do not have a **default** are not resilient to change and should have a **default** case that does **assert(false)** (see also Items 68 and 90):

```
// warning: missing "return"
int Fun( Color c ) {
  switch( c ) {
  case Red:    return 2;
  case Green:  return 0;
  case Blue:
  case Black:  return 1;
  }
}

// new version: eliminates warning
int Fun( Color c ) {
  switch( c ) {
  case Red:    return 2;
  case Green:  return 0;
  case Blue:
  case Black:  return 1;
  default:     assert( !"should never get here!" );   // !"string" evaluates to false
               return -1;
  }
}
```

Example 6: "Signed/unsigned mismatch." It is usually not necessary to compare or assign integers with different signedness. Change the types of the variables being compared so that the types agree. In the worst case, insert an explicit cast. (The compiler inserts that cast for you anyway, and warns you about doing it, so you're better off putting it out in the open.)

Exceptions

Sometimes, a compiler may emit a tedious or even spurious warning (i.e., one that is mere noise) but offer no way to turn it off, and it might be infeasible or unproductive busywork to rephrase the code to silence the warning. In these rare cases, as a team decision, avoid tediously working around a warning that is merely tedious: Disable that specific warning only, disable it as locally as possible, and write a clear comment documenting why it was necessary.

References

[Meyers97] §48 • [Stroustrup94] §2.6.2

2. Use an automated build system.

Summary

Push the (singular) button: Use a fully automatic ("one-action") build system that builds the whole project without user intervention.

Discussion

A one-action build process is essential. It must produce a dependable and repeatable translation of your source files into a deliverable package. There is a broad range of automated build tools available, and no excuse not to use one. Pick one. Use it.

We've seen organizations that neglect the "one-action" requirement. Some consider that a few mouse clicks here and there, running some utilities to register COM/CORBA servers, and copying some files by hand constitute a reasonable build process. But you don't have time and energy to waste on something a machine can do faster and better. You need a one-action build that is automated and dependable.

Successful builds should be silent, warning-free (see Item 1). The ideal build produces no noise and only one log message: "Build succeeded."

Have two build modes: Incremental and full. An incremental build rebuilds only what has changed since the last incremental or full build. Corollary: The second of two successive incremental builds should not write any output files; if it does, you probably have a dependency cycle (see Item 22), or your build system performs unnecessary operations (e.g., writes spurious temporary files just to discard them).

A project can have different forms of full build. Consider parameterizing your build by a number of essential features; likely candidates are target architecture, debug vs. release, and breadth (essential files vs. all files vs. full installer). One build setting can create the product's essential executables and libraries, another might also create ancillary files, and a full-fledged build might create an installer that comprises all your files, third-party redistributables, and installation code.

As projects grow over time, so does the cost of not having an automated build. If you don't use one from the start, you will waste time and resources. Worse still, by the time the need for an automated build becomes overwhelming, you will be under more pressure than at the start of the project.

Large projects might have a "build master" whose job is to care for the build system.

References

[Brooks95] §13, §19 • [Dewhurst03] §1 • [GnuMake] • [Stroustrup00] §9.1

3. Use a version control system.

(where more than one developer is involved)

Summary

The palest of ink is better than the best memory (Chinese proverb): Use a version control system (VCS). Never keep files checked out for long periods. Check in frequently after your updated unit tests pass. Ensure that checked-in code does not break the build.

Discussion

Nearly all nontrivial projects need more than one developer and/or take more than a week of work. On such projects, you *will* need to compare historical versions of the same file to determine when (and/or by whom) changes were introduced. You *will* need to control and manage source changes.

When there are multiple developers, those developers will make changes in parallel, possibly to different parts of the same file at the same time. You need tools to automate checkout/versioning of file and, in some cases, merging of concurrent edits. A VCS automates and controls checkouts, versioning, and merging. A VCS will do it faster and more correctly than you could do it by hand. And you don't have time to fiddle with administrivia—you have software to write.

Even a single developer has "oops!" and "huh?" moments, and needs to figure out when and why a bug or change was introduced. So will you. A VCS automatically tracks the history of each file and lets you "turn the clock back." The question isn't whether you will want to consult the history, but when.

Don't break the build. The code in the VCS must always build successfully.

The broad range of VCS offerings leaves no excuse not to use one. The least expensive and most popular is **cvs** (see References). It is a flexible tool, featuring TCP/IP access, optional enhanced security (by using the secure shell **ssh** protocol as a backend), excellent administration through scripting, and even a graphical interface. Many other VCS products either treat **cvs** as a standard to emulate, or build new functionality on top of it.

Exceptions

A project with one programmer that takes about a week from start to finish probably can live without a VCS.

References

[BetterSCM] • [Brooks95] §11, §13 • [CVS]

4.   Invest in code reviews.

Summary

Re-view code: More eyes will help make more quality. Show your code, and read others'. You'll all learn and benefit.

Discussion

A good code review process benefits your team in many ways. It can:

- Increase code quality through beneficial peer pressure.
- Find bugs, non-portable code (if applicable), and potential scaling problems.
- Foster better design and implementation through cross-breeding of ideas.
- Bring newer teammates and beginners up to speed.
- Develop common values and a sense of community inside the team.
- Increase meritocracy, confidence, motivation, and professional pride.

Many shops neither reward quality code and quality teams nor invest time and money encouraging them. We hope we won't have to eat our words a couple of years from now, but we feel that the tide is slowly changing, due in part to an increased need for safe and secure software. Code reviews help foster exactly that, in addition to being an excellent (and free!) method of in-house training.

Even if your employer doesn't yet support a code reviewing process, do increase management awareness (hint: to start, show them this book) and do your best to make time and conduct reviews anyway. It is time well spent.

Make code reviews a routine part of your software development cycle. If you agree with your teammates on a reward system based on incentives (and perhaps disincentives), so much the better.

Without getting too formalistic, it's best to get code reviews in writing—a simple e-mail can suffice. This makes it easier to track your own progress and avoid duplication.

When reviewing someone else's code, you might like to keep a checklist nearby for reference. We humbly suggest that one good list might be the table of contents of the book you are now reading. Enjoy!

In summary: We know we're preaching to the choir, but it had to be said. Your ego may hate a code review, but the little genius programmer inside of you loves it because it gets results and leads to better code and stronger applications.

References

[Constantine95] §10, §22, §33 • [McConnell93] §24 • [MozillaCRFAQ]

Design Style

Fools ignore complexity. Pragmatists suffer it. Some can avoid it. Geniuses remove it.

—Alan Perlis

But I also knew, and forgot, Hoare's dictum that
premature optimization is the root of all evil in programming.

—Donald Knuth,
The Errors of TeX [Knuth89]

It's difficult to fully separate Design Style and Coding Style. We have tried to leave to the next section those Items that generally crop up when actually writing code.

This section focuses on principles and practices that apply more broadly than just to a particular class or function. A classic case in point is the balance among simplicity and clarity (Item 6), avoiding premature optimization (Item 8), and avoiding premature pessimization (Item 9). Those three Items apply, not just at the function-coding level, but to the larger areas of class and module design tradeoffs and to far-reaching application architecture decisions. (They also apply to all programmers. If you think otherwise, please reread the above Knuth quote and note its citation.)

Following that, many of the other Items in this and the following section deal with aspects of dependency management—a cornerstone of software engineering and a recurring theme throughout the book. Stop and think of some random good software engineering technique—*any* good technique. Whichever one you picked, in one way or another it will be about reducing dependencies. Inheritance? Make code written to use the base class less dependent on the actual derived class. Minimize global variables? Reduce long-distance dependencies through widely visible data. Abstraction? Eliminate dependencies between code that manipulates concepts and code that implements them. Information hiding? Make client code less dependent on an entity's implementation details. An appropriate concern for dependency management is reflected in avoiding shared state (Item 10), applying information hiding (Item 11), and much more.

Our vote for the most valuable Item in this section goes to Item 6: Correctness, simplicity, and clarity come first. That they really, really must.

5.   Give one entity one cohesive responsibility.

Summary

Focus on one thing at a time: Prefer to give each entity (variable, class, function, namespace, module, library) one well-defined responsibility. As an entity grows, its scope of responsibility naturally increases, but its responsibility should not diverge.

Discussion

A good business idea, they say, can be explained in one sentence. Similarly, each program entity should have one clear purpose.

An entity with several disparate purposes is generally disproportionately harder to use, because it carries more than the sum of the intellectual overhead, complexity, and bugs of its parts. Such an entity is larger (often without good reason) and harder to use and reuse. Also, such an entity often offers crippled interfaces for any of its specific purposes because the partial overlap among various areas of functionality blurs the vision needed for crisply implementing each.

Entities with disparate responsibilities are typically hard to design and implement. "Multiple responsibilities" frequently implies "multiple personalities"—a combinatorial number of possible behaviors and states. Prefer brief single-purpose functions (see also Item 39), small single-purpose classes, and cohesive modules with clean boundaries.

Prefer to build higher-level abstractions from smaller lower-level abstractions. Avoid collecting several low-level abstractions into a larger low-level conglomerate. Implementing a complex behavior out of several simple ones is easier than the reverse.

Examples

*Example 1: **realloc**.* In Standard C, **realloc** is an infamous example of bad design. It has to do too many things: allocate memory if passed **NULL**, free it if passed a zero size, reallocate it in place if it can, or move memory around if it cannot. It is not easily extensible. It is widely viewed as a shortsighted design failure.

*Example 2: **basic_string**.* In Standard C++, **std::basic_string** is an equally infamous example of monolithic class design. Too many "nice-to-have" features were added to a bloated class that tries to be a container but isn't quite, is undecided on iteration vs. indexing, and gratuitously duplicates many standard algorithms while leaving little space for extensibility. (See Item 44's Example.)

References

[Henney02a] • *[Henney02b]* • *[McConnell93] §10.5* • *[Stroustrup00] §3.8, §4.9.4, §23.4.3.1* • *[Sutter00] §10, §12, §19, §23* • *[Sutter02] §1* • *[Sutter04] §37-40*

6.   Correctness, simplicity, and clarity come first.

Summary

KISS (Keep It Simple Software): Correct is better than fast. Simple is better than complex. Clear is better than cute. Safe is better than insecure (see Items 83 and 99).

Discussion

It's hard to overstate the value of simple designs and clear code. Your code's maintainer will thank you for making it understandable—and often that will be your future self, trying to remember what you were thinking six months ago. Hence such classic wisdom as:

> *Programs must be written for people to read, and only incidentally for machines to execute.* —Harold Abelson and Gerald Jay Sussman

> *Write programs for people first, computers second.* —Steve McConnell

> *The cheapest, fastest and most reliable components of a computer system are those that aren't there.* —Gordon Bell

> *Those missing components are also the most accurate (they never make mistakes), the most secure (they can't be broken into), and the easiest to design, document, test and maintain. The importance of a simple design can't be overemphasized.* —Jon Bentley

Many of the Items in this book naturally lead to designs and code that are easy to change, and clarity is the most desirable quality of easy-to-maintain, easy-to-refactor programs. What you can't comprehend, you can't change with confidence.

Probably the most common tension in this area is between code clarity and code optimization (see Items 7, 8, and 9). When—not if—you face the temptation to optimize prematurely for performance and thereby pessimize clarity, recall Item 8's point: It is far, far easier to make a correct program fast than it is to make a fast program correct.

Avoid the language's "dusty corners." Use the simplest techniques that are effective.

Examples

Example 1: Avoid gratuitous/clever operator overloading. One needlessly weird GUI library had users write **w + c;** to add a child control **c** to a widget **w**. (See Item 26.)

Example 2: Prefer using named variables, not temporaries, as constructor parameters. This avoids possible declaration ambiguities. It also often makes the purpose of your code clearer and thus is easier to maintain. It's also often safer (see Items 13 and 31).

References

[Abelson96] • *[Bentley00] §4* • *[Cargill92] pp. 91-93* • *[Cline99] §3.05-06* • *[Constantine95] §29* • *[Keffer95] p. 17* • *[Lakos96] §9.1, §10.2.4* • *[McConnell93]* • *[Meyers01] §47* • *[Stroustrup00] §1.7, §2.1, §6.2.3, §23.4.2, §23.4.3.2* • *[Sutter00] §40-41, §46* • *[Sutter04] §29*

7.   Know when and how to code for scalability.

Summary

Beware of explosive data growth: Without optimizing prematurely, keep an eye on asymptotic complexity. Algorithms that work on user data should take a predictable, and preferably no worse than linear, time with the amount of data processed. When optimization is provably necessary and important, and especially if it's because data volumes are growing, focus on improving big-Oh complexity rather than on micro-optimizations like saving that one extra addition.

Discussion

This Item illustrates one significant balance point between Items 8 and 9, "don't optimize prematurely" and "don't pessimize prematurely." That makes this a tough Item to write, lest it be misconstrued as "premature optimization." It is not that.

Here's the background and motivation: Memory and disk capacity continue to grow exponentially; for example, from 1988 to 2004 disk capacity grew by about 112% per year (nearly 1,900-fold growth per decade), whereas even Moore's Law is just 59% per year (100-fold per decade). One clear consequence is that whatever your code does today it may be asked to do tomorrow against more data—*much* more data. A bad (worse than linear) asymptotic behavior of an algorithm will sooner or later bring the most powerful system to its knees: Just throw enough data at it.

Defending against that likely future means we want to avoid "designing in" what will become performance pits in the face of larger files, larger databases, more pixels, more windows, more processes, more bits sent over the wire. One of the big success factors in future-proofing of the C++ standard library has been its performance complexity guarantees for the STL container operations and algorithms.

Here's the balance: It would clearly be wrong to optimize prematurely by using a less clear algorithm in anticipation of large data volumes that may never materialize. But it would equally clearly be wrong to pessimize prematurely by turning a blind eye to algorithmic complexity, a.k.a. "big-Oh" complexity, namely the cost of the computation as a function of the number of elements of data being worked on.

There are two parts to this advice. First, even before knowing whether data volumes will be large enough to be an issue for a particular computation, by default avoid using algorithms that work on user data (which could grow) but that don't scale well with data unless there is a clear clarity and readability benefit to using a less scalable algorithm (see Item 6). All too often we get surprised: We write ten pieces of code thinking they'll never have to operate on huge data sets, and then we'll turn out to be perfectly right nine of the ten times. The tenth time, we'll fall into a performance pit—we know it has happened to us, and we know it has happened or will happen to you. Sure, we go fix it and ship the fix to the customer, but it would be better to avoid such embarrassment and rework. So, all things being equal (including clarity and readability), do the following up front:

- *Use flexible, dynamically-allocated data instead of fixed-size arrays:* Arrays "larger than the largest I'll ever need" are a terrible correctness and security fallacy. (See Item 77.) Arrays are acceptable when sizes really are fixed at compile time.

- *Know your algorithm's actual complexity:* Beware subtle traps like linear-seeming algorithms that actually call other linear operations, making the algorithm actually quadratic. (See Item 81 for an example.)

- *Prefer to use linear algorithms or faster wherever possible:* Constant-time complexity, such as **push_back** and hash table lookup, is perfect (see Items 76 and 80). O(log N) logarithmic complexity, such as **set**/**map** operations and **lower_bound** and **upper_bound** with random-access iterators, is good (see Items 76, 85, and 86). O(N) linear complexity, such as **vector::insert** and **for_each**, is acceptable (see Items 76, 81, and 84).

- *Try to avoid worse-than-linear algorithms where reasonable:* For example, by default spend some effort on finding a replacement if you're facing a O(N log N) or O(N²) algorithm, so that your code won't fall into a disproportionately deep performance pit in the event that data volumes grow significantly. For example, this is a major reason why Item 81 advises to prefer range member functions (which are generally linear) over repeated calls of their single-element counterparts (which easily becomes quadratic as one linear operation invokes another linear operation; see Example 1 of Item 81).

- *Never use an exponential algorithm unless your back is against the wall and you really have no other option:* Search hard for an alternative before settling for an exponential algorithm, where even a modest increase in data volume means falling off a performance cliff.

Second, after measurements show that optimization is necessary and important, and especially if it's because data volumes are growing, focus on improving big-Oh complexity rather than on micro-optimizations like saving that one extra addition.

In sum: Prefer to use linear (or better) algorithms wherever possible. Avoid worse-than-linear polynomial algorithms where reasonable. Avoid exponential algorithms with all your might.

References

[Bentley00] §6, §8, Appendix 4 • *[Cormen01]* • *[Kernighan99] §7* • *[Knuth97a]* • *[Knuth97b]* • *[Knuth98]* • *[McConnell93] §5.1-4, §10.6* • *[Murray93] §9.11* • *[Sedgewick98]* • *[Stroustrup00] §17.1.2*

8.   Don't optimize prematurely.

Summary

Spur not a willing horse (Latin proverb): Premature optimization is as addictive as it is unproductive. The first rule of optimization is: Don't do it. The second rule of optimization (for experts only) is: Don't do it yet. Measure twice, optimize once.

Discussion

As [Stroustrup00] §6's introduction quotes so deliciously:

> *Premature optimization is the root of all evil.* —Donald Knuth [quoting Hoare]
>
> *On the other hand, we cannot ignore efficiency.* —Jon Bentley

Hoare and Knuth are, of course and as always, completely correct (see Item 6 and this Item). So is Bentley (see Item 9).

We define premature optimization as making designs or code more complex, and so less readable, in the name of performance when the effort is not justified by a proven performance need (such as actual measurement and comparison against goals) and thus by definition adds no proven value to your program. All too often, unneeded and unmeasured optimization efforts don't even make the program any faster.

Always remember:

> **It is far, far easier to make a correct program fast**
> **than it is to make a fast program correct.**

So, by default, don't focus on making code fast; focus first on making code as clear and readable as possible (see Item 6). Clear code is easier to write correctly, easier to understand, easier to refactor—and easier to optimize. Complications, including optimizations, can always be introduced later—and only if necessary.

There are two major reasons why premature optimizations frequently don't even make the program faster. First, we programmers are notoriously bad at estimating what code will be faster or smaller, and where the bottlenecks in our code will be. This includes the authors of this book, and it includes you. Consider: Modern computers feature an extremely complex computational model, often with several pipelined processing units working in parallel, a deep cache hierarchy, speculative execution, branch prediction... and that's just the CPU chip. On top of the hardware, compilers take their best guess at transforming your source code into machine code that exploits the hardware at its best. And on top of all that complication, it's... well, it's your guess. So if you go with nothing but guesswork, there is little chance your ill-targeted micro-optimizations will significantly improve things. So, optimization must be preceded by measurement; and measurement must be preceded by optimization goals. Until the need is proven, your focus should be on priority #1—writing code for humans. (When someone asks you to optimize, *do* demand proof.)

Second, in modern programs, increasingly many operations aren't CPU-bound anyway. They may be memory-bound, network-bound, disk-bound, waiting on a web service, or waiting on a database. At best, tuning application code in such operations only make the operations wait faster. It also means that the programmer wasted valuable time improving what didn't need improving instead of adding value by improving what did.

Of course, the day will come when you do need to optimize some code. When you do so, look first for an algorithmic optimization (see Item 7) and try to encapsulate and modularize the optimization (e.g., in a function or class; see Items 5 and 11), and clearly state in a comment the reason of the optimization and a reference to the algorithm used.

A common beginner's mistake is to write new code while obsessing—with pride!—over optimal execution at the cost of understandability. More often than not, this yields miles of spaghetti that, even if correct in the beginning, is hard to read and change. (See Item 6.)

It is not premature optimization to pass by reference (see Item 25), to prefer calling prefix ++ and -- (see Item 28), and use similar idioms that should just naturally flow out of our fingertips. These are not premature optimizations; they are simply avoiding premature pessimizations (see Item 9).

Examples

*Example: An **inline** irony.* Here is a simple demonstration of the hidden cost of a premature micro-optimization: Profilers are excellent at telling you, by function hit count, what functions you should have marked inline but didn't; profilers are terrible at telling you what functions you did mark inline but shouldn't have. Too many programmers "inline by default" in the name of optimization, nearly always trading higher coupling for at best dubious benefit. (This assumes that writing **inline** even matters on your compiler. See [Sutter00], [Sutter02], and [Sutter04].)

Exceptions

When writing libraries, it's harder to predict what operations will end up being used in performance-sensitive code. But even library authors run performance tests against a broad range of client code before committing to obfuscating optimizations.

References

[Bentley00] §6 • [Cline99] §13.01-09 • [Kernighan99] §7 • [Lakos96] §9.1.14 • [Meyers97] §33 • [Murray93] §9.9-10, §9.13 • [Stroustrup00] §6 introduction • [Sutter00] §30, §46 • [Sutter02] §12 • [Sutter04] §25

9.   Don't pessimize prematurely.

Summary

Easy on yourself, easy on the code: All other things being equal, notably code complexity and readability, certain efficient design patterns and coding idioms should just flow naturally from your fingertips and are no harder to write than the pessimized alternatives. This is not premature optimization; it is avoiding gratuitous pessimization.

Discussion

Avoiding premature optimization does not imply gratuitously hurting efficiency. By premature pessimization we mean writing such gratuitous potential inefficiencies as:

- Defining pass-by-value parameters when pass-by-reference is appropriate. (See Item 25.)
- Using postfix ++ when the prefix version is just as good. (See Item 28.)
- Using assignment inside constructors instead of the initializer list. (See Item 48.)

It is not a premature optimization to reduce spurious temporary copies of objects, especially in inner loops, when doing so doesn't impact code complexity. Item 18 encourages variables that are declared as locally as possible, but includes the exception that it can be sometimes beneficial to hoist a variable out of a loop. Most of the time that won't obfuscate the code's intent at all, and it can actually help clarify what work is done inside the loop and what calculations are loop-invariant. And of course, prefer to use algorithms instead of explicit loops. (See Item 84.)

Two important ways of crafting programs that are simultaneously clear and efficient are to use abstractions (see Items 11 and 36) and libraries (see Item 84). For example, using the standard library's **vector**, **list**, **map**, **find**, **sort** and other facilities, which have been standardized and implemented by world-class experts, not only makes your code clearer and easier to understand, but it often makes it faster to boot.

Avoiding premature pessimization becomes particularly important when you are writing a library. You typically can't know all contexts in which your library will be used, so you will want to strike a balance that leans more toward efficiency and reusability in mind, while at the same time not exaggerating efficiency for the benefit of a small fraction of potential callers. Drawing the line is your task, but as Item 7 shows, the bigger fish to focus on is scalability and not a little cycle-squeezing.

References

[Keffer95] pp.12-13 • [Stroustrup00] §6 introduction • [Sutter00] §6

10. Minimize global and shared data.

Summary

Sharing causes contention: Avoid shared data, especially global data. Shared data increases coupling, which reduces maintainability and often performance.

Discussion

This statement is more general than Item 18's specific treatment.

Avoid data with external linkage at namespace scope or as static class members. These complicate program logic and cause tighter coupling between different (and, worse, distant) parts of the program. Shared data weakens unit testing because the correctness of a piece of code that uses shared data is conditioned on the history of changes to the data, and further conditions the functioning of acres of yet-unknown code that subsequently uses the data further.

Names of objects in the global namespace additionally pollute the global namespace.

If you must have global, namespace-scope, or static class objects, be sure to initialize such objects carefully. The order of initialization of such objects in different compilation units is undefined, and special techniques are needed to handle it correctly (see References). The order-of-initialization rules are subtle; prefer to avoid them, but if you do have to use them then know them well and use them with great care.

Objects that are at namespace scope, static members, or shared across threads or processes will reduce parallelism in multithreaded and multiprocessor environments and are a frequent source of performance and scalability bottlenecks. (See Item 7.) Strive for "shared-nothing;" prefer communication (e.g., message queues) over data sharing.

Prefer low coupling and minimized interactions between classes. (See [Cargill92].)

Exceptions

The program-wide facilities **cin, cout**, and **cerr** are special and are implemented specially. A factory has to maintain a registry of what function to call to create a given type, and there is typically one registry for the whole program (but preferably it should be internal to the factory rather than a shared global object; see Item 11).

Code that does share objects across threads should always serialize all access to those shared objects. (See Item 12 and [Sutter04c].)

References

[Cargill92] pp. 126.136, 169-173 • [Dewhurst03] §3 • [Lakos96] §2.3.1 • [McConnell93] §5.1-4 • [Stroustrup00] §C.10.1 • [Sutter00] §47 • [Sutter02] §16, Appendix A • [Sutter04c] • [SuttHysl03]

11. Hide information.

Summary

Don't tell: Don't expose internal information from an entity that provides an abstraction.

Discussion

To minimize dependencies between calling code that manipulates an abstraction and the abstraction's implementation(s), data that is internal to the implementation must be hidden. Otherwise, calling code can access—or, worse, manipulate—that information, and the intended-to-be-internal information has leaked into the abstraction on which calling code depends. Expose an abstraction (preferably a domain abstraction where available, but at least a get/set abstraction) instead of data.

Information hiding improves a project's cost, schedule, and/or risk in two main ways:

- *It localizes changes:* Information hiding reduces the "ripple effect" scope of changes, and therefore their cost.
- *It strengthens invariants:* It limits the code responsible for maintaining (and, if it is buggy, possibly breaking) program invariants. (See Item 41.)

Don't expose data from any entity that provides an abstraction (see also Item 10). Data is just one possible incarnation of abstract, conceptual state. If you focus on concepts and not on their representations you can offer a suggestive interface and tweak implementation at will—such as caching vs. computing on-the-fly or using various representations that optimize certain usage patterns (e.g., polar vs. Cartesian).

A common example is to never expose data members of class types by making them **public** (see Item 41) or by giving out pointers or handles to them (see Item 42), but this applies equally to larger entities such as libraries, which must likewise not expose internal information. Modules and libraries likewise prefer to provide interfaces that define abstractions and traffic in those, and thereby allow communication with calling code to be safer and less tightly coupled than is possible with data sharing.

Exceptions

Testing code often needs white-box access to the tested class or module.

Value aggregates ("C-style **struct**s") that simply bundle data without providing any abstraction do not need to hide their data; the data is the interface. (See Item 41.)

References

[Brooks95] §19 • [McConnell93] §6.2 • [Parnas02] • [Stroustrup00] §24.4 • [SuttHysl04a]

12. Know when and how to code for concurrency.

Summary

Th$_{sa}$rea$_{fe}$d$_{ly}$: If your application uses multiple threads or processes, know how to minimize sharing objects where possible (see Item 10) and share the right ones safely.

Discussion

Threading is a huge domain. This Item exists because that domain is important and needs to be explicitly acknowledged, but one Item can't do it justice and we will only summarize a few essentials; see the References for many more details and techniques. Among the most important issues are to avoid deadlocks, livelocks, and malign race conditions (including corruption due to insufficient locking).

The C++ Standard says not one word about threads. Nevertheless, C++ is routinely and widely used to write solid multithreaded code. If your application shares data across threads, do so safely:

- *Consult your target platforms' documentation for local synchronization primitives:* Typical ones range from lightweight atomic integer operations to memory barriers to in-process and cross-process mutexes.

- *Prefer to wrap the platform's primitives in your own abstractions:* This is a good idea especially if you need cross-platform portability. Alternatively, you can use a library (e.g., pthreads [Butenhof97]) that does it for you.

- *Ensure that the types you are using are safe to use in a multithreaded program:* In particular, each type must at minimum:

  - *Guarantee that unshared objects are independent:* Two threads can freely use different objects without any special action on the caller's part.

  - *Document what the caller needs to do to use the same object of that type in different threads:* Many types will require you to serialize access to such shared objects, but some types do not; the latter typically either design away the locking requirement, or they do the locking internally themselves, in which case, you still need to be aware of the limits of what the internal locking granularity will do.

Note that the above applies regardless of whether the type is some kind of string type, or an STL container like a **vector**, or any other type. (We note that some authors have given advice that implies the standard containers are somehow special. They are not; a container is just another object.) In particular, if you want to use standard library components (e.g., **string**, containers) in a multi-threaded program, consult your standard library implementation's documentation to see whether that is supported, as described earlier.

When authoring your own type that is intended to be usable in a multithreaded program, you must do the same two things: First, you must guarantee that different threads can use different objects of that type without locking (note: a type with modifiable static data typically can't guarantee this). Second, you must document what users need to do in order to safely use the same object in different threads; the fundamental design issue is how to distribute the responsibility of correct execution (race- and deadlock-free) between the class and its client. The main options are:

- *External locking: Callers are responsible for locking.* In this option, code that uses an object is responsible for knowing whether the object is shared across threads and, if so, for serializing all uses of the object. For example, string types typically use external locking (or immutability; see the third option on the next page).

- *Internal locking: Each object serializes all access to itself, typically by locking every public member function, so that callers may not need to serialize uses of the object.* For example, producer/consumer queues typically use internal locking, because their whole *raison d'être* is to be shared across threads, and their interfaces are designed so that the appropriate level of locking is for the duration of individual member function calls (**Push, Pop**). More generally, note that this option is appropriate only when you know two things:

First, you must know up front that objects of the type will nearly always be shared across threads, otherwise you'll end up doing needless locking. Note that most types don't meet this condition; the vast majority of objects even in a heavily multithreaded program are never shared across threads (and this is good; see Item 10).

Second, you must know up front that per-member-function locking is at the right granularity and will be sufficient for most callers. In particular, the type's interface should be designed in favor of coarse-grained, self-sufficient operations. If the caller typically needs to lock several operations, rather than *an* operation, this is inappropriate; individually locked functions can only be assembled into a larger-scale locked unit of work by adding more (external) locking. For example, consider a container type that returns an iterator that could become invalid before you could use it, or provides a member algorithm like **find** that can return a correct answer that could become the wrong answer before you could use it, or has users who want to write **if(c.empty()) c.push_back(x);**. (See [Sutter02] for additional examples.) In such cases, the caller needs to perform external locking anyway in order to get a lock whose lifetime spans multiple individual member function calls, and so internal locking of each member function is needlessly wasteful.

So, internal locking is tied to the type's public interface: Internal locking becomes appropriate when the type's individual operations are complete in themselves; in other words, the type's level of abstraction is raised and expressed and encapsulated more precisely (e.g., as a producer-consumer queue rather than a plain **vector**). Combining primitive operations together to form coarser common operations is the approach needed to ensure meaningful but simple function calls. Where combinations of primitives can be arbitrary and you cannot capture the reasonable set of usage scenarios in one named operation, there are two alternatives: a) use a callback-based model (i.e., have the caller call a single member function, but pass in the task they want performed as a command or function object; see Items 87 to 89); or b) expose locking in the interface in some way.

- *Lock-free designs, including immutability (read-only objects): No locking needed.* It is possible to design types so that no locking at all is needed (see References). One common example is immutable objects, which do not need to be locked because they never change; for example, for an immutable string type, a string object is never modified once created, and every string operation results in the creation of a new string.

Note that calling code should not need to know about your types' implementation details (see Item 11). If your type uses under-the-covers data-sharing techniques (e.g., copy-on-write), you do not need to take responsibility for all possible thread safety issues, but you *must* take responsibility for restoring "just enough" thread safety to guarantee that calling code will be correct if it performs its usual duty of care: The type must be as safe to use as it would be if it didn't use covert implementation-sharing. (See [Sutter04c].) As noted, all properly written types must allow manipulation of distinct visible objects in different threads without synchronization.

Particularly if you are authoring a widely-used library, consider making your objects safe to use in a multithreaded program as described above, but without added overhead in a single-threaded program. For example, if you are writing a library containing a type that uses copy-on-write, and must therefore do at least some internal locking, prefer to arrange for the locking to disappear in single-threaded builds of your library (**#ifdef**s and no-op implementations are common strategies).

When acquiring multiple locks, avoid deadlock situations by arranging for all code that acquires the same locks to acquire them in the same order. (Releasing the locks can be done in any order.) One solution is to acquire locks in increasing order by memory address; addresses provide a handy, unique, application-wide ordering.

References

[Alexandrescu02a] • *[Alexandrescu04]* • *[Butenhof97]* • *[Henney00]* • *[Henney01]* • *[Meyers04]* • *[Schmidt01]* • *[Stroustrup00] §14.9* • *[Sutter02] §16* • *[Sutter04c]*

13. Ensure resources are owned by objects. Use explicit RAII and smart pointers.

Summary

Don't saw by hand when you have power tools: C++'s "resource acquisition is initialization" (RAII) idiom is *the* power tool for correct resource handling. RAII allows the compiler to provide strong and automated guarantees that in other languages require fragile hand-coded idioms. When allocating a raw resource, immediately pass it to an owning object. Never allocate more than one resource in a single statement.

Discussion

C++'s language-enforced constructor/destructor symmetry mirrors the symmetry inherent in resource acquire/release function pairs such as **fopen/fclose**, **lock/unlock**, and **new/delete**. This makes a stack-based (or reference-counted) object with a resource-acquiring constructor and a resource-releasing destructor an excellent tool for automating resource management and cleanup.

The automation is easy to implement, elegant, low-cost, and inherently error-safe. If you choose not to use it, you are choosing the nontrivial and attention-intensive task of pairing the calls correctly by hand, including in the presence of branched control flows and exceptions. Such C-style reliance on micromanaging resource deallocation is unacceptable when C++ provides direct automation via easy-to-use RAII.

Whenever you deal with a resource that needs paired acquire/release function calls, encapsulate that resource in an object that enforces pairing for you and performs the resource release in its destructor. For example, instead of calling a pair of **Open-Port/ClosePort** nonmember functions directly, consider:

```cpp
class Port {
public:
  Port( const string& destination );    // call OpenPort
  ~Port();                              // call ClosePort
  // ... ports can't usually be cloned, so disable copying and assignment ...
};

void DoSomething() {
  Port port1( "server1:80" );
  // ...
} // can't forget to close port1; it's closed automatically at the end of the scope

shared_ptr<Port> port2 = /*...*/;    // port2 is closed automatically when the
                                     // last shared_ptr referring to it goes away
```

You can also use libraries that implement the pattern for you (see [Alexandrescu00c]).

When implementing RAII, be conscious of copy construction and assignment (see Item 49); the compiler-generated versions probably won't be correct. If copying doesn't make sense, explicitly disable both by making them private and not defined (see Item 53). Otherwise, have the copy constructor duplicate the resource or reference-count the number of uses, and have the assignment operator do the same and ensure that it frees its originally held resource if necessary. A classic oversight is to free the old resource before the new resource is successfully duplicated (see Item 71).

Make sure that all resources are owned by objects. Prefer to hold dynamically allocated resources via smart pointers instead of raw pointers. Also, perform every explicit resource allocation (e.g., **new**) in its own statement that immediately gives the allocated resource to a manager object (e.g., **shared_ptr**); otherwise, you can leak resources because the order of evaluation of a function's parameters is undefined. (See Item 31.) For example:

```
void Fun( shared_ptr<Widget> sp1, shared_ptr<Widget> sp2 );
// ...
Fun( shared_ptr<Widget>(new Widget), shared_ptr<Widget>(new Widget) );
```

Such code is unsafe. The C++ Standard gives compilers great leeway to reorder the two expressions building the function's two arguments. In particular, the compiler can interleave execution of the two expressions: Memory allocation (by calling **operator new**) could be done first for both objects, followed by attempts to call the two **Widget** constructors. That very nicely sets things up for a leak because if one of the constructor calls throws an exception, then the *other* object's memory will never be released! (See [Sutter02] for details.)

This subtle problem has a simple solution: Follow the advice to never allocate more than one resource in a single statement, and perform every explicit resource allocation (e.g., **new**) in its own code statement that immediately gives the resource to an owning object (e.g., **shared_ptr**). For example:

```
shared_ptr<Widget> sp1(new Widget), sp2(new Widget);
Fun( sp1, sp2 );
```

See also Item 31 for other advantages to using this style.

Exceptions

Smart pointers can be overused. Raw pointers are fine in code where the pointed-to object is visible to only a restricted quantity of code (e.g., purely internal to a class, such as a **Tree** class's internal node navigation pointers).

References

[Alexandrescu00c] • [Cline99] §31.03-05 • [Dewhurst03] §24, §67 • [Meyers96] §9-10 • [Milewski01] • [Stroustrup00] §14.3-4, §25.7, §E.3, §E.6 • [Sutter00] §16 • [Sutter02] §20-21 • [Vandevoorde03] §20.1.4

Coding Style

One man's constant is another man's variable.

—Alan Perlis

In this section, we tighten our focus from general design issues to issues that arise most often during actual coding.

The rules and guidelines in this section target coding practices that aren't specific to a particular language area (e.g., functions, classes, or namespaces) but that improve the quality of your code. Many of these idioms are about getting your compiler to help you, including the powerful tool of declarative **const** (Item 15) and internal **#include** guards (Item 24). Others will help you steer clear of land mines (including some outright undefined behavior) that your compiler can't always check for you, including avoiding macros (Item 16) and uninitialized variables (Item 19). All of them help to make your code more reliable.

Our vote for the most valuable Item in this section goes to Item 14: Prefer compile- and link-time errors to run-time errors.

14. Prefer compile- and link-time errors to run-time errors.

Summary

Don't put off 'til run time what you can do at build time: Prefer to write code that uses the compiler to check for invariants during compilation, instead of checking them at run time. Run-time checks are control- and data-dependent, which means you'll seldom know whether they are exhaustive. In contrast, compile-time checking is not control- or data-dependent and typically offers higher degrees of confidence.

Discussion

The C++ language offers many opportunities to "accelerate" error detection by pushing it to compilation time. Exploiting these static checking capabilities offers you many advantages, including the following:

- *Static checks are data- and flow-independent:* Static checking offers guarantees that are independent of the program inputs or execution flow. In contrast, to make sure that your run-time checking is strong enough, you need to test it for a representative sample of all inputs. This is a daunting task for all but the most trivial systems.

- *Statically expressed models are stronger:* Oftentimes, a program that relies less on run-time checks and more on compile-time checks reflects a better design because the model the program creates is properly expressed using C++'s type system. This way, you and the compiler are partners having a consistent view of the program's invariants; run-time checks are often a fallback to do checking that could be done statically but cannot be expressed precisely in the language. (See Item 68.)

- *Static checks don't incur run-time overhead:* With static checks replacing dynamic checks, the resulting executable will be faster without sacrificing correctness.

One of C++'s most powerful static checking tools is its static type checking. The debate on whether types should be checked statically (C++, Java, ML, Haskell) or dynamically (Smalltalk, Ruby, Python, Lisp) is open and lively. There is no clear winner in the general case, and there are languages and development styles that favor either kind of checking with reportedly good results. The static checking crowd argues that a large category of run-time error handling can be thus easily eliminated, resulting in stronger programs. On the other hand, the dynamic checking camp says that compilers can only check a fraction of potential bugs, so if you need to write unit tests anyway you might as well not bother with static checking at all and get a less restrictive programming environment.

One thing is clear: Within the context of the statically typed language C++, which provides strong static checking and little automatic run-time checking, programmers should definitely use the type system to their advantage wherever possible (see also Items 90 through 100). At the same time, run-time checks are sensible for data- and flow-dependent checking (e.g., array bounds checking or input data validation) (see Items 70 and 71).

Examples

There are several instances in which you can replace run-time checks with compile-time checks.

Example 1: Compile-time Boolean conditions. If you are testing for compile-time Boolean conditions such as **sizeof(int) >= 8**, use static assertions instead of run-time tests. (But see also Item 91.)

Example 2: Compile-time polymorphism. Consider replacing run-time polymorphism (virtual functions) with compile-time polymorphism (templates) when defining generic functions or types. The latter yields code that is better checked statically. (See also Item 64.)

Example 3: Enums. Consider defining **enum**s (or, better yet, full-fledged types) when you need to express symbolic constants or restricted integral values.

Example 4: Downcasting. If you frequently use **dynamic_cast** (or, worse, an unchecked **static_cast**) to perform downcasting, it can be a sign that your base classes offer too little functionality. Consider redesigning your interfaces so that your program can express computation in terms of the base class.

Exceptions

Some conditions cannot be checked at compile time and require run-time checks. For these, prefer to use assertions to detect internal programming errors (see Item 68) and follow the advice in the rest of the error handling section for other run-time errors such as data-dependent errors (see Items 69 through 75).

References

[Alexandrescu01] §3 • [Boost] • [Meyers97] §46 • [Stroustrup00] §2.4.2 • [Sutter02] §4 • [Sutter04] §2, §19

15. Use const proactively.

Summary

const is your friend: Immutable values are easier to understand, track, and reason about, so prefer constants over variables wherever it is sensible and make **const** your default choice when you define a value: It's safe, it's checked at compile time (see Item 14), and it's integrated with C++'s type system. Don't cast away **const** except to call a const-incorrect function (see Item 94).

Discussion

Constants simplify code because you only have to look at where the constant is defined to know its value everywhere. Consider this code:

```
void Fun( vector<int>& v ) {
// ...

const size_t len = v.size();

// ... 30 more lines ...
}
```

When seeing **len**'s definition above, you gain instant confidence about **len**'s semantics throughout its scope (assuming the code doesn't cast away **const**, which it should not do; see below): It's a snapshot of **v**'s length at a specific point. Just by looking up one line of code, you know **len**'s semantics over its whole scope. Without the **const**, **len** might be later modified, either directly or through an alias. Best of all, the compiler will help you ensure that this truth remains true.

Note that **const** is not deep. For example, consider a class **C** that has a member of type **X***. In **C** objects that are **const**, the **X*** member is also **const**—but the **X** object that is pointed to is not. (See [Saks99].)

Implement logical constness with **mutable** members. When a **const** member function of a class legitimately needs to modify a member variable (i.e., when the variable does not affect the object's observable state, such as cached data), declare that member variable **mutable**. Note that if all private members are hidden using the Pimpl idiom (see Item 43), **mutable** is not needed on either the cached information or the unchanging pointer to it.

Yes, **const** is "viral"—add it in one place, and it wants to propagate throughout your code as you call other functions whose signatures aren't yet const-correct. This is a feature, not a bug, and this quality greatly increases **const**'s power even though it was unjustly demeaned in the days when **const** wasn't well understood and appreciated. Retrofitting an existing code base to make it const-correct takes effort, but it is worthwhile and likely to uncover latent bugs.

Const-correctness is worthwhile, proven, effective, and highly recommended. Understanding how and where a program's state changes is vital, and **const** documents that directly in code where the compiler can help to enforce it. Writing **const** appropriately helps you gain a better understanding of your design and makes your code sturdier and safer. If you find it impossible to make a member function **const**, you usually gain a better understanding of the ways in which that member function might modify an object's state. You might also understand which data members bridge the gap between physical constness and logical constness, as noted in the following Examples.

Never cast away **const** except to call a const-incorrect function, or in rare cases as a workaround for lack of **mutable** on older compilers.

Examples

*Example: Avoid **const** pass-by-value function parameters in function declarations.* The following two declarations are exactly equivalent:

```
void Fun( int x );

void Fun( const int x );        // redeclares the same function: top-level const is ignored
```

In the second declaration, the **const** is redundant. We recommend declaring functions without such top-level **const**s, so that readers of your header files won't get confused. However, the top-level **const** does make a difference in a function's *definition* and can be sensible there to catch unintended changes to the parameter:

```
void Fun( const int x ) {       // Fun's actual definition
  // ...

  ++x;                          // error: cannot modify a const value

  // ...
}
```

References

[Allison98] §10 • [Cline99] §14.02-12 • [Dewhurst03] §6, §31-32, §82 • [Keffer95] pp. 5-6 • [Koenig97] §4 • [Lakos96] §9.1.6, §9.1.12 • [Meyers97] §21 • [Murray93] §2.7 • [Stroustrup00] §7.2, §10.2.6, §16.3.1 • [Sutter00] §43

16. Avoid macros.

Summary

TO_PUT_IT_BLUNTLY: Macros are the bluntest instrument of C and C++'s abstraction facilities, ravenous wolves in functions' clothing, hard to tame, marching to their own beat all over your scopes. Avoid them.

Discussion

It's hard to find language that's colorful enough to describe macros, but we'll try. To quote from [Sutter04] §31:

> *Macros are obnoxious, smelly, sheet-hogging bedfellows for several reasons, most of which are related to the fact that they are a glorified text-substitution facility whose effects are applied during preprocessing, before any C++ syntax and semantic rules can even begin to apply.*

Lest there remain any ambiguity on this point, we note also that Bjarne Stroustrup has written:

> *I dislike most forms of preprocessors and macros. One of C++'s aims is to make C's preprocessor redundant (§4.4, §18) because I consider its actions inherently error prone. —[Stroustrup94] §3.3.1*

> *Macros are almost never necessary in C++. Use **const** (§5.4) or **enum** (§4.8) to define manifest constants [see Item 15], **inline** (§7.1.1) to avoid function-calling overhead [but see Item 8], **template**s (Chapter 13) to specify families of functions and types [see Items 64 through 67], and **namespace**s (§8.2) to avoid name clashes [see Items 57 through 59]. —[Stroustrup00] §1.6.1*

> *The first rule about macros is: Don't use them unless you have to. Almost every macro demonstrates a flaw in the programming language, in the program, or in the programmer. —[Stroustrup00] §7.8*

The main problem with C++ macros is that they seem much better at what they do than they really are. Macros ignore scopes, ignore the type system, ignore all other language features and rules, and hijack the symbols they **#define** for the remainder of a file. Macro invocations look like symbols or function calls, but are neither. Macros are not "hygienic," meaning that they can expand to significantly and surprisingly different things depending on the context in which they are used. The text substitution that macros perform makes writing even remotely proper macros a black art whose mastery is as unrewarding as it is tedious.

People who think that template-related errors are the worst to decipher probably haven't seen those caused by badly formed or badly used macros. Templates are part of C++'s type system and thus allow compilers to get better at handling them (which they do), whereas macros are forever divorced from the language and hence intractable. Worse, unlike a template, a macro might expand to some transmission line noise that undesirably compiles by pure chance. Finally, an error in a macro can only be reported after the macro is expanded and not when it is defined.

Even in the rare cases where you do legitimately write a macro (see Exceptions), never ever even consider starting to think about writing a macro that is a common word or abbreviation. Do **#undef**ine macros as soon as possible, always give them **SCREAMING_UPPERCASE_AND_UGLY** names, and avoid putting them in headers.

Examples

Example: Passing a template instantiation to a macro. Macros barely understand C's parentheses and square brackets well enough to balance them. C++, however, defines a new parenthetical construct, namely the < and > used in templates. Macros can't pair those correctly, which means that in a macro invocation

    MACRO(Foo<int, double>)

the macro thinks it is being passed two arguments, namely **Foo<int** and **double>**, when in fact the construct is one C++ entity.

Exceptions

Macros remain the only solution for a few important tasks, such as **#include** guards (see Item 24), **#ifdef** and **#if defined** for conditional compilation, and implementing **assert** (see Item 68).

For conditional compilation (e.g., system-dependent parts), avoid littering your code with **#ifdef**s. Instead, prefer to organize code such that the use of macros drives alternative implementations of one common interface, and then use the interface throughout.

You may want to use macros (cautiously) when the alternative is extreme copying and pasting snippets of code around.

We note that both [C99] and [Boost] include moderate and radical extensions, respectively, to the preprocessor.

References

[Boost] • [C99] • [Dewhurst03] §25-28 • [Meyers96] §1 • [Lakos96] §2.3.4 • [Stroustrup94] §3.3.1 • [Stroustrup00] §1.6.1, §7.8 • [Sutter02] §34-35 • [Sutter04] §31 • [Sutter04a]

17. Avoid magic numbers.

Summary

Programming isn't magic, so don't incant it: Avoid spelling literal constants like **42** or **3.14159** in code. They are not self-explanatory and complicate maintenance by adding a hard-to-detect form of duplication. Use symbolic names and expressions instead, such as **width * aspectRatio**.

Discussion

Names add information and introduce a single point of maintenance; raw numbers duplicated throughout a program are anonymous and a maintenance hassle. Constants should be enumerators or **const** values, scoped and named appropriately.

One **42** may not be the same as another **42**. Worse, "in-head" computations made by the programmer (e.g., "this **84** comes from doubling the **42** used five lines ago") make it tedious and error-prone to later replace **42** with another constant.

Prefer replacing hardcoded strings with symbolic constants. Keeping strings separate from the code (e.g., in a dedicated **.cpp** or resource file) lets non-programmers review and update them, reduces duplication, and helps internationalization.

Examples

Example 1: Important domain-specific constants at namespace level.

```
const size_t  PAGE_SIZE          = 8192,
              WORDS_PER_PAGE     = PAGE_SIZE / sizeof(int),
              INFO_BITS_PER_PAGE = 32 * CHAR_BIT;
```

Example 2: Class-specific constants. You can define static integral constants in the class definition; constants of other types need a separate definition or a short function.

```
// File widget.h
class Widget {
  static const int defaultWidth = 400;        // value provided in declaration
  static const double defaultPercent;         // value provided in definition
  static const char* Name() { return "Widget"; }
};

// File widget.cpp
const double Widget::defaultPercent = 66.67;  // value provided in definition
const int Widget::defaultWidth;               // definition required
```

References

[Dewhurst03] §2 • [Kernighan99] §1.5 • [Stroustrup00] §4.8, §5.4

18. Declare variables as locally as possible.

Summary

Avoid scope bloat, as with requirements so too with variables: Variables introduce state, and you should have to deal with as little state as possible, with lifetimes as short as possible. This is a specific case of Item 10 that deserves its own treatment.

Discussion

Variables whose lifetimes are longer than necessary have several drawbacks:

- *They make the program harder to understand and maintain:* For example, should code update the module-wide **path** string if it only changes the current drive?
- *They pollute their context with their name:* As a direct consequence of this, name-space-level variables, which are the most visible of all, are also the worst (see Item 10).
- *They can't always be sensibly initialized:* Never declare a variable before you can initialize it sensibly. Uninitialized variables are a pervasive source of bugs in all C and C++ programs, and they require our proactive attention because they can't always be detected by compilers (see Item 19).

In particular, older versions of C before [C99] required variables to be defined only at the beginning of a scope; this style is obsolete in C++. A serious problem with this restriction is that at the beginning of the scope you often don't yet have enough information to initialize variables with pertinent information. This leaves you with two choices—either initialize with some default blank value (e.g., zero), which is usually wasteful and can lead to errors if the variable ends up being used before it has a useful state, or leave them uninitialized, which is dangerous. An uninitialized variable of user-defined types will self-initialize to some blank value.

The cure is simple: Define each variable as locally as you can, which is usually exactly the point where you also have enough data to initialize it and immediately before its first use.

Exceptions

It can sometimes be beneficial to hoist a variable out of a loop. (See Item 9.)

Because constants don't add state, this Item does not apply to them. (See Item 17.)

References

[Dewhurst03] §3, §48, §66 • [Dewhurst03] §95 [McConnell93] §5.1-4, §10.1 • [Stroustrup00] §4.9.4, §6.3

19. Always initialize variables.

Summary

Start with a clean slate: Uninitialized variables are a common source of bugs in C and C++ programs. Avoid such bugs by being disciplined about cleaning memory before you use it; initialize variables upon definition.

Discussion

In the low-level efficiency tradition of C and C++ alike, the compiler is often not required to initialize variables unless you do it explicitly (e.g., local variables, forgotten members omitted from constructor initializer lists). Do it explicitly.

There are few reasons to ever leave a variable uninitialized. None is serious enough to justify the hazard of undefined behavior.

If you've used a procedural language (e.g., Pascal, C, Fortran, or Cobol) you might be used to defining variables in separation from the code that uses them, and then assigning them values later when they're about to be used. This approach is obsolete and not recommended (see Item 18).

A common misconception about uninitialized variables is that they will crash the program, so that those few uninitialized variables lying around here and there will be quickly revealed by simple testing. On the contrary, programs with uninitialized variables can run flawlessly for years if the bits in the memory happen to match the program's needs. Later, a call from a different context, a recompilation, or some change in another part of the program will cause failures ranging from inexplicable behavior to intermittent crashes.

Examples

Example 1: Using a default initial value or ?: to reduce mixing data flow with control flow.

```
// Not recommended: Doesn't initialize variable
int speedupFactor;
if( condition )
  speedupFactor = 2;
else
  speedupFactor = -1;

// Better: Initializes variable
int speedupFactor = -1;
if( condition )
  speedupFactor = 2;
```

```
// Better: Initializes variable
int speedupFactor = condition ? 2 : -1;
```

The better alternatives nicely leave no gap between definition and initialization.

Example 2: Replacing a complicated computational flow with a function. Sometimes a value is computed in a way that is best encapsulated in a function (see Item 11):

```
// Not recommended: Doesn't initialize variable
int speedupFactor;

if( condition ) {
  // ... code ...
  speedupFactor = someValue;
} else {
  // ... code ...
  speedupFactor = someOtherValue;
}

// Better: Initializes variable
int speedupFactor = ComputeSpeedupFactor();
```

Example 3: Initializing arrays. For large aggregate types such as arrays, proper initialization does not always mean having to really touch all the data. For example, say you use an API that forces you to use fixed arrays of **char** of size **MAX_PATH** (but see Items 77 and 78). If you are sure the arrays are always treated as null-terminated C strings, this immediate assignment is good enough:

```
// Acceptable: Create an empty path
char path[MAX_PATH]; path[0] = '\0';
```

The following safer initialization fills all the characters in the array with zero:

```
// Better: Create a zero-filled path
char path[MAX_PATH] = { '\0' };
```

Both variants above are recommended, but in general you should prefer safety to unneeded efficiency.

Exceptions

Input buffers and **volatile** data that is directly written by hardware or other processes does not need to be initialized by the program.

References

[Dewhurst03] §48 • [Stroustrup00] §4.9.5, §6.3

20. Avoid long functions. Avoid deep nesting.

Summary

Short is better than long, flat is better than deep: Excessively long functions and nested code blocks are often caused by failing to give one function one cohesive responsibility (see Item 5), and both are usually solved by better refactoring.

Discussion

Every function should be a coherent unit of work bearing a suggestive name (see Item 5 and the Discussion in Item 70). When a function instead tries to merge such small conceptual elements inside a long function body, it ends up doing too much.

Excessive straight-line function length and excessive block nesting depth (e.g., **if**, **for**, **while**, and **try** blocks) are twin culprits that make functions more difficult to understand and maintain, and often needlessly so.

Each level of nesting adds intellectual overhead when reading code because you need to maintain a mental stack (e.g., enter conditional, enter loop, enter **try**, enter conditional, …). Have you ever found a closing brace in someone's code and wondered which of the many **for**s, **while**s, or **if**s it matched? Prefer better functional decomposition to help avoid forcing readers to keep as much context in mind at a time.

Exercise common sense and reasonableness: Limit the length and depth of your functions. All of the following good advice also helps reduce length and nesting:

- *Prefer cohesion:* Give one function one responsibility (see Item 5).
- *Don't repeat yourself:* Prefer a named function over repeated similar code snippets.
- *Prefer &&:* Avoid nested consecutive **if**s where an **&&** condition will do.
- *Don't **try** too hard:* Prefer automatic cleanup via destructors over **try** blocks (see Item 13).
- *Prefer algorithms:* They're flatter than loops, and often better (see Item 84).
- *Don't **switch** on type tags.* Prefer polymorphic functions (see Item 90).

Exceptions

A function might be legitimately long and/or deep when its functionality can't be reasonably refactored into independent subtasks because every potential refactoring would require passing many local variables and context (rendering the result less readable rather than more readable). But if several such potential functions take similar arguments, they might be candidates for becoming members of a new class.

References

[Piwowarski82] • *[Miller56]*

21. Avoid initialization dependencies across compilation units.

Summary

Keep (initialization) order: Namespace-level objects in different compilation units should never depend on each other for initialization, because their initialization order is undefined. Doing otherwise causes headaches ranging from mysterious crashes when you make small changes in your project to severe non-portability even to new releases of the same compiler.

Discussion

When you define two namespace-level objects in different compilation units, which object's constructor is called first is not defined. Often (but not always) your tools might happen to initialize them in the order in which the compilation units' object files are linked, but this assumption is usually not reliable; even when it does hold, you don't want the correctness of your code to subtly depend on your makefile or project file. (For more on the evils of order dependencies, see also Item 59.)

Therefore, inside the initialization code of any namespace-level object, you can't assume that any other object defined in a different compilation unit has already been initialized. These considerations apply to dynamically initialized variables of primitive types, such as a namespace-level **bool reg_success = LibRegister("mylib");**

Note that, even before they are ever constructed using a constructor, namespace-level objects are statically initialized with all zeroes (as opposed to, say, automatic objects that initially contain garbage). Paradoxically, this zero-initialization can make bugs harder to detect, because instead of crashing your program swiftly the static zero-initialization gives your yet-uninitialized object an appearance of legitimacy. You'd think that that string is empty, that pointer is null, and that integer is zero, when in fact no code of yours has bothered to initialize them yet.

To avoid this problem, avoid namespace-level variables wherever possible; they are dangerous (see Item 10). When you do need such a variable that might depend upon another, consider the Singleton design pattern; used carefully, it might avoid implicit dependencies by ensuring that an object is initialized upon first access. Still, Singleton is a global variable in sheep's clothing (see again Item 10), and is broken by mutual or cyclic dependencies (again, zero-initialization only adds to the confusion).

References

[Dewhurst03] §55 • [Gamma95] • [McConnell93] §5.1-4 • [Stroustrup00] §9.4.1, §10.4.9

22. Minimize definitional dependencies. Avoid cyclic dependencies.

Summary

Don't be over-dependent: Don't **#include** a definition when a forward declaration will do.

Don't be co-dependent: Cyclic dependencies occur when two modules depend directly or indirectly on one another. A module is a cohesive unit of release (see page 103); modules that are interdependent are not really individual modules, but super-glued together into what's really a larger module, a larger unit of release. Thus, cyclic dependencies work against modularity and are a bane of large projects. Avoid them.

Discussion

Prefer forward declarations except where you really need a type's definition. You need a full definition of a class **C** in two main cases:

- *When you need to know the size of a **C** object:* For example, when allocating a **C** on the stack or as a directly-held member of another type.
- *When you need to name or call a member of **C**:* For example, when calling a member function.

In keeping with this book's charter, we'll set aside from the start those cyclic dependencies that cause compile-time errors; you've already fixed them by following good advice present in the literature and Item 1. Let's focus on cyclic dependencies that remain in compilable code, see how they trouble your code's quality, and what steps need be taken to avoid them.

In general, dependencies and their cycles should be thought of at module level. A module is a cohesive collection of classes and functions released together (see Item 5 and page 103). In its simplest form, a cyclic dependency has two classes that directly depend upon each other:

```
class Child;                    // breaks the dependency cycle

class Parent { // ...
  Child* myChild_;
};

class Child { // ...             // possibly in a different header
  Parent* myParent_;
};
```

Parent and **Child** depend upon each other. The code compiles, but we've set the stage for a fundamental problem: The two classes are not independent anymore, but have become interdependent. That is not necessarily bad, but it should only occur when both are part of the same module (developed by the same person or team and tested and released as a whole).

In contrast, consider: What if **Child** did not need to store a back link to its **Parent** object? Then **Child** could be released as its own separate, smaller module (and maybe under a different name) in total independence from **Parent**—clearly a more flexible design.

Things get only worse when dependency cycles span multiple modules, which are all stuck together with dependency glue to form a single monolithic unit of release. That's why cycles are the fiercest enemy of modularity.

To break cycles, apply the Dependency Inversion Principle documented in [Martin96a] and [Martin00] (see also Item 36): Don't make high-level modules depend on low-level modules; instead, make both depend on abstractions. If you can define independent abstract classes for either **Parent** or **Child**, you've broken the cycle. Otherwise, you must commit to making them parts of the same module.

A particular form of dependency that certain designs suffer from is transitive dependency on derived classes, which occurs when a base class depends on all of its descendants, direct and indirect. Some implementations of the Visitor design pattern leads to this kind of dependency. Such a dependency is acceptable only for exceptionally stable hierarchies. Otherwise, you may want to change your design; for example, use the Acyclic Visitor pattern [Martin98].

One symptom of excessive interdependencies is incremental builds that have to build large parts of the project in response to local changes. (See Item 2.)

Exceptions

Cycles among classes are not necessarily bad—as long as the classes are considered part of the same module, tested together, and released together. Naïve implementations of such patterns as Command and Visitor result in interfaces that are naturally interdependent. These interdependencies can be broken, but doing so requires explicit design.

References

[Alexandrescu01] §3 • [Boost] • [Gamma95] • [Lakos96] §0.2.1, §4.6-14, §5 • [Martin96a] • [Martin96b] • [Martin98] §7 • [Martin00] • [McConnell93] §5 • [Meyers97] §46 • [Stroustrup00] §24.3.5 • [Sutter00] §26 • [Sutter02] §37 • [Sutter03]

23. Make header files self-sufficient.

Summary

Behave responsibly: Ensure that each header you write is compilable standalone, by having it include any headers its contents depend upon.

Discussion

If one header file won't work unless the file that includes it also includes another header, that's gauche and puts unnecessary burden on that header file's users.

Years ago, some experts advised that headers should not include other headers because of the cost of opening and parsing a guarded header multiple times. Fortunately, this is largely obsolete: Many modern C++ compilers recognize header guards automatically (see Item 24) and don't even open the same header twice. Some also offer precompiled headers, which help to ensure that often-used, seldom-changed headers will not be parsed often.

But don't include headers that you *don't* need; they just create stray dependencies.

Consider this technique to help enforce header self-sufficiency: In your build, compile each header in isolation and validate that there are no errors or warnings.

Examples

Some subtler issues arise in connection with templates.

Example 1: Dependent names. Templates are compiled at the point where they are defined, except that any dependent names or types are not compiled until the point where the template is instantiated. This means that a **template<class T> class Widget** with a **std::deque<T>** member does not incur a compile-time error even when **<deque>** is not included, as long as nobody instantiates **Widget**. Given that **Widget** exists in order to be instantiated, its header clearly should **#include <deque>**.

Example 2: Member function templates, and member functions of templates, are instantiated only if used. Suppose that **Widget** doesn't have a member of type **std::deque<T>**, but **Widget**'s **Transmogrify** member function uses a **deque**. Then **Widget**'s callers can instantiate and use **Widget** just fine even if no one includes **<deque>**, as long as they don't use **Transmogrify**. By default, the **Widget** header should still **#include <deque>** because it is necessary for at least some callers of **Widget**. In rare cases where an expensive header is being included for few rarely used functions of a template, consider refactoring those functions as nonmembers supplied in a separate header that does include the expensive one. (See Item 44.)

References

[Lakos96] §3.2 • [Stroustrup00] §9.2.3 • [Sutter00] §26-30 • [Vandevoorde03] §9-10

24. Always write internal #include guards. Never write external #include guards.

Summary

Wear head(er) protection: Prevent unintended multiple inclusions by using **#include** guards with unique names for all of your header files.

Discussion

Each header file should be guarded by an internal **#include** guard to avoid redefinitions in case it is included multiple times. For example, a header file **foo.h** should follow the general form:

```
#ifndef FOO_H_INCLUDED_
#define FOO_H_INCLUDED_
// ... contents of the file ...
#endif
```

Observe the following rules when defining include guards:

- *Use a unique guard name:* Make sure it is unique at least within your application. We used a popular convention above; the guard name can include the application name, and some tools generate guard names containing random numbers.

- *Don't try to be clever:* Don't put any code or comments before and after the guarded portion, and stick to the standard form as shown. Today's preprocessors can detect include guards, but they might have limited intelligence and expect the guard code to appear exactly at the beginning and end of the header.

Avoid using the obsolete external include guards advocated in older books:

```
#ifndef FOO_H_INCLUDED_        // NOT recommended
#include "foo.h"
#define FOO_H_INCLUDED_
#endif
```

External include guards are tedious, are obsolete on today's compilers, and are fragile with tight coupling because the callers and header must agree on the guard name.

Exceptions

In very rare cases, a header file may be intended to be included multiple times.

References

[C++03, §2.1] • [Stroustrup00] §9.3.3

Functions and Operators

If you have a procedure with ten parameters, you probably missed some.

—Alan Perlis

Functions, including overloaded operators, are the fundamental units of work. As we will see later on in the section on Error Handling and Exceptions (and particularly in Item 70), this has a direct effect on how we reason about the correctness and safety of our code.

But first, let's consider some fundamental mechanics for writing functions, including operators. In particular, we'll focus on their parameters, their semantics, and their overloading.

Our vote for the most valuable Item in this section goes to Item 26: Preserve natural semantics for overloaded operators.

25. Take parameters appropriately by value, (smart) pointer, or reference.

Summary

Parameterize well: Distinguish among input, output, and input/output parameters, and between value and reference parameters. Take them appropriately.

Discussion

Choosing well among values, references, and pointers for parameters is good habit that maximizes both safety and efficiency.

Although efficiency should not be our primary up-front concern (see Item 8), neither should we write needlessly inefficient code when all other things, including clarity, are equal (see Item 9).

Prefer to follow these guidelines for choosing how to take parameters. For input-only parameters:

- Always **const**-qualify all pointers or references to input-only parameters.
- Prefer taking inputs of primitive types (e.g., **char**, **float**) and value objects that are cheap to copy (e.g., **Point**, **complex<float>**) by value.
- Prefer taking inputs of other user-defined types by reference to **const**.
- Consider pass-by-value instead of reference if the function requires a copy of its argument. This is conceptually identical to taking a reference to **const** plus doing a copy, and it can help compiler to better optimize away temporaries.

For output or input/output parameters:

- Prefer passing by (smart) pointer if the argument is optional (so callers can pass null as a "not available" or "don't care" value) or if the function stores a copy of the pointer or otherwise manipulates ownership of the argument.
- Prefer passing by reference if the argument is required and the function won't store a pointer to it or otherwise affect its ownership. This states that the argument is required and makes the caller responsible for providing a valid object.

Don't use C-style varargs (see Item 98).

References

[Alexandrescu03a] • [Cline99] §2.10-11, 14.02-12, 32.08 • [Dewhurst03] §57 • [Koenig97] §4 • [Lakos96] §9.1.11-12 • [McConnell93] §5.7 • [Meyers97] §21-22 • [Stroustrup94] §11.4.4 • [Stroustrup00] §5.5, §11.6, §16.3.4 • [Sutter00] §6, §46

26. Preserve natural semantics for overloaded operators.

Summary

Programmers hate surprises: Overload operators only for good reason, and preserve natural semantics; if that's difficult, you might be misusing operator overloading.

Discussion

Although anyone would agree (we hope) that one should not implement subtraction in an **operator+** implementation, other cases can be subtle. For example, does your **Tensor** class's **operator*** mean the scalar product or the vector product? Does **operator+=(Tensor& t, unsigned u)** add **u** to each of **t**'s elements, or will it resize **t**? In such ambiguous or counterintuitive cases, prefer using named functions instead of fostering cryptic code.

For value types (but not all types; see Item 32): "When in doubt, do as the **int**s do." [Meyers96] Mimicking the behavior of and relationships among operators on built-in types ensures that you don't surprise anyone. If your semantics of choice are likely to raise eyebrows, maybe operator overloading is not a good idea.

Programmers expect operators to come in bundles. If the expression **a @ b** is well formed for some operator **@** you define (possibly after conversions), ask: Can the caller also write **b @ a** without surprises? Can the caller write **a @= b**? (See Item 27.) If the operator has an inverse (e.g., **+** and **-**, or ***** and **/**), are both supported?

Named functions are less likely to have such assumed relationships, and therefore should be preferred for clearer code if there can be any doubt about semantics.

Exceptions

There are highly specialized libraries (e.g., parser generators and regular expression engines) that define domain-specific conventions for operators that are very different from their C++ meanings (e.g., a regular expression engine might use **operator*** to express "zero or more"). Prefer instead to find an alternative to unusual operator overloading (e.g., [C++TR104] regular expressions use strings, so that ***** can be used naturally without overloading operators). If after careful thought you choose to use operators anyway, make sure you define a coherent framework for your conventions and that you don't step on the toes of any built-in operator.

References

[Cline99] §23.02-06 • [C++TR104] §7 • [Dewhurst03] §85-86 • [Koenig97] §4 • [Lakos96] §9.1.1 • [Meyers96] §6 • [Stroustrup00] §11.1 • [Sutter00] §41

27. Prefer the canonical forms of arithmetic and assignment operators.

Summary

If you **a+b**, also **a+=b**: When defining binary arithmetic operators, provide their assignment versions as well, and write to minimize duplication and maximize efficiency.

Discussion

In general, for some binary operator @ (be it +, -, *, and so on), you should define its assignment version such that **a @= b** and **a = a @ b** have the same meaning (other than that the first form might be more efficient and only evaluates **a** once). The canonical way of achieving this goal is to define @ in terms of @=, as follows:

```
T& T::operator@=( const T& ) {
  // ... implementation ...
  return *this;
}

T operator@( const T& lhs, const T& rhs ) {
  T temp( lhs );
  return temp @= rhs;
}
```

The two functions work in tandem. The assignment form does the actual work and returns its left-hand parameter. The non-assignment version creates a temporary from **lhs**, modifies it by invoking the assignment form, and returns it.

Note that here **operator@** is a nonmember function, so that it will have the desirable property of accepting the same implicit conversions on its left-hand side and right-hand side parameters. (See Item 44.) For example, if you define a class **String** that has an implicit constructor taking a **char**, making **operator+(const String&, const String&)** a nonmember enables both **char + String** and **String + char** to work; a member version **String::operator+(const String&)** would only accept the latter. An efficiency-minded implementation might choose to define several nonmember overloads of **operator@** to avoid proliferation of temporaries resulted through conversions (see Item 29).

Where possible, make **operator@=** a nonmember function as well (see Item 44). In any case, put all nonmember operators in the same namespace as **T** so that they will be conveniently available to callers as well as to avoid name lookup surprises (see Item 57).

A variation is to have **operator@** accept its first parameter by value. This way, you arrange for the compiler itself to perform the copy for you implicitly, and this can give the compiler more leeway in applying optimizations:

```
T& operator@=( T& lhs, const T& rhs ) {
  // ... implementation ...
  return lhs;
}

T operator@( T lhs, const T& rhs ) {          // lhs taken by value
  return lhs @= rhs;
}
```

Another variation is to have **operator@** return a **const** value. This technique has the advantage that it disables nonsensical code such as **a + b = c**, but it does so at the cost of disabling some potentially useful constructs such as **a = (b + c).replace(pos, n, d)**—expressive code that, in one shot, concatenates strings **b** and **c**, replaces some characters, and assigns the final result to **a**.

Examples

*Example: An implementation of **+=** for strings.* When concatenating strings, it is useful to know the length in advance so as to allocate memory only once.

```
String& String::operator+=( const String& rhs ) {

  // ... implementation ...

  return *this;
}

String operator+( const String& lhs, const String& rhs ) {
  String temp;                                // initially empty
  temp.Reserve( lhs.size() + rhs.size() );    // allocate enough memory
  return (temp += lhs) += rhs;                // append the strings and return
}
```

Exceptions

In some cases (e.g., **operator*=** on complex numbers), an operator might mutate its left-hand side so significantly that it can be more advantageous to implement **operator*=** in terms of **operator*** rather than the reverse.

References

[Alexandrescu03a] • *[Cline99] §23.06* • *[Meyers96] §22* • *[Sutter00] §20*

28. Prefer the canonical form of ++ and --. Prefer calling the prefix forms.

Summary

If you **++c**, also **c++**: The increment and decrement operators are tricky because each has pre- and postfix forms, with slightly different semantics. Define **operator++** and **operator--** such that they mimic the behavior of their built-in counterparts. Prefer to call the prefix versions if you don't need the original value.

Discussion

An ancient joke about C++ was that the language is called C++ and not ++C because the language is improved (incremented), but many people still use it as C (the previous value). Fortunately, the joke is now obsolete, but it's a helpful illustration for understanding the difference between the two operator forms.

For **++** and **--**, the postfix forms return the original value, whereas the prefix forms return the new value. Prefer to implement the postfix form in terms of the prefix form. The canonical form is:

```
T& T::operator++() {          T& T::operator--() {          // the prefix form:
    // perform increment          // perform decrement      //  - do the work
    return *this;                 return *this;              //  - always return *this;
}                             }

T T::operator++(int) {        T T::operator--(int) {        // the postfix form:
    T old( *this );               T old( *this );           //  - remember old value
    ++*this;                      --*this;                  //  - call the prefix version
    return old;                   return old;               //  - return the old value
}                             }
```

In calling code, prefer using the prefix form unless you actually need the original value returned by the postfix version. The prefix form is semantically equivalent, just as much typing, and often slightly more efficient by creating one less object. This is not premature optimization; it is avoiding premature pessimization (see Item 9).

Exceptions

Expression template frameworks preserve the semantics via different means.

References

[Cline99] §23.07-08 • [Dewhurst03] §87 • [Meyers96] §6 • [Stroustrup00] §19.3 • [Sutter00] §6, §20

29. Consider overloading to avoid implicit type conversions.

Summary

Do not multiply objects beyond necessity (Occam's Razor): Implicit type conversions provide syntactic convenience (but see Item 40). But when the work of creating temporary objects is unnecessary and optimization is appropriate (see Item 8), you can provide overloaded functions with signatures that match common argument types exactly and won't cause conversions.

Discussion

If you're in the office and run out of paper, what do you do? Of course, you walk to your trusty photocopier and make several copies of a white sheet of paper.

As silly as it sounds, this is often what implicit conversions do: unnecessarily go through the trouble of creating temporaries, just to perform some trivial operation on them and toss them away (see Item 40). A common example is string comparison:

```
class String { // ...
  String( const char* text );                    // enables implicit conversion
};
bool operator==( const String&, const String& );

// ... somewhere in the code ...
if( someString == "Hello" ) { ... }
```

Having seen the definitions above, the compiler will compile the comparison as if you had written **someString == String("Hello")**. This can be quite wasteful, considering that you don't need to copy the characters just to read them. The solution to this problem is simple: define overloads that avoid the conversion. For example:

```
bool operator==( const String& lhs, const String& rhs );     // #1
bool operator==( const String& lhs, const char* rhs );       // #2
bool operator==( const char* lhs, const String& rhs );       // #3
```

That looks like a lot of code duplication, but in reality it is only "signature duplication" because all three typically use the same back-end function. You're unlikely to commit a premature optimization heresy (see Item 8) with such simple overloads, and it's *de bon goût* to provide them especially when designing a library when it's difficult to predict in advance what common types will be in performance-sensitive code.

References

[Meyers96] §21 • [Stroustrup00] §11.4, §C.6 • [Sutter00] §6

30. Avoid overloading &&, ||, or , (comma) .

Summary

Wisdom means knowing when to refrain: The built-in **&&**, **||**, and **,** (comma) enjoy special treatment from the compiler. If you overload them, they become ordinary functions with very different semantics (you *will* violate Items 26 and 31), and this is a sure way to introduce subtle bugs and fragilities. Don't overload these operators naïvely.

Discussion

The primary reason not to overload **operator&&**, **operator||**, or **operator,** (comma) is that you *cannot* implement the full semantics of the built-in operators in these three cases, and programmers commonly expect those semantics. In particular, the built-in versions evaluate left-to-right, and for **&&** and **||** also use short-circuit evaluation.

The built-in versions of **&&** and **||** first evaluate their left-hand expression, and if that fully determines the result (**false** for **&&**, **true** for **||**) then the right-hand expression doesn't need to be evaluated—and is guaranteed not to be. We all get so used to this handy feature that we routinely allow the correctness of the right-hand side depend on the success of the left-hand side:

```
Employee* e = TryToGetEmployee();
if( e && e->Manager() )
  // ...
```

This code's correctness relies on the fact that **e->Manager()** will not be evaluated if **e** is null. This is perfectly usual and fine—unless the **&&** used is an overloaded **operator&&**, because then the expression involving **&&** will follow function rules instead:

- Function calls always evaluate *all* arguments before execution.
- The *order* of evaluation of function arguments is unspecified. (See also Item 31.)

So let's look at a modernized version of the snippet above that uses smart pointers:

```
some_smart_ptr<Employee> e = TryToGetEmployee();
if( e && e->Manager() )
  // ...
```

Now, say this code happens to invoke an overloaded **operator&&** (provided by the author either of **some_smart_ptr** or of **Employee**). Then the code will still look fine to the reader, but will potentially (and disastrously) call **e->Manager()** when **e** is null.

Some other code won't dump core even in the presence of such eager evaluation, but becomes incorrect for a different reason if it depends on the order in which the two expressions are evaluated. The effects, of course, can be just as harmful. Consider:

```
if( DisplayPrompt() && GetLine() )
    // ...
```

If **operator&&** is a user-defined operator, it is unspecified whether **DisplayPrompt** or **GetLine** is called first. The program could inadvertently end up waiting for input from the user before displaying the explanatory prompt.

Of course, such code may seem to work with your current compiler and build settings. It's still fragile. Compilers can (and do) choose whatever order they find fit best for any particular call, taking into account concerns such as generated code size, available registers, expression complexity, and so on. So the same call might behave differently depending on the compiler version, the compiler switch settings, and even on the statements surrounding the call.

The same fragility occurs with the comma operator. Like **&&** and **||**, the built-in comma guarantees that its expressions will be evaluated left-to-right (unlike **&&** and **||**, it always evaluates both). A user-defined comma operator cannot guarantee left-to-right evaluation, usually with surprising results. For example, if the following code invokes a user-defined comma operator, it is unspecified whether **g** receives the value **0** or the value **1**.

```
int i = 0;
f( i++ ), g( i );                    // see also Item 31
```

Examples

*Example: Initialization library with overloaded **operator,** for sequence initialization.* One library helpfully tried to make it easier to add multiple values to a container in one shot by overloading the comma. For example, to append to a **vector<string> letters**:

```
set_cont(letters) += "a", "b";       // problematic
```

That's fine until the day the caller writes:

```
set_cont(letters) += getstr(), getstr(); // order unspecified when using overloaded ","
```

If **getstr** gets user console input, for example, and the user enters the strings **"c"** and **"d"** in that order, the strings can actually be applied in either order. That's a surprise, because this is not a problem for the built-in sequencing **operator,**:

```
string s; s = getstr(), getstr();        // order well-specified using built-in ","
```

Exceptions

An exception is expression template libraries, which by design capture all operators.

References

[Dewhurst03] §14 • [Meyers96] §7, §25 • [Murray93] §2.4.3 • [Stroustrup00] §6.2.2

31. Don't write code that depends on the order of evaluation of function arguments.

Summary

Keep (evaluation) order: The order in which arguments of a function are evaluated is unspecified, so don't rely on a specific ordering.

Discussion

In the early days of C, processor registers were a precious resource, and compilers were hard pressed to allocate them efficiently for complex expressions in high-level languages. To allow generation of faster code, the creators of C gave the register allocator an extra degree of freedom: When calling a function, the order of evaluation of its arguments was left unspecified. That motivation is arguably less strong with today's processors, but the fact remains that the order of evaluation is unspecified in C++ and, as it turns out, varies widely across compilers. (See also Item 30.)

This can cause big trouble to the unwary. Consider this code:

```
void Transmogrify( int, int );

int count = 5;
Transmogrify( ++count, ++count );          // order of evaluation unknown
```

All we can say for certain is that **count** will be **7** as soon as **Transmogrify**'s body is entered—but we can't say which of its arguments is **6** and which is **7**. This uncertainty applies to much less obvious cases, such as functions that modify their argument (or some global state) as a side effect:

```
int Bump( int& x ) { return ++x; }
Transmogrify( Bump(count), Bump(count) );  // still unknown
```

Per Item 10, avoid global and shared variables in the first place. But even if you avoid them, others' code might not. For example, some standard functions do have side effects (e.g., **strtok**, and the various overloads of **operator<<** that take an **ostream**).

The cure is simple—use named objects to enforce order of evaluation. (See Item 13.)

```
int bumped = ++count;
Transmogrify( bumped, ++count );           // ok
```

References

[Alexandrescu00c] • *[Cline99]* §31.03-05 • *[Dewhurst03]* §14-15 • *[Meyers96]* §9-10 • *[Stroustrup00]* §6.2.2, §14.4.1 • *[Sutter00]* §16 • *[Sutter02]* §20-21

Class Design and Inheritance

*The most important single aspect of software development
is to be clear about what you are trying to build.*

—Bjarne Stroustrup

What kinds of classes does your team prefer to design and build? Why?

Interestingly, most of the Items in this section are motivated primarily or exclusively by dependency management. For example, inheritance is the second-strongest relationship you can express in C++, second only to **friend**; it should come as no surprise, then, that it's important to use such a powerful tool judiciously, correctly, and well.

In this section, we focus on the key issues in class design, from minimalism to abstraction, from composition to inheritance, from virtual to nonvirtual, from **public** to **private**, from **new** to **delete**: How to get them right, how not to get them wrong, how to avoid the subtle pitfalls, and especially how to manage dependencies.

In the section after this one, we'll narrow our focus specifically to the Big Four special member functions: Default construction, copy construction, copy assignment, and destruction.

Our vote for the most valuable Item in this section goes to Item 33: Prefer minimal classes to monolithic classes.

32. Be clear what kind of class you're writing.

Summary

Know thyself: There are different kinds of classes. Know which kind you are writing.

Discussion

Different kinds of classes serve different purposes, and so follow different rules. Value classes (e.g., **std::pair**, **std::vector**) are modeled after built-in types. A value class:

- Has a public destructor, copy constructor, and assignment with value semantics.
- Has no virtual functions (including the destructor).
- Is intended to be used as a concrete class, not as a base class (see Item 35).
- Is usually instantiated on the stack or as a directly held member of another class.

Base classes are the building blocks of class hierarchies. A base class:

- Has a destructor that is public and virtual or else protected and nonvirtual (see Item 50), and a nonpublic copy constructor and assignment operator (see Item 53).
- Establishes interfaces through virtual functions.
- Is usually instantiated dynamically on the heap as part of a concrete derived class object, and used via a (smart) pointer.

Loosely, traits classes are templates that carry information about types. A traits class:

- Contains only **typedef**s and static functions. It has no modifiable state or virtuals.
- Is not usually instantiated (construction can normally be disabled).

Policy classes (normally templates) are fragments of pluggable behavior. A policy class:

- May or may not have state or virtual functions.
- Is not usually instantiated standalone, but only as a base or member.

Exception classes exhibit an unusual mix of value and reference semantics: They are thrown by value but should be caught by reference (see Item 73). An exception class:

- Has a public destructor and no-fail constructors (especially a no-fail copy constructor; throwing from an exception's copy constructor will abort your program).
- Has virtual functions, and often implements cloning (see Item 54) and visitation.
- Preferably derives virtually from **std::exception**.

Ancillary classes typically support specific idioms (e.g., RAII; see Item 13). They should be easy to use correctly and hard to use incorrectly (e.g., see Item 53).

References

[Abrahams01b] • *[Alexandrescu00a]* • *[Alexandrescu00b]* • *[Alexandrescu01]* §3 • *[Meyers96]* §13 • *[Stroustrup00]* §8.3.2, §10.3, §14.4.6, §25.1 • *[Vandevoorde03]* §15

33. Prefer minimal classes to monolithic classes.

Summary

Divide and conquer: Small classes are easier to write, get right, test, and use. They are also more likely to be usable in a variety of situations. Prefer such small classes that embody simple concepts instead of kitchen-sink classes that try to implement many and/or complex concepts (see Items 5 and 6).

Discussion

Designing fancy large classes is a typical mistake when starting object-oriented design. The prospect of having a class that offers complete and complex functionality in one shot can be quite alluring. However, designing smaller, minimal classes that can be easily combined is an approach that is more successful in practice for systems of any size, for many reasons:

- A minimal class embodies one concept at the right level of granularity. A monolithic class is likely to embody several separate concepts, and using one implies dragging the intellectual overhead of all others. (See Items 5 and 11.)

- A minimal class is easier to comprehend, and more likely to be used and reused.

- A minimal class is easier to deploy. A monolithic class must often be deployed as a bulky indivisible unit. For example, a monolithic **Matrix** class might attempt to implement and deploy exotic functionality such as computing the eigenvalues of a matrix—even when the majority of clients just want simple linear algebra. A better packaging would implement various functional areas as non-member functions operating on a minimal **Matrix** type. Then the functional areas can be tested and deployed in separation to the callers who need them. (See Item 44.)

- Monolithic classes dilute encapsulation. When a class has many member functions that don't need to be members but are—and therefore have gratuitous visibility to the class's private implementation—then the class's private data members become nearly as bad as public variables.

- Monolithic classes usually result from an attempt to predict and deliver a "complete" solution to a problem; in practice, they virtually never succeed. There's always something more that people want—and something less, for that matter.

- Monolithic classes are harder to make correct and error-safe because they often tackle multiple responsibilities. (See Items 5 and 44.)

References

[Cargill92] pp. 85-86, 152, 174-177 • [Lakos96] §0.2.1-2, §1.8, §8.1-2 • [Meyers97] §18 • [Stroustrup00] §16.2.2, §23.4.3.2, §24.4.3 • [Sutter04] §37-40

34. Prefer composition to inheritance.

Summary

Avoid inheritance taxes: Inheritance is the second-tightest coupling relationship in C++, second only to friendship. Tight coupling is undesirable and should be avoided where possible. Therefore, prefer composition to inheritance unless you know that the latter truly benefits your design.

Discussion

Inheritance is often overused, even by experienced developers. A sound rule of software engineering is to minimize coupling: If a relationship can be expressed in more than one way, use the weakest relationship that's practical.

Given that inheritance is nearly the strongest relationship we can express in C++, second only to friendship, it's only really appropriate when there is no equivalent weaker alternative. If you can express a class relationship using composition alone, you should prefer that.

In this context, "composition" means simply embedding a member variable of a type within another type. This way, you can hold and use the object in ways that allow you control over the strength of the coupling.

Composition has important advantages over inheritance:

- *Greater flexibility without affecting calling code:* A private data member is under your control. You can switch from holding it by value to holding by (smart) pointer or Pimpl (see Item 43) without breaking client code; you would only need to change the implementations of the class's own member functions that use it. If you decide you need different functionality, you can easily change the type of the member or the manner of holding it while keeping the class's public interface consistent. In contrast, if you begin with a public inheritance relationship, it is likely that clients have already come to depend on the inheritance; you have therefore committed your class to it and cannot easily change your base class decision later on. (See Item 37.)

- *Greater compile-time insulation, shorter compile times:* Holding an object by pointer (preferably a smart pointer), rather than as a direct member or base class, can also allow you to reduce header dependencies because declaring a pointer to an object doesn't require that object's full class definition. By contrast, inheritance always requires the full definition of the base class to be visible. A common technique is to aggregate all private members behind a single opaque pointer, called a Pimpl (see Item 43).

- *Less weirdness:* Inheriting from a type can cause name lookup to pull in functions and function templates defined in the same namespace as that type. This is very subtle and hard to debug. (See also Item 58.)

- *Wider applicability:* Some classes were not designed to be bases in the first place (and see Item 35). Most classes, however, can fulfill the role of a member.

- *Great robustness and safety:* The tighter coupling of inheritance makes it more difficult to write error-safe code. (See [Sutter02] §23.)

- *Less complexity and fragility:* Inheritance exposes you to additional complications, such as name hiding and other complications that can arise in the presence of later changes to the base class.

Of course, these are not arguments against inheritance *per se*. Inheritance affords a great deal of power, including substitutability and/or the ability to override virtual functions (see Items 36 through 39, and Exceptions below). But don't pay for what you don't need; unless you need inheritance's power, don't endure its drawbacks.

Exceptions

Do use public inheritance to model substitutability. (See Item 37.)

Even if you don't need to provide a substitutability relationship to all callers, you do need *nonpublic* inheritance if you need any of the following, in rough order from most common (the first two points) to exceedingly rare (the rest):

- If you need to override a virtual function.
- If you need access to a protected member.
- If you need to construct the used object before, or destroy it after, a base class.
- If you need to worry about virtual base classes.
- If you *know* you benefit from the empty base class optimization, including that it matters in this case and that your target compiler(s) actually perform it in this case. (See Item 8.)
- If you need controlled polymorphism. That is, if you need a substitutability relationship, but that relationship should be visible only to selected code (via friendship).

References

[Cargill92] pp. 49-65, 101-105 • [Cline99] §5.9-10, 8.11-12, 37.04 • [Dewhurst03] §95 • [Lakos96] §1.7, §6.3.1 • [McConnell93] §5 • [Meyers97] §40 • [Stroustrup00] §24.2-3 • [Sutter00] §22-24, §26-30 • [Sutter02] §23

35. Avoid inheriting from classes that were not designed to be base classes.

Summary

Some people don't want to have kids: Classes meant to be used standalone obey a different blueprint than base classes (see Item 32). Using a standalone class as a base is a serious design error and should be avoided. To add behavior, prefer to add nonmember functions instead of member functions (see Item 44). To add state, prefer composition instead of inheritance (see Item 34). Avoid inheriting from concrete base classes.

Discussion

Using inheritance when it is not needed betrays a misplaced faith in the power of object orientation. In C++, you need to do specific things when defining base classes (see also Items 32, 50, and 54), and very different and often contrary things when designing standalone classes. Inheriting from a standalone class opens your code to a host of problems, very few of which will be ever flagged by your compiler.

Beginners sometimes derive from value classes, such as a **string** class (the standard one or another), to "add more functionality." However, defining free (nonmember) functions is vastly superior to creating **super_string** for the following reasons:

- Nonmember functions work well within existing code that already manipulates **string**s. If instead you supply a **super_string**, you force changes throughout your code base to change types and function signatures to **super_string**.

- Interface functions that take a **string** now need to: a) stay away from **super_string**'s added functionality (unuseful); b) copy their argument to a **super_string** (wasteful); or c) cast the **string** reference to a **super_string** reference (awkward and potentially illegal).

- **super_string**'s member functions don't have any more access to **string**'s internals than nonmember functions because **string** probably doesn't have **protected** members (remember, it wasn't meant to be derived from in the first place).

- If **super_string** hides some of **string**'s functions (and redefining a nonvirtual function in a derived class is not overriding, it's just hiding), that could cause widespread confusion in code that manipulates **string**s that started their life converted automatically from **super_string**s.

So, prefer to add functionality via new nonmember functions (see Item 44). To avoid name lookup problems, make sure you put them in the same namespace as the type they are meant to extend (see Item 57). Some people dislike nonmember functions because the invocation syntax is **Fun(str)** instead of **str.Fun()**, but this is just a matter of syntactic habit and familiarity. (Then there's the sound bite, attributed to the legendary Alan Perlis, that too much syntactic sugar causes cancer of the semicolon.)

What if **super_string** wants to inherit from **string** to add more *state*, such as encoding or a cached word count? Public inheritance is still not recommended, because **string** is not protected against slicing (see Item 54) and so any copying of a **super_string** to a **string** will silently chop off all of the carefully maintained extra state.

Finally, inheriting from a class with a public nonvirtual destructor risks littering your code with undefined behavior by **delete**-ing pointers to **string** that actually point to **super_string** objects (see Item 50). This undefined behavior might seem to be tolerated by your compiler and memory allocator, but it leaves you in the dark swamp of silent errors, memory leaks, heap corruptions, and porting nightmares.

Examples

Example 1: Composition instead of public or private inheritance. What if you do need a **localized_string** that is "almost like **string**, but with some more state and functions and some tweaks to existing **string** functions," and many functions' implementations will be unchanged? Then implement it in terms of **string** safely by using containment instead of inheritance (which prevents slicing and undefined polymorphic deletion), and add passthrough functions to make unchanged functions visible:

```
class localized_string {
public:
  // ... provide passthroughs to string member function that we want to
  // retain unchanged (e.g., define insert that calls impl_.insert) ...

  void clear();                          // mask/redefine clear()

  bool is_in_klingon() const;            // add functionality
private:
  std::string impl_;
  // ... add extra state  ...
};
```

Admittedly, it's tedious to have to write passthrough functions for the member functions you want to keep, but such an implementation is vastly better and safer than using public or nonpublic inheritance.

*Example 2: **std::unary_function**.* Although **std::unary_function** has no virtual functions, it is indeed designed to be a base class, and is not outlawed by this Item. (But **unary_function** could be improved by giving it a protected destructor; see Item 50.)

References

[Dewhurst03] §70, §93 • [Meyers97] §33 • [Stroustrup00] §24.2-3, §25.2

36. Prefer providing abstract interfaces.

Summary

Love abstract art: Abstract interfaces help you focus on getting an abstraction right without muddling it with implementation or state management details. Prefer to design hierarchies that implement abstract interfaces that model abstract concepts.

Discussion

Prefer to define and inherit from abstract interfaces. An abstract interface is an abstract class made up entirely of (pure) virtual functions and having no state (member data) and usually no member function implementations. Note that avoiding state in abstract interfaces simplifies the entire hierarchy design (see [Meyers96] for examples).

Prefer to follow the Dependency Inversion Principle (DIP; see [Martin96a] and [Martin00]). The DIP states that:

- High-level modules should not depend upon low-level modules. Rather, both should depend upon abstractions.
- Abstractions should not depend upon details. Rather, details should depend upon abstractions.

Respecting the DIP implies that hierarchies should be rooted in abstract classes, not concrete classes. (See Item 35.) The abstract base classes must worry about defining functionality, not about implementing it. Put another way: Push policy up and implementation down.

The Dependency Inversion Principle has three fundamental design benefits:

- *Improved robustness:* The less stable parts of a system (implementations) depend on more stable parts (abstractions). A robust design is one in which changes have localized effect. In a fragile system, on the other hand, a small change ripples in unfortunate ways through unexpected parts of the system. This is exactly what happens with designs that have concrete base classes.
- *Greater flexibility:* Designs based on abstract interfaces are generally more flexible. If the abstractions are properly modeled, it is easy to devise new implementations for new requirements. On the contrary, a design that depends on many concrete details is rigid, in that new requirements lead to core changes.
- *Good modularity:* A design relying on abstractions has good modularity because its dependencies are simple: Highly changeable parts depend on stable parts, not vice versa. At the other extreme, a design that has interfaces mixed with im-

plementation details is likely to sport intricate webs of dependency that make it hard to reapply as a unit to plug into another system.

The related Law of Second Chances states: "The most important thing to get right is the interface. Everything else can be fixed later. Get the interface wrong, and you may never be allowed to fix it." [Sutter04]

Typically, choose a public virtual destructor to enable polymorphic deletion (per Item 50), unless you use an object broker such as COM or CORBA that uses an alternate memory management mechanism.

Be wary about using multiple inheritance of classes that are not abstract interfaces. Designs that use multiple inheritance can be very expressive, but are harder to get right and easier to get wrong. In particular, state management is particularly hard in designs using multiple inheritance.

As noted in Item 34, inheriting from a type can also cause name lookup coupling: subtly pulling in functions from the namespace of that type. (See also Item 58.)

Examples

Example: Backup program. In naïve designs, high-level components depend on low-level details. For example, an ill-designed backup program might have an archiving component that depends directly on types or routines that read the directory structure and others that write data on the tape. Adapting such a program to a new file system and backup hardware would incur significant redesign.

If the logic of the backup system is designed around well-designed abstractions of a file system and backup device, no redesign is needed—only new implementations of the abstract interfaces must be added and plugged into the system. As should be natural, new requirements are met by new code; new requirements should not cause rework on existing code.

Exceptions

The empty base optimization is one instance when inheritance (preferably nonpublic) is used for purely optimization purposes. (But see Item 8.)

It would appear that policy-based designs have a high-level component depend on implementation details (the policies). However, that is only a use of static polymorphism. The abstract interfaces are there, except that they are implicit, not explicitly stated via pure virtual functions.

References

[Alexandrescu01] • *[Cargill92] pp. 12-15, 215-218* • *[Cline99] §5.18-20, 21.13* • *[Lakos96] §6.4.1* • *[Martin96a]* • *[Martin00]* • *[Meyers96] §33* • *[Stroustrup00] §12.3-4, §23.4.3.2, §23.4.3.5, §24.2-3, §25.3, §25.6* • *[Sutter04] §17*

37. Public inheritance is substitutability. Inherit, not to reuse, but to be reused.

Summary

Know what: Public inheritance allows a pointer or reference to the base class to actually refer to an object of some derived class, without destroying code correctness and without needing to change existing code.

Know why: Don't inherit publicly to reuse code (that exists in the base class); inherit publicly in order to be reused (by existing code that already uses base objects polymorphically).

Discussion

Despite two decades of object-oriented design knowledge, the purpose and practice of public inheritance are still frequently misunderstood, and many uses of inheritance are flawed.

Public inheritance must always model "is-a" ("works-like-a") according to the Liskov Substitution Principle (see [Liskov88]): All base contracts must be fulfilled, and so all overrides of virtual member functions must require no more and promise no less than their base versions if they are to successfully fulfill the base's contract. Code using a pointer or reference to a **Base** must behave correctly even when that pointer or reference actually points to a **Derived**.

Misuse of inheritance destroys correctness. Incorrectly implemented inheritance most typically goes astray by failing to obey the explicit or implicit contract that the base class establishes. Such contracts can be subtle, and when they cannot be expressed directly in code the programmer must take extra care. (Some patterns help to declare more intent in code; see Item 39.)

To distill a frequently cited example: Consider that two classes **Square** and **Rectangle** each have virtual functions for setting their height and width. Then **Square** cannot correctly inherit from **Rectangle**, because code that uses a modifiable **Rectangle** will assume that **SetWidth** does not change the height (whether **Rectangle** explicitly documents that contract or not), whereas **Square::SetWidth** cannot preserve that contract and its own squareness invariant at the same time. But **Rectangle** cannot correctly inherit from **Square** either, if clients of **Square** assume for example that a **Square**'s area is its width squared, or if they rely on some other property that doesn't hold for **Rectangle**s.

The "is-a" description of public inheritance is misunderstood when people use it to draw irrelevant real-world analogies: A square "is-a" rectangle (mathematically) but a **Square** is not a **Rectangle** (behaviorally). Consequently, instead of "is-a," we prefer to say "works-like-a" (or, if you prefer, "usable-as-a") to make the description less prone to misunderstanding.

Public inheritance is indeed about reuse, but not the way many programmers seem to think. As already pointed out, the purpose of public inheritance is to implement substitutability (see [Liskov88]). The purpose of public inheritance is *not* for the derived class to reuse base class code to implement itself in terms of the base class's code. Such an is-implemented-in-terms-of relationship can be entirely proper, but should be modeled by composition—or, in special cases only, by nonpublic inheritance (see Item 34).

Put another way: When dynamic polymorphism is correct and appropriate, composition is selfish; inheritance is generous.

A new derived class is a new special case of an existing general abstraction. Existing (dynamically) polymorphic code that uses a **Base&** or **Base*** by calling **Base**'s virtual functions should be able to seamlessly use objects of **MyNewDerivedType** that inherits from **Base**. The new derived type adds new functionality to the existing code, which does not need to be changed but can seamlessly increase its functionality when new derived objects are plugged in.

New requirements should naturally be met by new code; new requirements should not cause rework on existing code. (See Item 36.)

Before object orientation, it has always been easy for new code to call existing code. Public inheritance specifically makes it easier for existing code to seamlessly and safely call new code. (So do templates, which provide static polymorphism that can blend well with dynamic polymorphism; see Item 64.)

Exceptions

Policy classes and mixins add behavior by public inheritance, but this is not abusing public inheritance to model is-implemented-in-terms-of.

References

[Cargill92] pp. 19-20 • [Cline99] §5.13, §7.01-8.15 • [Dewhurst03] §92 • [Liskov88] • [Meyers97] §35 • [Stroustrup00] §12.4.1, §23.4.3.1, §24.3.4 • [Sutter00] §22-24

38. Practice safe overriding.

Summary

Override responsibly: When overriding a virtual function, preserve substitutability; in particular, observe the function's pre- and post-conditions in the base class. Don't change default arguments of virtual functions. Prefer explicitly redeclaring overrides as **virtual**. Beware of hiding overloads in the base class.

Discussion

Although derived classes usually add more state (i.e., data members), they model *subsets*, not supersets, of their base classes. In correct inheritance, a derived class models a special case of a more general base concept (see Item 37).

This has direct consequences for correct overriding: Respecting the inclusion relationship implies substitutability—operations that apply to entire sets should apply to any of their subsets as well. After the base class guarantees the preconditions and postconditions of an operation, any derived class must respect those guarantees. An override can ask for *less* and provide *more*, but it must never require more or promise less because that would break the contract that was promised to calling code.

Defining a derived override that can fail (e.g., throws an exception; see Item 70) is correct only if the base class did not advertise that the operation always succeeds. For example, say **Employee** offers a virtual member function **GetBuilding** intended to return an encoding of the building where the **Employee** works. What if we want to write a **RemoteContractor** derived class that overrides **GetBuilding** to sometimes throw an exception or return a null building encoding? That is valid only if **Employee**'s documentation specifies that **GetBuilding** might fail and **RemoteContractor** reports the failure in an **Employee**-documented way.

When overriding, never change default arguments. They are not part of the function's signature, and client code will unwittingly pass different arguments to the function, depending on what node of the hierarchy they have access to. Consider:

```
class Base {
  // ...
  virtual void Foo( int x = 0 );
};

class Derived : public Base {
  // ...
  virtual void Foo( int x = 1 );      // poor form, and surprise-inducing
};
```

```
Derived *pD = new Derived;
pD->Foo();                          // invokes pD->Foo(1)

Base *pB = pD;
pB->Foo();                          // invokes pB->Foo(0)
```

It can be surprising to callers that the same object's member function silently takes different arguments depending on the static type they happen to access it through.

Prefer to add the redundant **virtual** when overriding a function. It makes the intent clearer to the reader.

Beware of inadvertently hiding overloads in the base class. For example:

```
class Base{ //...
  virtual void Foo( int );
  virtual void Foo( int, int );
  void Foo( int, int, int );
};

class Derived : public Base { //...
  virtual void Foo( int );      // overrides Base::Foo(int), but hides the others
};

Derived d;
d.Foo( 1 );                    // ok
d.Foo( 1, 2 );                 // error (oops?)
d.Foo( 1, 2, 3 );              // error (oops?)
```

If the base class's overloads should be visible, write a **using** declaration to redeclare them in the derived class:

```
class Derived : public Base { //...
  virtual void Foo( int );      // overrides Base::Foo(int)
  using Base::Foo;              // bring the other Base::Foo overloads into scope
};
```

Examples

Example: **Ostrich**. If class **Bird** defines the virtual function **Fly** and you derive a new class **Ostrich** (a notoriously flightless bird) from **Bird**, how do you implement **Ostrich::Fly**? The answer is, "It depends." If **Bird::Fly** guarantees success (i.e., provides the no-fail guarantee; see Item 71) because flying is an essential part of the **Bird** model, then **Ostrich** is not an adequate implementation of that model.

References

[Dewhurst03] §73-74, §78-79 • [Sutter00] §21 • [Keffer95] p. 18

39. Consider making virtual functions nonpublic, and public functions nonvirtual.

Summary

In base classes with a high cost of change (particularly ones in libraries and frameworks): Prefer to make public functions nonvirtual. Prefer to make virtual functions private, or protected if derived classes need to be able to call the base versions. (Note that this advice does not apply to destructors; see Item 50.)

Discussion

Most of us have learned through bitter experience to make class members private by default unless we really need to expose them. That's just good encapsulation. This wisdom is applied most frequently to data members (see Item 41), but it applies equally to all members, including virtual functions.

Particularly in OO hierarchies that are expensive to change, prefer full abstraction: Prefer to make public functions nonvirtual, and prefer to make virtual functions private (or protected if derived classes need to be able to call the base versions). This is the Nonvirtual Interface (NVI) pattern. (NVI is similar to other patterns, notably Template Method [Gamma95], but has a distinct motivation and purpose.)

A public virtual function inherently has two different and competing responsibilities, aimed at two different and competing audiences:

- *It specifies interface:* Being public, it is directly part of the interface the class presents to the rest of the world.

- *It specifies implementation detail:* Being virtual, it provides a hook for derived classes to replace the base implementation of that function (if any); it is a customization point.

Because these two responsibilities have different motives and audiences, they can be (and frequently are) in conflict, and then one function by definition cannot fulfill both responsibilities perfectly. That a public virtual function inherently has two significantly different jobs and two competing audiences is a sign that it's not separating concerns well—including that it is inherently violating Items 5 and 11—and that we should consider a different approach.

By separating public functions from virtual functions, we achieve the following significant benefits:

- *Each interface can take its natural shape:* When we separate the public interface from the customization interface, each can easily take the form it naturally wants to take instead of trying to find a compromise that forces them to look identical. Often, the two interfaces want different numbers of functions and/or different parameters; for example, outside callers may call a single public **Process** function that performs a logical unit of work, whereas customizers may prefer to override only certain parts of the processing, which is naturally modeled by independently overridable virtual functions (e.g., **DoProcessPhase1**, **DoProcessPhase2**) so that derived classes aren't forced to override everything. (This latter example specifically is the Template Method pattern arrived at from a different route.)

- *The base class is in control:* The base class is now in complete control of its interface and policy and can enforce interface preconditions and postconditions (see Items 14 and 68), insert instrumentation, and do any similar work all in a single convenient reusable place—the nonvirtual interface function. This "prefactoring" for separation thus promotes good class design.

- *The base class is robust in the face of change:* We are free to change our minds later and add pre- and postcondition checking, or separate processing into more steps, or refactor, or implement a fuller interface/implementation separation using the Pimpl idiom (see Item 43), or make other modifications to the base class's customizability, without affecting any of the code that uses or inherits from the class. Note that it is much easier to start with NVI (even if the public function is just a one-line passthrough to the virtual function) and then later add checking or instrumentation, because that can then be done without breaking any code that uses or inherits from the class. It is much harder to start with a public virtual function and later have to break it apart, which necessarily breaks either the code that uses the class or the code that inherits from the class, depending on whether we choose to keep the original function as the virtual function or as the public function, respectively.

See also Item 54.

Exceptions

NVI does not apply to destructors because of their special order of execution (see Item 50).

NVI does not directly support covariant return types for callers. If you need covariance that is visible to calling code without using **dynamic_cast** downcasts (see also Item 93), it's easier to make the virtual function public.

References

[Allison98] §10 • [Dewhurst03] §72 • [Gamma95] • [Keffer95 pp. 6-7] • [Koenig97] §11 • [Sutter00] §19, §23 • [Sutter04] §18

40. Avoid providing implicit conversions.

Summary

Not all change is progress: Implicit conversions can often do more damage than good. Think twice before providing implicit conversions to and from the types you define, and prefer to rely on explicit conversions (**explicit** constructors and named conversion functions).

Discussion

Implicit conversions have two main problems:

- They can fire in the most unexpected places.
- They don't always mesh well with the rest of the language.

Implicitly converting constructors (constructors that can be called with one argument and are not declared **explicit**) interact poorly with overloading and foster invisible temporary objects that pop up all over. Conversions defined as member functions of the form **operator T** (where **T** is a type) are no better—they interact poorly with implicit constructors and can allow all sorts of nonsensical code to compile. Examples are embarrassingly numerous (see References). We mention only two (see Examples).

In C++, a conversion sequence can include at most one user-defined conversion. However, when built-in conversions are added to the mix, the results can be extremely confusing. The solution is simple:

- By default, write **explicit** on single-argument constructors (see also Item 54):

  ```
  class Widget { // ...
    explicit Widget( unsigned int widgetizationFactor );
    explicit Widget( const char* name, const Widget* other = 0 );
  };
  ```

- Use named functions that offer conversions instead of conversion operators:

  ```
  class String { // ...
    const char* as_char_pointer() const;        // in the grand c_str tradition
  };
  ```

See also the discussion of **explicit** copy constructors in Item 54.

Examples

Example 1: Overloading. Say you have a **Widget::Widget(unsigned int)** that can be invoked implicitly, and a **Display** function overloaded for **Widget**s and **double**s. Consider the following overload resolution surprise:

```
void Display( double );              // displays a double
void Display( const Widget& );       // displays a Widget

Display( 5 );                        // oops: creates and displays a Widget
```

Example 2: Errors that work. Say you provide **operator const char*** for a **String** class:

```
class String {
  // ...
public:
  operator const char*();            // deplorable form
};
```

Suddenly, a lot of silly expressions now compile. Assume **s1**, **s2** are **String**s:

```
int x = s1 - s2;                     // compiles; undefined behavior
const char* p = s1 - 5;              // compiles; undefined behavior
p = s1 + '0';                        // compiles; doesn't do what you'd expect
if( s1 == "0" ) { ... }              // compiles; doesn't do what you'd expect
```

The standard **string** wisely avoids an **operator const char*** for exactly this reason.

Exceptions

When used sparingly and with care, implicit conversions can make calling code short and intuitive. The standard **std::string** defines an implicit constructor that takes a **const char***. This works fine because the designers took some precautions:

- There is no automatic conversion *to* **const char***; that conversion is provided through two named functions, **c_str** and **data**.

- All comparison operators defined for **std::string** (e.g., **==**, **!=**, **<**) are overloaded to compare a **const char*** and a **std::string** in any order (see Item 29). This avoids the creation of hidden temporary variables.

Even so, there can still be some weirdness with overloaded functions:

```
void Display( int );
void Display( std::string );

Display( NULL );                     // calls Display(int)
```

This result might be surprising. (Incidentally, if it did call **Display(std::string)**, the code would have exhibited undefined behavior because it's illegal to construct a **std::string** from a null pointer, but its constructor isn't required to check for the null.)

References

[Dewhurst03] §36-37 • [Lakos96] §9.3.1 • [Meyers96] §5 • [Murray93] §2.4 • [Sutter00] §6, §20, §39

41. Make data members private, except in behaviorless aggregates (C-style structs).

Summary

They're none of your caller's business: Keep data members private. Only in the case of simple C-style **struct** types that aggregate a bunch of values but don't pretend to encapsulate or provide behavior, make all data members public. Avoid mixes of public and nonpublic data, which almost always signal a muddled design.

Discussion

Information hiding is key to good software engineering (see Item 11). Prefer making all data members private; private data is the best means that a class can use to preserve its invariants now, and to keep preserving them in the face of future changes.

Public data is bad if a class models an abstraction and must therefore maintain invariants. Having public data means that part of your class's state can vary uncontrollably, unpredictably, and asynchronously with the rest of its state. It means that an abstraction is sharing responsibility for maintaining one or more invariants with the unbounded set of all code that uses the abstraction, and that is obviously, fundamentally, and indefensibly flawed. Reject such designs outright.

Protected data has all the drawbacks of public data, because having protected data still means that an abstraction is sharing the responsibility of maintaining some invariant with an unbounded set of code—in this case, with the unbounded set of current and future derived classes. Further, any code can read and modify protected data as easily as public data by deriving a new class and using that to get at the data.

Mixing public and nonpublic data members in the same class is confusing and inconsistent. Private data demonstrates that you have invariants and some intent to preserve them; mixing it with public data means a failure to decide clearly whether the class really is supposed to be an abstraction or not.

Nonprivate data members are almost always inferior to even simple passthrough get/set functions, which allow for robust versioning.

Consider hiding a class's private members using the Pimpl idiom. (See Item 43.)

Examples

Example 1: Proper encapsulation. Most classes (e.g., **Matrix**, **File**, **Date**, **BankAccount**, **Security**) should have all private data members and expose adequate interfaces. Allowing calling code to manipulate their internals directly would directly work against the abstraction they provide and the invariants they must sustain.

A **Node** aggregate, as commonly used in the implementation of a **List** class, typically contains some data and two pointers to **Node**: **next_** and **prev_**. **Node**'s members don't need to be hidden from **List**. But now consider Example 3.

Example 2: TreeNode. Consider a **Tree<T>** container implemented in terms of **TreeNode<T>**, an aggregate used within **Tree** that holds previous/next/parent pointers and a **T** object payload. **TreeNode**'s members can all be public because they don't need to be hidden from **Tree**, which directly manipulates them. But **Tree** should hide **TreeNode** altogether (e.g., as a private nested class, or defined only in **Tree**'s implementation file), because it is an internal detail of **Tree** that callers shouldn't depend on or manipulate. Finally, **Tree** does *not* hide the contained **T** objects, because the payload is the caller's responsibility; containers use the iterator abstraction to expose the contained objects while hiding internal structures.

Example 3: Getters and setters. If there is no better domain abstraction available, public and protected data members (e.g., **color**) can at least be made private and hidden behind get and set functions (e.g., **GetColor**, **SetColor**); these provide a minimal abstraction and robust versioning.

Using functions raises the level of discourse about "color" from that of a concrete state to that of an abstract state that we are free to implement as we want: We can change to an internal color encoding other than **int**, add code to update the display when changing color, add instrumentation, and make many other changes without breaking calling code. At worst, callers just recompile (i.e., we preserve source-level compatibility); at best, they don't have to recompile or relink at all (if the change also preserves binary compatibility). Neither source nor binary compatibility is possible for such changes if the starting design has a public **color** member variable to which calling code becomes tightly coupled.

Exceptions

Get/set functions are useful, but a class consisting mostly of gets/sets is probably poorly designed: Decide whether it wants to provide an abstraction or be a **struct**.

Value aggregates (also called "C-style **struct**s") simply keep a bunch of data together but do not actually add significant behavior or attempt to model an abstraction and enforce invariants; they are not meant to be abstractions. Their data members should all be public because the data members *are* the interface. For example, **std::pair<T,U>** is used by the standard containers to aggregate two otherwise unrelated elements of type **T** and **U**, and **pair** itself doesn't add behavior or invariants.

References

[Dewhurst03] §80 • [Henricson97] pg. 105 • [Koenig97] §4 • [Lakos96] §2.2 • [Meyers97] §20 • [Murray93] §2.3 • [Stroustrup00] §10.2.8, §15.3.1.1, §24.4.2-3 • [SuttHysl04a]

42. Don't give away your internals.

Summary

Don't volunteer too much: Avoid returning handles to internal data managed by your class, so clients won't uncontrollably modify state that your object thinks it owns.

Discussion

Consider:

```
class Socket {
public:
  // ... constructor that opens handle_, destructor that closes handle_, etc. ...
  int GetHandle() const { return handle_; }     // avoid this
private:
  int handle_;                                  // perhaps an OS resource handle
};
```

Data hiding is a powerful abstraction and modularity device (see Items 11 and 41). But hiding data and then giving away handles to it is self-defeating, just like locking your house and leaving the keys in the lock. This is because:

- *Clients now have two ways to implement functionality:* They can use your class's abstraction (**Socket**) or directly manipulate the implementation that your class relies on (the socket's C-style handle). In the latter case, the object is unaware of significant changes to the resource it thinks it owns. Now the class cannot reliably enrich or embellish functionality (e.g., proxying, logging, collecting statistics) because clients can bypass the embellished, controlled implementation—and any of the invariants it thinks it's adding, which makes correct error handling next to impossible (see Item 70).

- *The class cannot change the underlying implementation of its abstraction because clients depend on it:* If **Socket** is later upgraded to support a different protocol with a different set of low-level primitives, calling code that fetches the underlying **handle_** and manipulates it incorrectly will be silently broken.

- *The class cannot enforce its invariants because calling code can alter state unbeknownst to the class:* For example, someone could close the handle being used by a **Socket** object without going through a **Socket** member function, thus rendering the object invalid.

- Client code can store the handles that your class returns, and attempt to use them after your class's code has invalidated them.

A common mistake is to forget that **const** is shallow and doesn't propagate through pointers (see Item 15). For example, **Socket::GetHandle** is a **const** member; as far as the compiler is concerned, returning **handle_** preserves constness just fine. However, raw calls to system functions using **handle_**'s value can certainly modify data that **handle_** refers to indirectly.

The following pointer example is similar, although we'll see that the situation is slightly better because at least a **const** return type can reduce accidental misuses:

```
class String {
  char* buffer_;
public:
  char* GetBuffer() const { return buffer_; }   // bad: should return const char*
  // ...
};
```

Even though **GetBuffer** is **const**, this code is technically valid and legal. Clearly, a client can use this **GetBuffer** to change a **String** object in quite major ways without explicit casting and therefore accidentally; for example, **strcpy(s.GetBuffer(), "Very Long String...")** is legal code; in practice, every compiler we tried compiles it without a warning. Returning **const char*** instead from this member function would at least cause a compile-time error for such misuses so they could not occur accidentally; such calling code would have to write an explicit cast (see Items 92 to 95).

Even returning pointers to **const** does not eliminate all accidental misuses, because another problem with giving away object internals has to do with the internals' validity. In the above **String** example, calling code might store the pointer returned by **GetBuffer**, then perform an operation that causes the **String** to grow (and move) its buffer, and finally (and apocalyptically) try to use the saved-and-now-invalidated dangling pointer to a buffer that no longer exists. Thus, if you do think you have a good reason to yield such internal state, you must still document in detail how long the returned value remains valid and what operations will invalidate it (compare this with the standard library's explicit iterator validity guarantees; see [C++03]).

Exceptions

Sometimes classes must provide access to internal handles for compatibility reasons, such as interfacing with legacy code or other systems. For example, **std::basic_string** offers access to its internal handle via the **data** and the **c_str** member functions for compatibility with functions that expect C-style pointers—but that presumably do not store those pointers or try to write through them! Such backdoor access functions are a necessary evil that should be used rarely and cautiously, and the conditions under which the handle remains valid must be carefully documented.

References

[C++03] §23 • [Dewhurst03] §80 • [Meyers97] #29 • [Saks99] • [Stroustrup00] §7.3 • [Sutter02] §9

43. Pimpl judiciously.

Summary

Overcome the language's separation anxiety: C++ makes private members inaccessible, but not invisible. Where the benefits warrant it, consider making private members truly invisible using the Pimpl idiom to implement compiler firewalls and increase information hiding. (See Items 11 and 41.)

Discussion

When it makes sense to create a "compiler firewall" that completely insulates calling code from a class's private parts, use the Pimpl idiom: Hide them behind an opaque pointer (a pointer, preferably an appropriate smart pointer, to a class that is declared but not yet defined). For example:

```
class Map {
  // ...
private:
  struct Impl;
  shared_ptr<Impl> pimpl_;
};
```

The eponymous Pimpl should be used to store all private members, both member data and private member functions. This allows you to make arbitrary changes to your class's private implementation details without any recompilation of calling code—an independence and liberty that is the hallmark of the idiom. (See Item 41.)

Note: Do declare the Pimpl using two declarations as shown. It would be legal, but have a different meaning, to combine the two lines and forward-declare the type and a pointer to it in one statement with **struct Impl* pimpl;**—but then **Impl** is in the enclosing namespace and not a nested type within your class.

There are at least three reasons you might use Pimpl, and they all stem from C++'s distinction between accessibility (whether you can call or use something) and visibility (whether you can see it and therefore depend on its definition). In particular, all private members of a class are inaccessible outside member functions and friends, but are visible to the entire world—to all code that sees the class's definition.

The first consequence of this is potentially longer build times due to processing unnecessary type definitions. For private data members held by value, and for private member functions' parameters taken by value or used in visible function implementations, types must be defined even if they can never be needed in this compilation unit. This can lead to longer build times. For example:

```
class C {
  // ...

private:
  AComplicatedType act_;
};
```

The header file containing class **C**'s definition must also **#include** the header containing the definition for **AComplicatedType**, which in turn transitively includes every header that **AComplicatedType** might need, and so on. If the headers are extensive, compilation times can be noticeably affected.

The second consequence is creating ambiguity and name hiding for code that is trying to call a function. Even though private member functions can never be called from outside the class and its friends, they do participate in name lookup and overload resolution and so can render calls invalid or ambiguous. C++ performs name lookup and then overload resolution *before* accessibility checking. That's why visibility gets priority:

```
int Twice( int );            // 1

class Calc {
public:
  string Twice( string );    // 2

private:
  char* Twice( char* );      // 3

  int Test() {
    return Twice( 21 );      // A: error, 2 and 3 are unviable (1 would be viable,
  }                          // but it can't be considered because it's hidden)
};

Calc c;
c.Twice( "Hello" );          // B: error, 3 is inaccessible (2 would be fine, but it
                             // can't be considered because 3 is a better match)
```

On line A, the workaround is to explicitly qualify the call as **::Twice(21)** to force lookup to select the global function. On line B, the workaround is to add an explicit cast as **c.Twice(string("Hello"))** to force overload resolution to select the intended function. Some of these calling issues can be worked around in other ways than the Pimpl idiom, for example by never writing private overloads for member functions, but not all of the issues resolved by Pimpl have such alternative workarounds.

The third consequence is its impact on error handling and safety. Consider Tom Cargill's Widget example:

```
class Widget { // ...
public:
  Widget& operator=( const Widget& );

private:
  T1 t1_;
  T2 t2_;
};
```

In short, we cannot write **operator=** to give the strong guarantee or even the minimum required (basic) guarantee if **T1** or **T2** operations might fail in a way that is not reversible (see Item 71). The good news is that the following simple transformation always works to enable at least the basic guarantee for error-safe assignment, and usually the strong guarantee as long as the needed **T1** and **T2** operations (notably construction and destruction) don't have side effects: Hold the member objects by pointer instead of by value, preferably all behind a single Pimpl pointer.

```
class Widget { // ...
public:
  Widget& operator=( const Widget& );

private:
  struct Impl;
  shared_ptr<Impl> pimpl_;
};

Widget& Widget::operator=( const Widget& ) {
  shared_ptr<Impl> temp( new Impl( /*...*/ ) );

  // change temp->t1_ and temp->t2_; if it fails then throw, else commit using:

  pimpl_ = temp;
  return *this;
}
```

Exceptions

Only add complexity, including Pimpls, when you know you benefit from the extra level of indirection. (See Items 6 and 8.)

References

[Coplien92] §5.5 • [Dewhurst03] §8 • [Lakos96] §6.4.2 • [Meyers97] §34 • [Murray93] §3.3 • [Stroustrup94] §2.10, §24.4.2 • [Sutter00] §23, §26-30 • [Sutter02] §18, §22 • [Sutter04] §16-17

44. Prefer writing nonmember nonfriend functions.

Summary

Avoid membership fees: Where possible, prefer making functions nonmember nonfriends.

Discussion

Nonmember nonfriend functions improve encapsulation by minimizing dependencies: The body of the function cannot come to depend on the nonpublic members of the class (see Item 11). They also break apart monolithic classes to liberate separable functionality, further reducing coupling (see Item 33). They improve genericity, because it's hard to write templates that don't know whether or not an operation is a member for a given type (see Item 67).

Use this algorithm to determine whether a function should be a member and/or friend:

> *// If you have no choice then you have no choice; make it a member if it must be:*
> If the function is one of the operators =, ->, [], or (), which must be members:
> > Make it a member.
>
> *// If it can be a nonmember **non**friend, or benefits from being a nonmember friend, do it:*
> Else if: a) the function needs a different type as its left-hand argument (as do operators >> or <<, for example); *or* b) it needs type conversions on its leftmost argument; *or* c) it can be implemented using the class's public interface alone:
> > Make it a nonmember (and friend if needed in cases a) and b)).
> > If it needs to behave virtually:
> > > Add a virtual member function to provide the virtual behavior, and implement the nonmember in terms of that.
>
> Else: Make it a member.

Examples

*Example: **basic_string**.* The standard **basic_string** is a needlessly monolithic class with 103 member functions—of which 71 could be written as nonmember nonfriends without loss of efficiency. Many of them duplicate functionality already available as algorithms, or are themselves algorithms that would be useful more widely if they weren't buried inside **basic_string**. (See Items 5 and 32, and [Sutter04].)

References

[Lakos96] §3.6.1, §9.1.2 • [McConnell93] §5.1-4 • [Murray93] §2.6 • [Meyers00] • [Stroustrup00] §10.3.2, §11.3.2, §11.3.5, §11.5.2, §21.2.3.1 • [Sutter00] §20 • [Sutter04] §37-40

45. Always provide new and delete together.

Summary

They're a package deal: Every class-specific overload **void* operator new(*parms*)** must be accompanied by a corresponding overload **void operator delete(void*, *parms*)**, where ***parms*** is a list of extra parameter types (of which the first is always **std::size_t**). The same goes for the array forms **new[]** and **delete[]**.

Discussion

You rarely need to provide a custom **new** or **delete**, but if you need one you usually need both. If you define a class-specific **T::operator new** to do some special allocation, it's very likely you need to define a class-specific **T::operator delete** as well to do the corresponding special deallocation.

That much may be somewhat basic, but there is a subtler reason for this Item: The compiler might be yearning for an overload of **T::operator delete** even when you never actually invoke it. That's why you always need to provide **operator new** and **operator delete** (and **operator new[]** and **operator delete[]**) in pairs.

Say you define a class with customized allocation:

```
class T {
  // ...

  static void* operator new(std::size_t);
  static void* operator new(std::size_t, CustomAllocator&);

  static void operator delete(void*, std::size_t);
};
```

You establish a simple protocol for allocation and deallocation:

- Callers can allocate objects of type **T** with either the default allocator (using **new T**) or the custom allocator (using **new(alloc) T** where **alloc** is an object of type **CustomAllocator**).
- The only **operator delete** that callers can ever invoke is the default **operator delete(size_t)**, so of course you implement such that it correctly deallocates memory allocated either way.

So far, so good.

However, the compiler still needs to covertly call another overload of **delete**, namely **T::operator delete(size_t, CustomAllocator&)**. This is because the statement

```
T* p = new(alloc) T;
```

really expands into something like

```
// compiler-generated code for T* p = new(alloc) T;
//
void* __compilerTemp = T::operator new(sizeof(T), alloc);
T* p;
try {
  p = new (__compilerTemp) T;        // construct a T at address __compilerTemp
}
catch(...) {                         // constructor failed, attention here...
  T::operator delete(__compilerTemp, sizeof(T), alloc);
  throw;
}
```

So, quite logically, the compiler automatically inserts code to call the corresponding **T::operator delete** for the overloaded **T::operator new** if the allocation succeeds but the constructor fails. The "corresponding" signature is **void operator delete(void*, *whatever-parameters-new-takes*)**.

Here comes the fly-in-the-ointment part. The C++ Standard (in [C++03] §5.3.4(17)) specifies that the code above will be generated if and only if that overload of **operator delete** actually exists. Otherwise, the code does not invoke any **operator delete** at all in the case of a constructor failure. In other words: If the constructor fails, memory *will* leak. Of six popular compilers tested at the time of this writing, only two issued a warning in such situations.

That's why every overload **void* operator new(*parms*)** must be accompanied by its corresponding overload **void operator delete(void*, *parms*)**—because the compiler wants to call them itself.

Exceptions

The in-place form of **operator new**

```
void* T::operator new(size_t, void* p) { return p; }
```

does not need a corresponding **operator delete** because there is no real allocation going on. All compilers we tested issue no spurious warnings concerning the absence of **void T::operator delete(void*, size_t, void*)**.

References

[C++03] §5.3.4 • [Stroustrup00] §6.2.6.2, §15.6 • [Sutter00] §36

46. If you provide any class-specific new, provide all of the standard forms (plain, in-place, and nothrow).

Summary

Don't hide good **new**s: If a class defines any overload of **operator new**, it should provide overloads of all three of plain, in-place, and non-throwing **operator new**. If you don't, they'll be hidden and unavailable to users of your class.

Discussion

You rarely need to provide a custom **new** or **delete**, but if you need them you usually don't want to hide the built-in signatures.

In C++, after you define a name in a scope (e.g., in a class scope), it will hide the same name in all enclosing scopes (e.g., in base classes or enclosing namespaces), and overloading never happens across scopes. And when said name is **operator new**, you need to be extra cautious lest you make life hard for your class's clients.

Say you define a class-specific **operator new**:

```
class C {
  // ...
  static void* operator new(size_t, MemoryPool&);// hides three normal forms
};
```

Then, if someone tries to write an expression as boring as plain old **new C**, the compiler will reject it on grounds that it can't find plain old **operator new**. Declaring the **C::operator new** overload that takes a **MemoryPool** hides all other overloads, including the familiar built-in global versions that we all know and love, to wit:

```
void* operator new(std::size_t);                   // plain new
void* operator new(std::size_t, std::nothrow_t) throw();  // nothrow new
void* operator new(std::size_t, void*);            // in-place new
```

Alternatively, perhaps your class provides a class-specific version of one of these three operators **new**. In that case, by declaring one of them your class will by default also mask the other two:

```
class C {
  // ...
  static void* operator new(size_t, void*);  // hides other two normal forms
};
```

Prefer to have class **C** explicitly bring into scope all three of the standard variants of **operator new**. Normally, all should have the same visibility. (The visibility can still be made **private** for individual forms, such as if you want to explicitly disable the plain or non-throwing **operator new**, but the purpose of this Item is to remind you not to hide them inadvertently.)

Note that you should always avoid hiding in-place **new** because STL containers use it extensively.

The only remaining trick is that exposing the hidden operators **new** needs to be done in two different ways in two different circumstances. If your class's base class also defines **operator new**, all you need to do to "unhide" **operator new** is:

```
class C : public B { // ...
public:
  using B::operator new;
};
```

Otherwise, if there is no base class version or the base class doesn't define **operator new**, you will need to write some short forwarding functions (because you can't employ **using** to pull names from the global namespace):

```
class C { // ...
public:
  static void* operator new(std::size_t s) {
    return ::operator new(s);
  }

  static void* operator new(std::size_t s, std::nothrow_t nt) throw() {
    return ::operator new(s, nt);
  }

  static void* operator new(std::size_t s, void* p) {
    return ::operator new(s, p);
  }
};
```

The advice above also applies to the array forms of **operator new[]** and **operator delete[]**.

Avoid calling the **new (nothrow)** version in client code, but provide it to save some clients from surprises if they happen to use it.

References

[Dewhurst03] §60 • [Sutter04] §22-23

Construction, Destruction, and Copying

Just because the standard provides a cliff in front of you,
you are not necessarily required to jump off it.

—Norman Diamond

There is enough to be said about the Big Four special member functions that you will probably be unsurprised to see that they rate having their own section. Herein we collect knowledge and best practices related to default construction, copy construction, copy assignment, and destruction.

One of the reasons you need to be careful with these functions is that, given half a chance, the compiler will write them for you. Another reason is that C++ by default treats classes as value-like types, but not all types are value-like (see Item 32). Know when to write (or disable) these special member functions explicitly, and follow the rules and guidelines in this section to help ensure that you get correct, extensible, and error-safe code.

Our vote for the most valuable Item in this section goes to Item 51: Destructors, deallocation, and **swap** never fail.

47. Define and initialize member variables in the same order.

Summary

Agree with your compiler: Member variables are always initialized in the order they are declared in the class definition; the order in which you write them in the constructor initialization list is ignored. Make sure the constructor code doesn't confusingly specify a different order.

Discussion

Consider the code below:

```
class Employee {
  string email_, firstName_, lastName_;

public:
  Employee( const char* firstName, const char* lastName )
    : firstName_(firstName), lastName_(lastName)
    , email_(firstName_ + "." + lastName_ + "@acme.com") {}
};
```

This code harbors a bug that's as pernicious as it is hard to spot. Because **email_** is declared before **first_** and **last_** in the class definition, it will be initialized first and will attempt to use the other not-yet-initialized fields. Worse, if the constructor's definition is in a separate file, the long-distance influence that the order of member variable declarations has over the constructor's correctness will be even harder to spot.

The reason for this language design decision is to ensure there is a unique order to destroy members; otherwise, the destructor would have to destroy objects in different orders, depending on the constructor that built the object. The bookkeeping overhead for that was deemed unacceptable.

The solution is to always write member initializers in the same order in which the members are declared. That way, any illegal dependency will become obvious. Better yet, strive to not have one member's initialization depend on other members.

Many compilers (but not all) will issue a warning if you break this rule.

References

[Cline99] §22.03-11 • [Dewhurst03] §52-53 • [Koenig97] §4 • [Lakos96] §10.3.5 • [Meyers97] §13 • [Murray93] §2.1.3 • [Sutter00] §47

48. Prefer initialization to assignment in constructors.

Summary

Set once, use everywhere: In constructors, using initialization instead of assignment to set member variables prevents needless run-time work and takes the same amount of typing.

Discussion

Constructors generate initialization code under the covers. Consider:

```
class A {
  string s1_, s2_;
public:
  A() { s1_ = "Hello, "; s2_ = "world"; }
};
```

In reality, constructor's code is generated as if you wrote:

```
A() : s1_(), s2_() { s1_ = "Hello, "; s2_ = "world"; }
```

That is, the objects not explicitly initialized by you are automatically initialized using their default constructors, and then assigned to using their assignment operators. Most often, the assignment operator of a nontrivial object needs to do slightly more than a constructor because it needs to deal with an already-constructed object.

Say what you mean: Initialize member variables in the initializer list, with code that better expresses intent and in addition, as a perk, is usually smaller and faster:

```
A() : s1_("Hello, "), s2_("world") { }
```

This isn't premature optimization; it's avoiding premature pessimization. (See Item 9.)

Exceptions

Always perform unmanaged resource acquisition, such as a **new** expression whose result is not immediately passed to a smart pointer constructor, in the constructor body and not in initializer lists (see [Sutter02]). Of course, it's better to not have such unsafe unowned resources in the first place (see Item 13).

References

[Dewhurst03] §51, §59 • [Keffer95] pp.13-14 • [Meyers97] §12 • [Murray93] §2.1.31 • [Sutter00] §8, §47 • [Sutter02] §18

49. Avoid calling virtual functions in constructors and destructors.

Summary

Virtual functions only "virtually" always behave virtually: Inside constructors and destructors, they don't. Worse, any direct or indirect call to an unimplemented *pure virtual* function from a constructor or destructor results in undefined behavior. If your design wants virtual dispatch into a derived class from a base class constructor or destructor, you need other techniques such as post-constructors.

Discussion

In C++, a complete object is constructed one base class at a time.

Say we have a base class **B** and a class **D** derived from **B**. When constructing a **D** object, while executing **B**'s constructor, the dynamic type of the object under construction is **B**. In particular, a call to a virtual function **B::Fun** will hit **B**'s definition of **Fun**, regardless of whether **D** overrides it or not; and that's a good thing, because calling a **D** member function when the **D** object's members haven't even been initialized yet would lead to chaos. Only after the construction of **B** has completed is **D**'s constructor body executed and its identity as a **D** established. As a rule of thumb, keep in mind that during **B**'s construction there is no way to tell whether the **B** is a stand-alone object or a base part of some other further-derived object; virtually-acting virtual functions would be such a "way."

To add insult to injury, a call from a constructor to a pure virtual function that isn't defined at all has, well, undefined behavior. Such code is therefore not only confusing, but it is also more fragile in face of maintenance.

On the other hand, some designs ask for "post-construction," that is, a virtual function that must be invoked right after the full object has been constructed. Some techniques for this are shown in the References. Here's a non-exhaustive list of options:

- *Pass the buck:* Just document that user code must call the post-initialization function right after constructing an object.

- *Post-initialize lazily:* Do it during the first call of a member function. A Boolean flag in the base class tells whether or not post-construction has taken place yet.

- *Use virtual base class semantics:* Language rules dictate that the constructor most-derived class decides which base constructor will be invoked; you can use that to your advantage. (See [Taligent94].)

- *Use a factory function:* This way, you can easily force a mandatory invocation of a post-constructor function. (See Examples.)

No post-construction technique is perfect. The worst dodge the whole issue by simply asking the caller to invoke the post-constructor manually. Even the best require a different syntax for constructing objects (easy to check at compile time) and/or co-operation from derived class authors (impossible to check at compile time).

Examples

Example: Using a factory function to insert a post-constructor call. Consider:

```
class B {                                       // hierarchy root
protected:
  B() { /* ... */ }

  virtual void PostInitialize() { /* ... */ }   // called right after construction

public:
  template<class T>
  static shared_ptr<T> Create() {               // interface for creating objects
    shared_ptr<T> p( new T );
    p->PostInitialize();
    return p;
  }
};

class D : public B { /* ... */ };               // some derived class

shared_ptr<D> p = D::Create<D>();               // creating a D object
```

This rather fragile design sports the following tradeoffs:

- Derived classes such as **D** must not expose a public constructor. Otherwise, **D**'s users could create **D** objects that don't invoke **PostInitialize**.

- Allocation is limited to **operator new**. **B** can, however, override **new** (see Items 45 and 46).

- **D** must define a constructor with the same parameters that **B** selected. Defining several overloads of **Create** can assuage this problem, however; and the overloads can even be templated on the argument types.

- If the requirements above are met, the design guarantees that **PostInitialize** has been called for any fully constructed **B**-derived object. **PostInitialize** doesn't need to be virtual; it can, however, invoke virtual functions freely.

References

[Alexandrescu01] §3 • *[Boost]* • *[Dewhurst03] §75* • *[Meyers97] §46* • *[Stroustrup00] §15.4.3* • *[Taligent94]*

50. Make base class destructors public and virtual, or protected and nonvirtual.

Summary

To delete, or not to delete; that is the question: If deletion through a pointer to a base **Base** should be allowed, then **Base**'s destructor must be public and virtual. Otherwise, it should be protected and nonvirtual.

Discussion

This simple guideline illustrates a subtle issue and reflects modern uses of inheritance and object-oriented design principles.

For a base class **Base**, calling code might try to **delete** derived objects through pointers to **Base**. If **Base**'s destructor is public and nonvirtual (the default), it can be accidentally called on a pointer that actually points to a derived object, in which case the behavior of the attempted deletion is undefined. This state of affairs has led older coding standards to impose a blanket requirement that all base class destructors must be virtual. This is overkill (even if it is the common case); instead, the rule should be to make base class destructors virtual if and only if they are public.

To write a base class is to define an abstraction (see Items 35 through 37). Recall that for each member function participating in that abstraction, you need to decide:

- Whether it should behave virtually or not.
- Whether it should be publicly available to all callers using a pointer to **Base** or else be a hidden internal implementation detail.

As described in Item 39, for a normal member function, the choice is between allowing it to be called via a **Base*** nonvirtually (but possibly with virtual behavior if it invokes virtual functions, such as in the NVI or Template Method patterns), virtually, or not at all. The NVI pattern is a technique to avoid public virtual functions.

Destruction can be viewed as just another operation, albeit with special semantics that make nonvirtual calls dangerous or wrong. For a base class destructor, therefore, the choice is between allowing it to be called via a **Base*** virtually or not at all; "nonvirtually" is not an option. Hence, a base class destructor is virtual if it can be called (i.e., is public), and nonvirtual otherwise.

Note that the NVI pattern cannot be applied to the destructor because constructors and destructors cannot make deep virtual calls. (See Items 39 and 55.)

Corollary: Always write a destructor for a base class, because the implicitly generated one is public and nonvirtual.

Examples

Either clients should be able to **delete** polymorphically using a pointer to **Base**, or they shouldn't. Each alternative implies a specific design:

- *Example 1: Base classes with polymorphic deletion.* If polymorphic deletion should be allowed, the destructor must be public (else calling code can't call it) and it must be virtual (else calling it results in undefined behavior).

- *Example 2: Base classes without polymorphic deletion.* If polymorphic deletion shouldn't be allowed, the destructor must be nonpublic (so that calling code can't call it) and should be nonvirtual (because it needn't be virtual).

Policy classes are frequently used as base classes for convenience, not for polymorphic behavior. It is recommended to make their destructors protected and nonvirtual.

Exceptions

Some component architectures (e.g., COM and CORBA) don't use a standard deletion mechanism, and foster different protocols for object disposal. Follow the local patterns and idioms, and adapt this guideline as appropriate.

Consider also this rare case:

- **B** is both a base class and a concrete class that can be instantiated by itself (and so the destructor must be public for **B** objects to be created and destroyed).

- Yet **B** also has no virtual functions and is not meant to be used polymorphically (and so although the destructor is public it does not need to be virtual).

Then, even though the destructor has to be public, there can be great pressure to not make it virtual because as the first virtual function it would incur all the run-time type overhead when the added functionality should never be needed.

In this rare case, you could make the destructor public and nonvirtual but clearly document that further-derived objects must not be used polymorphically as **B**'s. This is what was done with **std::unary_function**.

In general, however, avoid concrete base classes (see Item 35). For example, **unary_function** is a bundle-of-typedefs that was never intended to be instantiated standalone. It really makes no sense to give it a public destructor; a better design would be to follow this Item's advice and give it a protected nonvirtual destructor.

References

[Cargill92] pp. 77-79, 207 • [Cline99] §21.06, 21.12-13 • [Henricson97] pp. 110-114 • [Koenig97] Chapters 4, 11 • [Meyers97] §14 • [Stroustrup00] §12.4.2 • [Sutter02] §27 • [Sutter04] §18

51. Destructors, deallocation, and swap never fail.

Summary

Everything they attempt shall succeed: Never allow an error to be reported from a destructor, a resource deallocation function (e.g., **operator delete**), or a swap function. Specifically, types whose destructors may throw an exception are flatly forbidden from use with the C++ standard library.

Discussion

These are key functions that must not fail because they are necessary for the two key operations in transactional programming: to back out work if problems are encountered during processing, and to commit work if no problems occur. If there's no way to safely back out using no-fail operations, then no-fail rollback is impossible to implement. If there's no way to safely commit state changes using a no-fail operation (notably, but not limited to, swap), then no-fail commit is impossible to implement.

Consider the following advice and requirements found in the C++ Standard:

> *If a destructor called during stack unwinding exits with an exception, **terminate** is called (15.5.1). So destructors should generally catch exceptions and not let them propagate out of the destructor.* —[C++03] §15.2(3)

> *No destructor operation defined in the C++ Standard Library* [including the destructor of any type that is used to instantiate a standard library template] *will throw an exception.* —[C++03] §17.4.4.8(3)

Destructors are special, and the compiler invokes them automatically in various contexts. If you write a class—let's call it **Nefarious**—whose destructor might fail (usually by throwing an exception; see Item 72), you incur the following consequences:

- *Nefarious objects are hard to use safely in normal functions:* You can't reliably instantiate automatic **Nefarious** objects in a scope if that scope might be exited through an exception. If that happened, **Nefarious**'s destructor (automatically invoked) might attempt to throw an exception as well, which would result in sudden death of your entire program via **std::terminate**. (See also Item 75.)

- *Classes with Nefarious members or bases are also hard to use safely:* **Nefarious**' poor behavior extends to any class of which **Nefarious** is a member or a base class.

- *You can't reliably create global or static Nefarious objects either:* Any exception its destructor might throw can't be caught.

- *You can't reliably create arrays of* **Nefarious**: In short, the behavior of arrays is undefined in the presence of destructors that throw because there is no reasonable rollback behavior that could ever be devised. (Just think: What code can the compiler generate for constructing an array of ten **Nefarious** objects where, if the fourth object's constructor throws, the code has to give up and in its cleanup mode tries to call the destructors of the already-constructed objects… and one or more of those destructors throws? There is no satisfactory answer.)
- *You can't use* **Nefarious** *objects in standard containers:* You can't store **Nefarious** objects in standard containers or use them with any other part of the standard library. The standard library forbids all destructors used with it from throwing.

Deallocation functions, including specifically overloaded **operator delete** and **operator delete[]**, fall into the same category, because they too are used during cleanup in general, and during exception handling in particular, to back out of partial work that needs to be undone.

Besides destructors and deallocation functions, common error-safety techniques rely also on swap operations never failing—in this case, not because they are used to implement a guaranteed rollback, but because they are used to implement a guaranteed commit. For example, here is an idiomatic implementation of **operator=** for a type **T** that performs copy construction followed by a call to a no-fail **Swap**:

```
T& T::operator=( const T& other ) {
  T temp( other );
  Swap( temp );
}
```

(See also Item 56.)

Fortunately, when releasing a resource, the scope for failure is definitely smaller. If using exceptions as the error reporting mechanism, make sure such functions handle all exceptions and other errors that their internal processing might generate. (For exceptions, simply wrap everything sensitive that your destructor does in a **try/catch(...)** block.) This is particularly important because a destructor might be called in a crisis situation, such as failure to allocate a system resource (e.g., memory, files, locks, ports, windows, or other system objects).

When using exceptions as your error handling mechanism, prefer documenting this behavior by declaring these functions with a commented empty exception specification of */* throw() */*. (See Item 75.)

References

[C++03] §15.2(3), §17.4.4.8(3) • *[Meyers96] §11* • *[Stroustrup00] §14.4.7, §E.2-4* • *[Sutter00] §8, §16* • *[Sutter02] §18-19*

52. Copy and destroy consistently.

Summary

What you create, also clean up: If you define any of the copy constructor, copy assignment operator, or destructor, you might need to define one or both of the others.

Discussion

If you need to define any of these three functions, it means you need it to do more than its default behavior—and the three are asymmetrically interrelated. Here's how:

- *If you write/disable either the copy constructor or the copy assignment operator, you probably need to do the same for the other:* If one does "special" work, probably so should the other because the two functions should have similar effects. (See Item 53, which expands on this point in isolation.)

- *If you explicitly write the copying functions, you probably need to write the destructor:* If the "special" work in the copy constructor is to allocate or duplicate some resource (e.g., memory, file, socket), you need to deallocate it in the destructor.

- *If you explicitly write the destructor, you probably need to explicitly write or disable copying:* If you have to write a nontrivial destructor, it's often because you need to manually release a resource that the object held. If so, it is likely that those resources require careful duplication, and then you need to pay attention to the way objects are copied and assigned, or disable copying completely.

In many cases, holding properly encapsulated resources using RAII "owning" objects can eliminate the need to write these operations yourself. (See Item 13.)

Prefer compiler generated special members; only these can be classified as "trivial," and at least one major STL vendor heavily optimizes for classes having trivial special members. This is likely to become common practice.

Exceptions

When any of the special functions are declared only to make them private or virtual, but without special semantics, it doesn't imply that the others are needed.

In rare cases, classes that have members of strange types (e.g., references, **std::auto_ptr**s) are an exception because they have peculiar copy semantics. In a class holding a reference or an **auto_ptr**, you likely need to write the copy constructor and the assignment operator, but the default destructor already does the right thing. (Note that using a reference or **auto_ptr** member is almost always wrong.)

References

[Cline99] §30.01-14 • [Koenig97] §4 • [Stroustrup00] §5.5, §10.4 • [SuttHysl04b]

53. Explicitly enable or disable copying.

Summary

Copy consciously: Knowingly choose among using the compiler-generated copy constructor and assignment operator, writing your own versions, or explicitly disabling both if copying should not be allowed.

Discussion

A common mistake (and not only among beginners) is to forget to think about copy and assignment semantics when defining a class. This happens often with small helper classes such as those meant for RAII support (see Item 13).

Ensure that your class provides sensible copying, or none at all. The choices are:

- *Explicitly disable both:* If copying doesn't make sense for your type, disable both copy construction and copy assignment by declaring them as private unimplemented functions:

  ```
  class T { // ...
  private:                        // make T non-copyable
    T( const T& );                // not implemented
    T& operator=( const T& );     // not implemented
  };
  ```

- *Explicitly write both:* If copying and copy assignment is warranted for **T** objects, but correct copying behavior differs from what the compiler-generated versions will do, then write the functions yourself and make them nonprivate.

- *Use the compiler-generated versions, preferably with an explicit comment:* Otherwise, if copying makes sense and the default behavior is correct, don't declare them yourself and just let the compiler-generated versions kick in. Prefer to comment that the default behavior is correct, so that readers of your code will know that you didn't miss one of the other two options by accident.

Note that disabling copying and copy assignment means that you cannot put **T** objects into standard containers. That's not necessarily a bad thing; very likely, you wouldn't want to hold such **T** objects in a container anyway. (You can still put them in containers by holding them via a smart pointer; see Item 79.)

Bottom line: Be proactive about these two operations because the compiler has the tendency to generously generate them, and the compiler-generated versions are often unsafe by default for non-value-like types. (See also Item 32.)

References

[Dewhurst03] §88 • [Meyers97] §11 • [Stroustrup00] §11.2.2

54. Avoid slicing. Consider Clone instead of copying in base classes.

Summary

Sliced bread is good; sliced objects aren't: Object slicing is automatic, invisible, and likely to bring wonderful polymorphic designs to a screeching halt. In base classes, consider disabling the copy constructor and copy assignment operator, and instead supplying a virtual **Clone** member function if clients need to make polymorphic (complete, deep) copies.

Discussion

When you build class hierarchies, usually the intent is to get polymorphic behavior. You want objects, once created, to preserve their type and identity. This goal conflicts with C++'s usual object copy semantics because the copy constructor is not virtual and cannot be made virtual. Consider:

```cpp
class B { /* ... */ };
class D : public B { /* ... */ };

void Transmogrify( B obj );          // oops: takes an object by value
void Transubstantiate( B& obj ) {    // ok: takes a reference
  Transmogrify( obj );               // oops: slices the object
  // ...
}

D d;
Transubstantiate( d );
```

The programmer's intent is to manipulate **B** and **B**-derived objects polymorphically. However, by mistake (fatigue? too little caffeine?) the programmer either forgot to write an **&** in **Transmogrify**'s signature, or intended to create a copy but did it the wrong way. The code will compile fine, but when **Transmogrify** is called the passed-in **D** object will, well, transmogrify into a **B**. This is because a by-value pass involves a call to **B::B(const B&)**, that is, **B**'s copy constructor, and the **const B&** passed in will be the automatically converted reference to **d**. Wiping away all the dynamic, polymorphic behavior that prompted you to use inheritance in the first place is most likely what you don't want.

If as the author of **B** you do want to allow slicing, but you don't want callers to slice easily or by accident, here's one option we mention for completeness but do not recommend in code that needs to be portable: You can make **B**'s copy constructor **explicit**. This can help avoid implicit slicing, but it also prevents all pass-by-value (this can be good for base classes, which shouldn't be instantiable anyway; see Item 35):

```
// Making the copy constructor explicit (has side effects, needs improvement)
class B { // ...
public:
  explicit B( const B& rhs );
};

class D : public B { /* ... */ };
```

Calling code can still slice if it really wants to, but has to be, well, explicit about it:

```
void Transmogrify( B obj );              // note: now can't ever be called (!)

void Transmogrify2( const B& obj ) { // an idiom to explicitly say "I want to take
  B b( obj );                            // obj by value anyway (and possibly slice it)"
  // ...
}

B b;                                     // base classes shouldn't be concrete (see
D d;                                     // Item 35), but let's imagine that B is

Transmogrify( b );                       // now an error (or should be; see note)
Transmogrify( d );                       // now an error (or should be; see note)
Transmogrify2( d );                      // ok
```

Note: As of this writing, some compilers incorrectly accept one or both of these calls to **Transmogrify**. This idiom is standard, but it's not (yet) completely portable.

There is a better way that portably achieves the goal of preventing slicing and delivers more value to boot. Let's say that functions like **Transmogrify** really do want to take a full deep copy without knowing the actual derived type of the object it's being given. The more general idiomatic solution is to make the copy constructor for base classes **protected** (so that a function like **Transmogrify** won't call it accidentally) and rely on a virtual **Clone** function instead:

```
// Adding Clone (first cut, better but still needs improvement)
class B { // ...
public:
  virtual B* Clone() const = 0;

protected:
  B( const B& );
};
```

```
class D : public B { // ...
public:
  virtual D* Clone() const { return new D(*this); }

protected:
  D( const D& rhs ) : B( rhs ) { /* ... */ }
};
```

Now, trying to slice will (portably) generate a compile-time error, and making **Clone** a pure virtual function forces immediately-derived classes to override it. Unfortunately, this solution still has two problems that the compiler cannot detect: A further-derived class in the hierarchy can still forget to implement **Clone**, and an override of **Clone** could implement it improperly so that the copy is not the same type as the original. **Clone** should apply the Nonvirtual Interface pattern (NVI; see Item 39), which separates **Clone**'s **public** and **virtual** natures and lets you plant a valuable assertion:

```
class B { // ...
public:
  B* Clone() const {                                      // nonvirtual
    B* p = DoClone();
    assert( typeid(*p) == typeid(*this) && "DoClone incorrectly overridden" );
    return p;                                  // check DoClone's returned type
  }

protected:
  B( const B& );

private:
  virtual B* DoClone() const = 0;
};
```

Clone is now the nonvirtual interface used by all calling code. Derived classes only need to override **DoClone**. The **assert** will flag any copy that doesn't have the same type as the original, thus signaling that some derived class forgot to override the **DoClone** function; **assert**s are, after all, to report such programming errors (see Items 68 and 70).

Exceptions

Some designs might require that the copy constructors of base classes are left public (e.g., when part of your hierarchy is a third-party library). In that case, prefer passing by (smart) pointer to passing by reference; as Item 25 shows, passing by pointer is much less vulnerable to slicing and unwanted temporary construction.

References

[Dewhurst03] §30, §76, §94 • [Meyers96] §13 • [Meyers97] §22 • [Stroustrup94] §11.4.4 • [Stroustrup00] §12.2.3

55. Prefer the canonical form of assignment.

Summary

Your assignment: When implementing **operator=**, prefer the canonical form—nonvirtual and with a specific signature.

Discussion

Prefer to declare copy assignment for a type **T** with one of the following signatures (see [Stroustrup00] and [Alexandrescu03a]):

```
T& operator=( const T& );        // classic
T& operator=( T );               // potentially optimizer-friendly (see Item 27)
```

Settle for the second version if you would need to make a copy of the argument inside your operator anyway, such as the **swap**-based idiom featured in Item 56.

Avoid making any assignment operator virtual (see [Meyers96] §33 and [Sutter04] §19). If you think you need virtual behavior for assignment, reread those citations first. If that doesn't dissuade you and you still think you need virtual assignment, prefer to provide a named function instead (e.g., **virtual void Assign(const T&);**).

Don't return **const T&**. Although this has the benefit of preventing odd code like **(a=b)=c**, it has the drawback that you wouldn't be able to put **T** objects into standard library containers; the containers require that assignment return a plain **T&**.

Always make copy assignment error-safe, and prefer to provide the strong guarantee. (See Item 71.)

Ensure the assignment operator is safe for self-assignment. Avoid writing a copy assignment operator that relies on a check for self-assignment in order to work properly; often, that reveals a lack of error safety. If you write the copy assignment operator using the swap idiom (see Item 56), it will automatically be both strongly error-safe and safe for self-assignment; if self-assignment is frequent due to reference aliasing or other reasons, it's okay to still check for self-assignment anyway as an optimization check to avoid needless work.

Explicitly invoke all base assignment operators and assign all data members ([Meyers97] §16); note that swapping automatically take cares of all these things. Return ***this** ([Meyers97] §15).

References

[Alexandrescu03a] • *[Cargill92] pp41-42, 95* • *[Cline99] §24.01-12* • *[Koenig97] §4* • *[Meyers96] §33* • *[Meyers97] §17* • *[Murray93] §2.2.1* • *[Stroustrup00] §10.4.4.1, §10.4.6.3* • *[Sutter00] §13, §38, §41* • *[Sutter04] §19*

56. Whenever it makes sense, provide a no-fail swap (and provide it correctly).

Summary

swap is both a lightweight and a workhorse: Consider providing a **swap** function to efficiently and infallibly swap the internals of this object with another's. Such a function can be handy for implementing a number of idioms, from smoothly moving objects around to implementing assignment easily to providing a guaranteed commit function that enables strongly error-safe calling code. (See also Item 51.)

Discussion

A **swap** function typically looks like this, where **U** is some user-defined type:

```
class T { // ...
public:
  void swap( T& rhs ) {
    member1_.swap( rhs.member1_ );
    std::swap( member2_, rhs.member2_ );
  }
private:
  U member1_;
  int member2_;
};
```

For primitive types and for standard containers, **std::swap** will do. Other classes might implement swapping as a member function under various names.

Consider using **swap** to implement copy assignment in terms of copy construction. The following implementation of **operator=** provides the strong guarantee (see Item 71), although at the price of creating an extra object, which can be inappropriate if there are more efficient ways to perform error-safe assignment for **T** objects:

```
T& T::operator=( const T& other ) {   // good: Variant #1 (traditional)
  T temp( other );
  swap( temp );
  return *this;
}

T& T::operator=( T temp ) {           // good: Variant #2 (see Item 27)
  swap( temp );                       // note: temp passed by value
  return *this;
}
```

What if **U** does not implement a no-fail swap function, as is the case with many legacy classes, and you still need **T** to support a swap function? All is not lost:

- If **U**'s copy constructor and copy assignment don't fail (as, again, might be the case with legacy classes), **std::swap** will work fine on **U** objects.
- If **U**'s copy constructor might fail, you can store a (smart) pointer to **U** instead of a direct member. Pointers are easily swappable. They do incur the additional overhead of one extra dynamic storage allocation and one extra access indirection, but if you store all such members in a single Pimpl object you'll incur the overhead only once for all private members. (See Item 43.)

Never use the trick of implementing copy assignment in terms of copy construction by using an explicit destructor followed by placement **new**, even though this trick still crops up regularly in C++ forums. (See also Item 99.) That is, never write:

```
T& T::operator=( const T& rhs ) {          // bad: an anti-idiom
  if( this != &rhs ) {
    this->~T();                            // this technique is evil
    new (this) T( rhs );                   // (see [Sutter00] §41)
  }
  return *this;
}
```

Prefer to provide a nonmember swap function in the same namespace as your type when objects of your type have a way to exchange their values more efficiently than via brute-force assignment, such as if they have their own **swap** or equivalent function (see Item 57). Additionally, consider specializing **std::swap** for your own nontemplate types:

```
namespace std {
  template<> void swap( MyType& lhs, MyType& rhs) {     // for MyType objects,
    lhs.swap( rhs );                                     // use MyType::swap
  }
}
```

The standard does not allow you to do this when **MyType** is itself a template class. Fortunately, this specialization is just a nice-to-have; the primary technique is to provide a type-customized swap as a nonmember in the same namespace as the type.

Exceptions

Swapping is valuable for classes with value semantics. It is less often useful for base classes because you use those classes through pointers anyway. (See Items 32 and 54.)

References

[C++03] §17.4.3.1(1) • [Stroustrup00] §E.3.3 • [Sutter00] §12-13, §41

Namespaces and Modules

Systems have sub-systems and sub-systems have sub-systems
and so on ad infinitum—which is why we're always starting over.

—Alan Perlis

The namespace is an important tool for managing names and reducing name collisions. So is a module, which is additionally an important tool for managing releases and versioning. We define a module as any cohesive unit of release (see Item 5) maintained by the same person or team; typically, a module is also consistently compiled with the same compiler and switch settings. Modules exist at many levels of granularity that range widely in size; a module can be as small as a single object file that delivers a single class, to a single shared or dynamic library generated from multiple source files whose contents form a subsystem inside a larger application or are released independently, to as large as a huge library composed of many smaller modules (e.g., shared libraries, DLLs, or other libraries) and containing thousands of types. Even though such entities as shared libraries and dynamic libraries are not mentioned directly in the C++ Standard, C++ programmers routinely build and use libraries, and good modularization is a fundamental part of successful dependency management (see for example Item 11).

It's hard to imagine a program of any significant size that doesn't use both namespaces and modules. In this section, we cover basic guidelines on using these two related management and bundling tools with a view to how they interact well or badly with the rest of the C++ language and run-time environment. These rules and guidelines show how to maximize the "well" and avoid the "badly."

Our vote for the most valuable Item in this section goes to Item 58: Keep types and functions in separate namespaces unless they're specifically intended to work together.

57. Keep a type and its nonmember function interface in the same namespace.

Summary

Nonmembers are functions too: Nonmember functions that are designed to be part of the interface of a class **X** (notably operators and helper functions) must be defined in the same namespace as the **X** in order to be called correctly.

Discussion

Both public member functions and nonmember functions form part of the public interface of a class. The Interface Principle states: For a class **X**, all functions (including nonmember functions) that both "mention" **X** and are "supplied with" **X** in the same namespace are logically part of **X**, because they form part of **X**'s interface. (See Item 44 and [Sutter00].)

The C++ language is explicitly designed to enforce the Interface Principle. The reason why argument-dependent lookup (ADL, also known as Koenig lookup) was added to the language was to ensure that code that uses an object **x** of type **X** can use its nonmember function interface (e.g., **cout << x**, which invokes the nonmember **operator<<** for **X**) as easily as it can use member functions (e.g., **x.f()**, which requires no special lookup because **f** is clearly to be looked up in the scope of **X**). ADL ensures that nonmember functions that take **X** objects and that are supplied with **X**'s definition can participate as first-class members of **X**'s interface, just like **X**'s direct member functions naturally do.

In particular, the primary motivating example for ADL was the case where **X** is **std::string** (see [Sutter00]).

Consider a class **X**, defined in namespace **N**:

```
class X {
public:
  void f();
};

X operator+( const X&, const X& );
```

Callers will typically want to write code like this, where **x1**, **x2**, and **x3** are objects of type **X**:

```
x3 = x1 + x2;
```

If the **operator+** is declared in the same namespace as **X**, there's no problem, and such code always just works, because the supplied **operator+** will be looked up using ADL.

If the **operator+** is not declared in the same namespace as **X**, the caller's code fails to work. The caller has two workarounds to make it work. The first is to use explicit qualification:

```
x3 = N::operator+( x1, x2 );
```

This is deplorable and shameful because it requires the user to give up natural operator syntax, which is the point of operator overloading in the first place. The only other option is to write a **using** statement:

```
using N::operator+;
// or: using namespace N;

x3 = x1 + x2;
```

Writing either of the indicated **using** statements is perfectly acceptable (see Item 59), but the caller doesn't have to jump through these hoops when the author of **X** does the right thing and puts **operator+** for **X** objects into the same namespace as **X**.

For the flip side of this issue, see Item 58.

Examples

Example 1: Operators. The streaming **operator<<** and **operator>>** for objects of some class type **X** are perhaps the most compelling examples of functions that are clearly part of the interface of the class **X**, but which are always nonmember functions (this is of necessity, because the left-hand argument is a stream, not an **X**). The same argument applies to other nonmember operators on **X** objects. Make sure that your operators appear in the same namespace as the class on which they operate. When you have the option, prefer making operators and all other functions nonmember nonfriends (see Item 44).

Example 2: Other functions. If the author of **X** supplies named helper functions that take **X** objects, they should be supplied in the same namespace, otherwise calling code that uses **X** objects will not be able to use the named functions without explicit qualification or a **using** statement.

References

[Stroustrup00] §8.2, §10.3.2, §11.2.4 • [Sutter00] §31-34

58. Keep types and functions in separate namespaces unless they're specifically intended to work together.

Summary

Help prevent name lookup accidents: Isolate types from unintentional argument-dependent lookup (ADL, also known as Koenig lookup), and encourage intentional ADL, by putting them in their own namespaces (along with their directly related nonmember functions; see Item 57). Avoid putting a type into the same namespace as a templated function or operator.

Discussion

By following this advice, you will avoid having to track down hard-to-diagnose errors in your code and avoid having to know about excessively subtle language details that you, well, should never have to know about.

Consider this actual example that was posted publicly to a newsgroup:

```
#include <vector>

namespace N {
  struct X { };

  template<typename T>
  int* operator+( T , unsigned ) { /* do something */ }
}

int main() {
  std::vector<N::X> v(5);
  v[0] ;
}
```

The statement **v[0];** compiles on some standard library implementations but not on others. To make a very long story moderately less long (take a deep breath): The exceedingly subtle problem is that inside most implementations of **vector<T>::operator[]** lurks code like **v.begin() + n**, and the name lookup for that **operator+** function *might* reach out into the namespace (here **N**) of the type that **vector** is instantiated with (here **X**). Whether it reaches out into **N** like that depends on how **vector<T>::iterator** happens to be defined in that release of that standard library implementation—but if it does look into **N**, then it will find **N::operator+**. Finally, depending on the types involved, the compiler might just discover that **N::operator+** is a better match than the **std::operator+** for **vector<T>::iterator**s that was provided (and intended to be called) in that standard library implementation. (One way that the standard library implementation could protect itself from this is to not write code like **v.begin() + n** in that way, which injects an unintentional point of customization: Either arrange for **v.begin()**'s type to not depend in any way on the template parameter, or rewrite the call to **operator+** as a qualified call. See Item 65.)

In short, you'll almost certainly never figure out what's going on from the error message—if you're lucky enough to get an error message, that is, because you might happen to hit the worst of all possible worlds where **N::operator+** is chosen but unfortunately turns out to be compilable, although completely unintended and wildly wrong.

If you think you haven't been bit by this, just think back: Can you remember a time when you wrote code that used the standard library (for example) and got mysterious and incomprehensible compiler errors? And you kept slightly rearranging your code and recompiling, and rearranging some more and compiling some more, until the mysterious compile errors went away, and then you happily continued on—with at best a faint nagging curiosity about why the compiler didn't like the only-ever-so-slightly different arrangement of the code you wrote at first? We've all had those days, and the odds are decent that the mystery culprit was some form of the aforementioned problem, where ADL pulled in names from other namespaces inappropriately just because types from those namespaces were being used nearby.

This problem is not unique to uses of the standard library. It can and does happen in C++ with the use of any type that is defined in the same namespace as functions—especially templated functions, and most especially operators—that aren't specifically related to that type. Don't do that.

Bottom line: You shouldn't have to know this stuff. The easiest way to avoid this whole category of problems is to in general avoid putting nonmember functions that are not part of the interface of a type **X** into the same namespace as **X**, and especially never ever put templated functions or operators into the same namespace as a user-defined type.

Note: Yes, the C++ standard library puts algorithms and other function templates, such as **copy** and **distance**, into the same namespace as lots of types, such as **pair** and **vector**. It puts *everything* into a single namespace. That's unfortunate, and it causes exactly these kinds of very subtle problems. We know better now. Learn from the past. Don't do that.

For the flip side of this issue, see Item 57.

References

[Stroustrup00] §10.3.2, §11.2.4 • [Sutter00] §34 • [Sutter02] §39-40

59. Don't write namespace usings in a header file or before an #include.

Summary

Namespace **using**s are for your convenience, not for you to inflict on others: Never write a **using** declaration or a **using** directive before an **#include** directive.

Corollary: In header files, don't write namespace-level **using** directives or **using** declarations; instead, explicitly namespace-qualify all names. (The second rule follows from the first, because headers can never know what other header **#include**s might appear after them.)

Discussion

In short: You can and should use namespace **using** declarations and directives liberally *in your implementation files after* **#include** *directives* and feel good about it. Despite repeated assertions to the contrary, namespace **using** declarations and directives are not evil and they do not defeat the purpose of namespaces. Rather, they are what make namespaces usable.

Namespaces deliver the powerful advantage of unambiguous name management. Most of the time, different programmers don't choose the very same name for a type or function; but on the off chance that they do so, and that the two pieces of code end up being used together, having those names in separate namespaces prevents them from colliding. (We don't, after all, want the global namespace pollution experienced by default in languages like C.) In the rare case when there is such an actual ambiguity, calling code can explicitly qualify a name to say which one it wants. But the vast majority of the time there is no ambiguity: And that is why namespace **using** declarations and directives are what make namespaces usable, because they greatly reduce code clutter by freeing you from having to tediously qualify every name every time (which would be onerous, and frankly people just won't put up with it) and still letting you qualify names only in those rare cases when you need to resolve an actual ambiguity.

But **using** declarations and directives are for your coding convenience, and you shouldn't use them in a way that affects someone else's code. In particular, don't write them anywhere they could be followed by someone else's code: Specifically, don't write them in header files (which are meant to be included in an unbounded number of implementation files, and you shouldn't mess with the meaning of that other code) or before an **#include** (you really don't want to mess with the meaning of code in someone else's header).

Most people understand viscerally why a **using** directive (e.g., **using namespace A;**) causes pollution when it can affect code that follows and that isn't aware of it: Because it imports one namespace wholesale into another, including even those names that haven't been seen yet, it's fairly obvious that it can easily change the meaning of code that follows.

But here's the common trap: Many people think that **using** *declarations* issued at namespace level (for example, **using N::Widget;**) are safe. They are not. They are at least as dangerous, and in a subtler and more insidious way. Consider:

```
// snippet 1
namespace A {
  int f(double);
}

// snippet 2
namespace B {
  using A::f;
  void g();
}

// snippet 3
namespace A {
  int f(int);
}

// snippet 4
void B::g() {
  f(1);                          // which overload is called?
}
```

The dangerous thing happening here is that the **using** declaration *takes a snapshot* of whatever entities named **f** in namespace **A** have been seen by the time the **using** declaration is encountered. So, from within **B**, which overloads are visible depends on where these code snippets exist and in what order they are combined. (At this point, your internal "but order dependencies are evil!" klaxon should be blaring.) The second overload, **f(int)**, would be a better match for the call **f(1)**, but **f(int)** will be invisible to **B::g** if its declaration comes after the **using** declaration.

Consider two specific cases. First, let's say that snippets 1, 2, and 3 are in three distinct header files **s1.h**, **s2.h**, and **s3.h**, and snippet 4 in an implementation file **s4.cpp** that includes those header files to pull the relevant declarations. Then, we have an unfortunate phenomenon: The semantics of **B::g** depends on the *order* in which the headers were included in **s4.cpp**! In particular:

- If **s3.h** comes before **s2.h**, **B::g** will call **A::f(int)**.
- Else if **s1.h** comes before **s2.h**, **B::g** will call **A::f(double)**.
- Else **B::g** won't compile at all.

At least in the preceding case, there's still one well-defined order, and the answer will be exactly one of the three listed alternatives.

But now it gets much worse: Let's instead say that snippets 1, 2, 3, and 4 are in four distinct header files **s1.h**, **s2.h**, **s3.h**, and **s4.h**. Now life is even more unfortunate: The semantics of **B::g** depends on the order in which the headers were included, not only in **s4.h** itself, but in any code that includes **s4.h**! In particular, an implementation file **client_code.cpp** might try to include the headers in any order:

- If **s3.h** comes before **s2.h**, **B::g** will call **A::f(int)**.
- Else if **s1.h** comes before **s2.h**, **B::g** will call **A::f(double)**.
- Else **B::g** won't compile at all.

This is worse because two implementation files can include the headers *in different orders*. Consider what happens if **client_code_1.cpp** includes **s1.h**, **s2.h**, and **s4.h** in that order, but **client_code_2.cpp** includes **s3.h**, **s2.h**, and **s4.h** in that order. Then, **B::g** violates the One Definition Rule (ODR) because it has two inconsistent and incompatible implementations that can't both be right—one that tries to call **A::f(int)** and one that tries to call **A::f(double)**.

So don't write namespace **using** declarations or **using** directives in a header file, or before an **#include** directive in an implementation file. You are liable to affect the meaning of later code by causing namespace pollution, by taking an incomplete snapshot of the names that you want to import, or both. (Note the qualifier "*namespace* **using** declarations or **using** directives." This doesn't apply to writing class member **using** declarations to bring in base class member names as needed.)

In all headers, and in all implementation files before the last **#include**, always explicitly namespace-qualify all names. In implementation files after all **#include**s, you can and should write namespace **using** declarations and directives liberally. This is the right way to reconcile code brevity with modularity.

Exceptions

Migrating a large project from an old, pre-ANSI/ISO implementation of the standard library (one that puts all of its symbols in the global namespace) to an updated one (where most everything is in namespace **std**) might force you to carefully put a **using** directive in a header file. The way to do that is described in [Sutter02].

References

[Stroustrup00] §9.2.1 • [Sutter02] §39-40

60. Avoid allocating and deallocating memory in different modules.

Summary

Put things back where you found them: Allocating memory in one module and deallocating it in a different module makes your program fragile by creating a subtle long-distance dependency between those modules. They must be compiled with the same compiler version and same flags (notably debug vs. **NDEBUG**) and the same standard library implementation, and in practice the module allocating the memory had better still be loaded when the deallocation happens.

Discussion

Library writers want to improve the quality of their libraries, and as a direct consequence the internal data structures and algorithms used by the standard memory allocator can significantly vary from one version to the next. Furthermore, various compiler switches (e.g., turning debugging facilities on and off) can change the inner workings of the memory allocator significantly.

Therefore, make very few assumptions about deallocation functions (e.g., **::operator delete** or **std::free**) when you cross module boundaries—especially boundaries of modules that you can't guarantee will be compiled with the same C++ compiler and the same build options. Often, it is the case that various modules are in the same makefile and compiled with the same options, but comfort often leads to forgetfulness. Especially when it comes to dynamically linked libraries, large projects distributed across large teams, or the challenging "hot swapping" of modules, you should pay maximum attention to allocate and deallocate within the same module or subsystem.

A good way to ensure that deletion is performed by the appropriate function is to use the **shared_ptr** facility (see [C++TR104]). **shared_ptr** is a reference-counted smart pointer that can capture its "deleter" at construction time. The deleter is a function object (or a straight pointer to function) that performs deallocation. Because the said function object, or pointer to function, is part of the **shared_ptr** object's state, the module allocating the object can at the same time specify the deallocation function, and that function will be called correctly even if the point of deallocation is somewhere within another module—admittedly at a slight cost. (Correctness is worth the cost; see also Items 5, 6, and 8.) Of course, the original module must remain loaded.

References

[C++TR104]

61. Don't define entities with linkage in a header file.

Summary

Repetition causes bloat: Entities with linkage, including namespace-level variables or functions, have memory allocated for them. Defining such entities in header files results in either link-time errors or memory waste. Put all entities with linkage in implementation files.

Discussion

While starting to use C++, we all learn quite quickly that header files like

```
// avoid defining entities with external linkage in a header
int fudgeFactor;
string hello("Hello, world!");
void foo() { /* ... */ }
```

are liable to cause link-time errors complaining of duplicate symbols as soon as such a header is included by more than one source file. The reason is simple: Each source file actually defines and allocates space for **fudgeFactor** and **hello** and **foo**'s body, and when the time comes to put it all together (linking), the linker is faced with several symbols bearing the same name and competing for visibility.

The solution is simple—put just the declarations in the header:

```
extern int fudgeFactor;
extern string hello;
void foo();                    // "extern" is optional with function declarations
```

The actual definitions go in a single implementation file:

```
int fudgeFactor;
string hello("Hello, world!");
void foo() { /* ... */ }
```

Also, do not define namespace-level **static** entities in a header. For example:

```
// avoid defining entities with static linkage in a header
static int fudgeFactor;
static string hello("Hello, world!");
static void foo() { /* ... */ }
```

Such misuse of **static** is more dangerous than just defining global entities in the header. With global entities, at least the linker is liable to promptly uncover the duplication. But static data and functions are legal to duplicate because the compiler recognizes that you are asking for a private copy in each source file. So, if you define static data and static functions in a header and include that header in 50 files, the bodies of the functions and the space for the data will be duplicated 50 times in the final executable code (except in the presence of some modern linkers that merge together identical function bodies and **const** data when such merging is safe). Needless to say, global data (such as the static **fudgeFactor**) is not really global because each source file ends up manipulating its own copy, independent of all other copies in the program.

Don't try to get around this by (ab)using unnamed namespaces in header files because the effects would be just as unpleasant:

```
// in a header file, this is just as bad as static
namespace {
  int fudgeFactor;
  string hello("Hello, world!");
  void foo() { /* ... */ }
}
```

Exceptions

The following entities with external linkage can go in header files:

- *Inline functions:* These have external linkage, but the linker is guaranteed not to reject multiple copies. Other than that, they behave exactly like regular functions. In particular, the address of an inline function is guaranteed to be unique throughout a program.

- *Function templates:* Similar to inline functions, instantiations behave just like regular functions except that duplicate copies are acceptable (and had better be identical). Of course, a good compilation framework eliminates the unnecessary copies.

- *Static data members of class templates:* These can be particularly rough on the linker, but that's not your problem—you just define them in your header file and let your compiler and linker deal with it.

Also, a global data initialization technique known as "Schwarz counters" or "nifty counters" prescribes planting static (or unnamed-namespace) data in a header file. Jerry Schwarz made the technique popular by using it to initialize the standard I/O streams **cin**, **cout**, **cerr**, and **clog**.

References

[Dewhurst03] §55 • [Ellis90] §3.3 • [Stroustrup00] §9.2, §9.4.1

62. Don't allow exceptions to propagate across module boundaries.

Summary

Don't throw stones into your neighbor's garden: There is no ubiquitous binary standard for C++ exception handling. Don't allow exceptions to propagate between two pieces of code unless you control the compiler and compiler options used to build both sides; otherwise, the modules might not support compatible implementations for exception propagation. Typically, this boils down to: Don't let exceptions propagate across module/subsystem boundaries.

Discussion

The C++ Standard does not specify the way exception propagation has to be implemented, and there isn't even a *de facto* standard respected by most systems. The mechanics of exception propagation vary not only with the operating system and compiler used, but also with the compiler options used to build each module of your application with a given compiler on a given operating system. Therefore, an application must prevent exception handling incompatibilities by shielding the boundaries of each of its major modules, meaning each unit for which the developer can ensure that the same compiler and options are consistently used.

At a minimum, your application must have catch-all **catch(...)** seals in the following places, most of which apply directly to modules:

- *Around **main**:* Catch and log any otherwise uncaught exception that's about to end your program ignominiously.

- *Around callbacks from code you don't control:* Operating systems and libraries offer frameworks in which you pass a pointer to a function to be invoked later (e.g., when an asynchronous event occurs). Don't allow exceptions to propagate out of your callback, because it's very possible that the code invoking your callback does not use the same exception handling mechanism. For that matter, it might not even have been written in C++.

- *Around thread boundaries:* Ultimately, a thread is created from within the bowels of the operating system. Make sure your thread mainline function doesn't surprise the system by passing it an exception.

- *Around module interface boundaries:* Your subsystem will expose some public interface for the rest of the world to use. If the subsystem is packaged as a separate library, prefer to confine exceptions inside and use ye olde staid-but-stable error codes for signaling errors to the outer world. (See Item 72.)

- *Inside destructors:* Destructors don't throw (see Item 51). Destructors that call functions that might throw exceptions need to protect themselves against leaking those exceptions.

Ensure that each module consistently uses a single error handling strategy internally (preferably C++ exceptions; see Item 72) and a single error handling strategy in its interface (e.g., error codes for a C API); the two might happen to be the same, but they usually aren't. Error handling strategies change only on module boundaries. Make clear how to interface the strategies between modules (e.g., how to interact with COM or CORBA, or to always catch exceptions at a C API boundary). A good solution is to define central functions that translate between exceptions and error codes returned by a subsystem. This way, you can easily translate incoming errors from peer modules into your internally used exceptions and ease integration.

Using two strategies instead of one may sound like overkill and you might be tempted to forgo exceptions and only use the good old error codes throughout. But don't forget that exception handling has real ease-of-use and robustness advantages, is idiomatic C++, and can't be avoided in nontrivial C++ programs (because the standard language and library throw exceptions), so you should prefer to use exception handling when you can. For more details, see Item 72.

A word of caution: Some operating systems use the C++ exception mechanism to piggyback low-level, system-specific errors, such as dereferencing a null pointer. Consequently, a **catch(...)** clause can catch more things than just straight C++ exceptions, and so your program might be in a twilight zone by the time the **catch(...)** is executing. Consult your system's documentation and either be prepared for handling such low-level exceptions in the smartest way you can devise, or use system-specific calls to disable such piggybacking at the start of your application. Replacing **catch(...)** with a series of **catch(E1&) { /*...*/ } catch(E2&) { /*...*/ } ... catch(E*n*&) { /*...*/ }** for each known base exception type **E*i*** is not a scalable solution because you'd need to update the caught list whenever you add a new library (using its own exception hierarchy) to your application.

Using **catch(...)** in places other than those listed in this Item is often a sign of bad design, because it means you are eager to catch absolutely all exceptions without necessarily having specific knowledge about how to handle them (see Item 74). A good program doesn't have many catch-alls and, indeed, not many **try**/**catch** statements at all; ideally, errors are propagated smoothly throughout, translated across module boundaries (a necessary evil), and handled at strategically placed boundaries.

References

[Stroustrup00] §3.7.2, §14.7 • [Sutter00] §8-17 • [Sutter02] §17-23 • [Sutter04] §11-13

63. Use sufficiently portable types in a module's interface.

Summary

Take extra care when living on the edge (of a module): Don't allow a type to appear in a module's external interface unless you can ensure that all clients understand the type correctly. Use the highest level of abstraction that clients can understand.

Discussion

The more widely distributed your library, and the less control you have over the build environment of all of its clients, the fewer the types that the library can reliably use in its external interface. Interfacing across modules involves binary data exchange. Alas, C++ doesn't specify standard binary interfaces; widely distributed libraries in particular might need to rely on built-in types like **int** and **char** to interface with the outer world. Even compiling the same type using different build options on the same compiler can cause binary-incompatible versions of the type.

Typically, either you control the compiler and options used to build the module and all its clients, and you can use any type—or you don't, and you can use only platform-provided types and C++ built-in types (even then, document the size and representation you expect for the latter). In particular, never mention standard library types in the interface of a module unless all other modules that use it will be compiled at the same time and with the same standard library source image.

There is a tradeoff between the problems of using types that can't be correctly understood by all clients, and the problems of using a low level of abstraction. Abstraction is important; if some clients understand only low-level types, and you must therefore use those, consider also supplying alternate operations that use higher-level types. Consider a **SummarizeFile** function that takes the file to be processed as a parameter. There are three common options for the parameter: It can be a **char*** that points to a C-style string containing the file's name; a **string** that contains the file's name; or an **istream** or a custom **File** object. Each of these choices is a tradeoff:

- *Option 1: **char***.* Clearly the **char*** type is accessible to the widest audience of clients. Unfortunately, it is also the lowest-level option; in particular, it is less robust (e.g., the caller and callee must explicitly decide who allocates the memory and who deallocates it), more open to errors (e.g., the file might not exist), and less secure (e.g., to classic buffer overrun attacks).
- *Option 2: **string**.* The **string** type is accessible to the more restricted audience of clients that are written in C++ and compiled using the same standard library implementation, the same compiler, and compatible compiler settings. In exchange, it is more robust (e.g., callers and callees can be less explicit about

memory management; but see Item 60) and more secure (e.g., **string** grows its buffer as needed, and is not inherently as susceptible to buffer overrun attacks). But this option is still relatively low-level, and thus open to errors that have to be checked for explicitly (e.g., the file might not exist).

- *Option 3:* **istream** *or* **File**. If you're going to jump to class types anyway, thereby requiring clients to be written in C++ using the same compiler and switches, use a strong abstraction: An **istream** (or custom **File** object that wraps **istream** to avoid a direct dependency on one standard library implementation) raises the level of abstraction and makes the API much more robust. The function knows that it's getting a **File** or a suitable input stream, does not need to manage memory for string filenames, and is immune to many accidental and deliberate errors possible with the other options. Few checks remain: The **File** must be open, and the contents must be in the right format, but that's about all that can go wrong.

Even when you choose to use a lower-level abstraction in a module's external interface, always use the highest level of abstraction internally and translate to the lower-level abstraction at the module's boundary. For example, if you will have non-C++ clients, you might use opaque **void*** or **int** handles to client code, but still use objects internally, and cast only at the module's interface to translate between the two.

Examples

Example: Using **std::string** *in a module interface.* Say a module wants to provide this API:

    std::string Translate(const std::string&);

For libraries used internally in one team or company, this is usually fine. But if you need to dynamically link this module together with a caller that has a different implementation of **std::string** (sporting a different memory layout), strange things will happen because the client and the module can't understand each others' strings.

We have seen developers try to get around this by wrapping **std::string** with their own **CustomString**, only to be shocked when they continue to encounter the very same problem because they don't control the build process of all callers.

One solution is to rely on portable (probably built-in) types, either instead of or in addition to the function that takes a **string**. For example:

    void Translate(const char* src, char* dest, size_t destSize);

Using a lower-level abstraction is more portable, but always adds complexity; e.g., here, both the caller and the callee have to explicitly deal with possible truncation if the buffer is not big enough. (Note that this version uses a caller-allocated buffer to avoid the pitfall of allocating and deallocating memory in different modules; see Item 60.)

References

[McConnell93] §6 • [Meyers01] §15

Templates and Genericity

And likewise: Your intro here.

Our vote for the most valuable Item in this section goes to Item 64: Blend static and dynamic polymorphism judiciously.

64. Blend static and dynamic polymorphism judiciously.

Summary

So much more than a mere sum of parts: Static and dynamic polymorphism are complementary. Understand their tradeoffs, use each for what it's best at, and mix them to get the best of both worlds.

Discussion

Dynamic polymorphism comes in the form of classes with virtual functions and instances manipulated indirectly (through pointers or references). Static polymorphism involves template classes and template functions.

Polymorphism means that a given value can have more than one type, and a given function can accept arguments of types other than the exact types of its parameters. "Polymorphism is a way of gaining some of the freedom of dynamic type checking without giving up the benefits of static type checking." —[Webber03]

The strength of polymorphism is that the same piece of code can operate on different types, even types that were not known at the time the code was written. Such "post-hoc applicability" is the cornerstone of polymorphism because it amplifies the usefulness and reusability of code (see Item 37). (Contrast that with monomorphic code that rigidly operates only on the concrete types it was meant to work with.)

Dynamic polymorphism via public inheritance lets a value have more than one type. For example, a **Derived* p** can be viewed as a pointer not only to a **Derived**, but to an object of any type **Base** that's a direct or indirect base of **Derived** (the *subsumption* property). Dynamic polymorphism is also referred to as *inclusion polymorphism* because the set modeled by **Base** includes the specializations modeled by **Derived**.

Due to its characteristics, dynamic polymorphism in C++ is best at:

- *Uniform manipulation based on superset/subset relationships:* Different classes that hold a superset/subset (base/derived) relationship can be treated uniformly. A function that works on **Employee** objects works also on **Secretary** objects.
- *Static type checking:* All types are checked statically in C++.
- *Dynamic binding and separate compilation:* Code that uses classes in a hierarchy can be compiled apart from the code of the entire hierarchy. This is possible because of the indirection that pointers provide (both to objects and to functions).
- *Binary interfacing:* Modules can be linked either statically or dynamically, as long as the linked modules lay out the virtual tables the same way.

Static polymorphism via templates also lets a value have more than one type. Inside a **template<class T> void f(T t) { /*...*/ }**, t can have any type that can be substituted inside **f** to render compilable code. This is called an "implicit interface," in contrast to a base class's explicit interface. It achieves the same goal of polymorphism—writing code that operates on multiple types—but in a very different way.

Static polymorphism is best at:

- *Uniform manipulation based on syntactic and semantic interface:* Types that obey a syntactic and semantic interface can be treated uniformly. Interfaces are syntactic and implicit (not signature-based and explicit), and so allow any type substitution that fits a given syntax. For example, given the statement **int i = p->f(5)**: If **p** is a pointer to a **Base** class type, this calls a specific interface function, such as perhaps a **virtual int f(int)**. But if **p** is of a generic type, this call can bind to a myriad of things, including that it might invoke an overloaded **operator->** that returns a type defining the function **X f(double)** where **X** is convertible to **int**.

- *Static type checking:* All types are checked statically.

- *Static binding (prevents separate compilation):* All types are bound statically.

- *Efficiency:* Compile-time evaluation and static binding allow optimizations and efficiencies not available with dynamic binding.

Decide on your priorities, and use each type of polymorphism for its strengths.

Prefer to blend both kinds of polymorphism to combine their benefits while trying not to combine their drawbacks:

- *Static helps dynamic:* Use static polymorphism to implement dynamically polymorphic interfaces. For example, you might have an abstract base class **Command** and define various implementations as **template</*...*/> class ConcreteCommand : public Command**. Examples include implementing the Command and Visitor design patterns (see [Alexandrescu01] and [Sutter04]).

- *Dynamic helps static:* Offer a generic, comfortable, statically bound interface, but internally dispatch dynamically, so you offer a uniform object layout. Good examples are discriminated union implementations (see [Alexandrescu02b] and [Boost]) and **tr1::shared_ptr**'s **Deleter** parameter (see [C++TR104]).

- *Any other blend:* A bad blend that combines the weaknesses of both is worse than either alone; a good blend that combines the benefits of both is better than either alone. For example, don't put virtual functions into a class template unless you want *all* virtual functions to be instantiated every time (this is in sharp contrast to nonvirtual functions of templated types). The code size hit can be astronomical, and you may overconstrain your generic type by instantiating functionality that is never needed. The standard facets made this mistake. Don't make it again.

References

[Alexandrescu01] §10 • [Alexandrescu02b] • [C++TR104] • [Gamma95] • [Musser01] §1.2-3, §17 • [Stroustrup00] §24.4.1 • [Sutter00] §3 • [Sutter02] §1 • [Sutter04] §17, §35 • [Vandevoorde03] §14 • [Webber03] §8.6

65. Customize intentionally and explicitly.

Summary

Intentional is better than accidental, and explicit is better than implicit: When writing a template, provide points of customization knowingly and correctly, and document them clearly. When using a template, know how the template intends for you to customize it for use with your type, and customize it appropriately.

Discussion

A common pitfall when writing template libraries is providing *unintentional* points of customization—that is, points where a caller's code can get looked up and used inside your template, but you didn't mean for a caller's code to get involved. It's easy to do: Just call another function or operator the normal way (unqualified), and if one of its arguments happens to be of a template parameter type (or a related type) then ADL will pick it up. Examples abound: See Item 58 for an example.

Instead, be intentional: Know the three major ways to provide points of customization in a template, decide which one you want to use at a given point in your template, and code it correctly. Then, check to verify that that you didn't accidentally also code a customization hook in places where you didn't mean to.

The first way to provide a point of customization is the usual "implicit interface" (see Item 64) approach where your template simply relies on a type's having an appropriate member with a given name:

```
// Option 1: Provide a point of customization by requiring T to provide "foo-ability"
// as a member function with a given name, signature, and semantics.
template<typename T>
void Sample1( T t ) {
  t.foo();                  // foo is a point of customization

  typename T::value_type x; // another example: providing a point of custom-
}                           //   ization to look up a type (usually via typedef)
```

To implement Option 1, the author of **Sample1** must:

- *Call the function with member notation:* Just use the natural member syntax.
- *Document the point of customization:* The type must provide an accessible member function **foo** that can be called with given arguments (here, none).

The second option is to use the "implicit interface" method, but with a nonmember function that is looked up via argument-dependent lookup (i.e., it is expected to be in the namespace of the type with which the template is instantiated); this is a major motivation for the language's ADL feature (see Item 57). Your template is relying on a type's having an appropriate *non*member with a given name:

// Option 2: Provide a point of customization by requiring T to provide "foo-ability"
// as a nonmember function, typically looked up by ADL, with a given name, signature,
// and semantics. (This is the only option that doesn't also work to look up a type.)
```
template<typename T>
void Sample2( T t ) {
    foo( t );              // foo is a point of customization

    cout << t;             // another example: operator<< with operator nota-
}                          //   tion is the same kind of point of customization
```

To implement Option 2, the author of **Sample2** must:

- *Call the function with* unqualified *nonmember notation (including natural operator notation in the case of operators) and ensure the template itself doesn't have a member function with the same name:* It is essential for the template *not* to qualify the call to **foo** (e.g., don't write **SomeNamespace::foo(t)**) or to have its own member function of the same name, because either of those would turn off ADL and thus prevent name lookup from finding the function in the namespace of the type **T**.

- *Document the point of customization:* The type must provide a nonmember function **foo** that can be called with given arguments.

Options 1 and 2 have similar advantages and applicability: The user can write the customization function once for his type in a place where other template libraries could also pick it up, thus avoiding writing lots of little adapters, one for each template library. The corresponding drawback is that the semantics would have to be reasonably broadly applicable so as to make sense for all those potential uses. (Note that operators in particular fall into this category; this is another reason for Item 26.)

The third option is to use specialization, so that your template is relying on a type's having specialized (if necessary) another *class* template you provide:

// Option 3: Provide a point of customization by requiring T to provide "foo-ability"
// by specializing SampleTraits<> and provide a (typically static) function with a
// given name, signature, and semantics.
```
template<typename T>
void Sample3( T t ) {
    S3Traits<T>::foo( t );          // S3Traits<>::foo is a point of customization

    typename S3Traits<T>::value_type x; // another example: providing a point of custom-
}                                       //   ization to look up a type (usually via typedef)
```

In Option 3, making the user write an adapter ensures that custom code for this library is isolated inside this library. The corresponding drawback is that this can be cumbersome; if several template libraries need the same common functionality, the user has to write multiple adapters, one for each library.

To implement this option, the author of **Sample3** must:

- *Provide a default class template in the template's own namespace:* Don't use a function template, which can't be partially specialized and leads to overloads and order dependencies. (See also Item 66.)
- *Document the point of customization:* The user must specialize **S3Traits** in the template library's namespace for his own type, and document all of **S3Traits**'s members (e.g., **foo**) and their semantics.

Under all options, always clearly document also the semantics required of **foo**, notably any essential actions (postconditions) **foo** must guarantee, and failure semantics (what happens, including how errors are reported, if the actions don't succeed).

If the point of customization must be customizable also for built-in types, use Option 2 or Option 3.

Prefer Option 1 or Option 2 for common operations that really are services provided by the type. Here's a litmus test: Could other template libraries use this facility too? And are these generally accepted semantics for this name? If so, this option is probably appropriate.

Prefer Option 3 for less-common operations whose meaning can be expected to vary. You can then happily make the same names mean whatever you want in any given namespace, without confusion or collision.

A template with multiple points of customization can choose a different appropriate strategy for each point of customization. The point is that it must consciously choose and document exactly one strategy for each point of customization, document the requirements including expected postconditions and failure semantics, and implement the chosen strategy correctly.

To avoid providing points of customization unintentionally:

- *Put any helper functions your template uses internally into their own nested namespace, and call them with explicit qualification to disable ADL:* When you want to call your own helper function and pass an object of the template parameter type, and that call should not be a point of customization (i.e., you always intend *your* helper to be called, not some other function), prefer to put the helper in a nested namespace and explicitly turn off ADL by qualifying the call or putting the function name in parentheses:

    ```
    template<typename T>
    void Sample4( T t ) {
      S4Helpers::bar( t );    // disables ADL: bar is not a point of customization
      (bar)( t );             // alternative
    }
    ```

- *Avoid depending on dependent names:* Informally, a dependent name is a name that somehow mentions a template parameter. Many compilers do not support the "two-phase lookup" for dependent names mandated by the C++ Standard, and this means that template code that uses dependent names will behave differently on different compilers unless it takes care to be explicit when using dependent names. Particular care is required in the presence of *dependent base classes*, which occur when a class template inherits from one of its template parameters (e.g., **T** in the case **template<typename T> class C : T { };**) or from a type that is built up from one of its template parameters (e.g., **X<T>** in the case **template<typename T> class C : X<T> { };**).

In short, when referring to any member of a dependent base class, always explicitly qualify with the base class name or with **this->**, which you can think of just as a magical way of forcing all compilers to do what you actually meant:

```
template<typename T>
class C : X<T> {
  typename X<T>::SomeType s;  // use base's nested type or typedef

public:
  void f() {
    X<T>::baz();              // call base member function
    this->baz();              // alternative
  }
};
```

The C++ standard library generally favors relying on Option 2 (e.g., **ostream_iterator**s look up **operator<<**, and **accumulate** looks up **operator+**, in your type's namespace). It also uses Option 3 in some places (e.g., **iterator_traits**, **char_traits**), particularly because those traits must be specializable for built-in types.

Note that, unfortunately, the C++ standard library fails to clearly specify the points of customization of some algorithms. For example, it clearly says that the three-parameter version of **accumulate** must call a user's **operator+** using Option 2. But it doesn't say whether **sort** must call a user's **swap** (thereby providing an intentional point of customization using Option 2), whether it *may* call a user's **swap**, or whether it calls any **swap** at all; today, some implementations of **sort** do pull in a user-defined **swap** while others don't. This Item's point has only been learned relatively recently, and now the standards committee is fixing the current inadequate specification by removing such fuzziness from the standard. We know better now. Learn from the past. Don't make the same mistakes. (For more options, see Item 66.)

References

[Stroustrup00] §8.2, §10.3.2, §11.2.4 • [Sutter00] §31-34 • [Sutter04d]

66. Don't specialize function templates.

Summary

Specialization is good only when it can be done correctly: When extending someone else's function template (including **std::swap**), avoid trying to write a specialization; instead, write an overload of the function template, and put it in the namespace of the type(s) the overload is designed to be used for. (See Item 57.) When you write your own function template, avoid encouraging direct specialization of the function template itself.

Discussion

It's okay to overload function templates. Overload resolution considers all primary templates equally, and that's why it works as you would naturally expect from your experience with normal C++ function overloading: Whatever templates are visible are considered for overload resolution, and the compiler simply picks the best match.

Unfortunately, it's a lot less intuitive to specialize function templates. There are two basic reasons:

- *You can't specialize function templates partially, only totally:* Code that looks like partial specialization is really just overloading instead.
- *Function template specializations never participate in overloading:* Therefore, any specializations you write will not affect which template gets used, and this runs counter to what most people would intuitively expect. After all, if you had written a nontemplate function with the identical signature instead of a function template specialization, the nontemplate function would always be selected because it's always considered to be a better match than a template.

If you're writing a function template, prefer to write it as a single function template that should never be specialized or overloaded, and implement the function template entirely in terms of a class template. This is the proverbial extra level of indirection that steers you well clear of the limitations and dark corners of function templates. This way, programmers using your template will be able to partially specialize and explicitly specialize the class template to their heart's content without affecting the expected operation of the function template. This nicely avoids both the limitation that function templates can't be partially specialized, as well as the sometimes surprising effect that function template specializations don't overload. Problem solved.

If you're using someone else's plain old function template that doesn't use this technique (i.e., a function template that is not implemented in terms of a class template), and you want to write your own special-case version that should participate in overloading, don't write it as a specialization; just make it an overloaded nontemplate function. (See also Items 57 and 58.)

Examples

Example: ***std::swap***. The basic swap template swaps two values **a** and **b** by creating a **temp** copy of **a**, assigning **a** = **b**, and assigning **b** = **temp**. How can you extend it for your own types? For example, let's say you have your own type **Widget** in your own namespace **N**:

```
namespace N {
  class Widget { /* ... */ };
}
```

Suppose that you have a more efficient way to swap two **Widget** objects. To enable it for use with the standard library, should you provide an overload of **swap** (in the same namespace as **Widget**; see Item 57) or specialize **std::swap** directly? The standard is unclear, and existing practice varies considerably (see Item 65). Today, in practice, on some implementations a correct answer is to provide an overload in the same namespace as **Widget**. For the above nontemplate **Widget**:

```
namespace N {
  void swap( Widget&, Widget& );
}
```

But note that if **Widget** is instead a template,

```
namespace N {
  template<typename T> class Widget { /*...*/ };
}
```

then specializing **std::swap** isn't even possible, because there's no such thing as a partial specialization of a function template. The best you can do is add the overload:

```
namespace ??? {
  template<typename T> void swap( Widget<T>&, Widget<T>& );
}
```

but this is problematic because if you put it in the namespace of **Widget**, then many implementations won't find it, but the standard forbids you from putting it in **std**. Catch-22. This problem would not exist if the standard either specified that overloads in the namespace of the type will be found, or allowed you to add overloads to namespace **std**, or (getting back to the point of this Item) specified **swap** to be implemented in terms of a class template that you *could* partially specialize.

References

[Austern99] §A.1.4 • [Sutter04] §7 • [Vandevoorde03] §12

67. Don't write unintentionally nongeneric code.

Summary

Commit to abstractions, not to details: Use the most generic and abstract means to implement a piece of functionality.

Discussion

When writing code, use the most abstract means available that get the job done. Think in terms of what operations put the least "capabilities strain" on the interfaces they operate on. This habit makes your code more generic, and therefore more reusable and more resilient to changes in its surroundings.

On the contrary, code that gratuitously commits to details is rigid and fragile:

- *Use* != *instead of* < *to compare iterators:* Using != is more general and so applies to a larger class of objects; using < asks for ordering, and only random-access iterators can implement **operator<**. If you use **operator!=** your code will "port" easily to other kinds of iterators, such as forward and bidirectional iterators.

- *Prefer iteration to indexed access:* Most containers don't support indexed access; for example, **list** can't implement it efficiently. But all containers support iterators. Iteration is a better approach because it is more general, and it can still be used in conjunction with indexed access as needed.

- *Use* **empty()** *instead of* **size()** *== 0:* "Empty/non-empty" is a more primitive concept than "exact size." For example, you might not know the size of a stream but can always talk about emptiness, and the same applies to input iterators. Some containers, such as **list**, naturally implement **empty** more efficiently than **size**.

- *Use the highest class in the hierarchy that offers the functionality you need:* When programming with dynamic polymorphic classes, don't depend on details you don't need and that tie you to specific derived classes.

- *Write const-correct code (see Item 15):* Taking **const&** parameters puts less strain on the caller because **const&** covers constant and non-constant objects alike.

Exceptions

In some cases, indexing instead of iteration enables compilers to do better optimization. Before you're tempted to make use of this, make sure you really need it and that your compiler really does it. (See Item 8).

References

[Koenig97] §12.7, §17-18 • [Meyers01] §4 • [Stroustrup00] §13, §17.1.1 • [Sutter04] §1, §5, §34

Error Handling and Exceptions

Error handling is a difficult task for which the programmer needs all the help that can be provided.

—Bjarne Stroustrup,
[Stroustrup94] §16.2

There are two ways to write error-free programs; only the third one works.

—Alan Perlis

The question isn't whether or not we will make programming errors; the question is whether or not we will arrange for our compiler and tools to find them for us.

This section documents hard-won wisdom and best practices, some of them gained only after years and mountains of pain. Follow these rules and guidelines. Stick to them. When it comes to writing robust, safe, and secure software, we need all the help we can get.

Our vote for the most valuable Item in this section goes to Item 69: Establish a rational error handling policy, and follow it strictly.

68. Assert liberally to document internal assumptions and invariants.

Summary

Be assertive! Use **assert** or an equivalent liberally to document assumptions internal to a module (i.e., where the caller and callee are maintained by the same person or team) that must always be true and otherwise represent programming errors (e.g., violations of a function's postconditions detected by the caller of the function). (See also Item 70.) Ensure that assertions don't perform side effects.

Discussion

> *It's hard enough to find an error in your code when you're looking for it; it's even harder when you've assumed your code is error-free.* —Steve McConnell

It is hard to overestimate the power of assertions. The **assert** macro and alternatives such as compile-time (and, less preferably, run-time) assertion templates are invaluable tools for detecting and debugging programming errors during a project's development. Of all such tools, they arguably have the best complexity/effectiveness ratio. The success of a project can be conditioned at least in part by the effectiveness with which developers use assertions in their code.

Assertions commonly generate code in debug mode only (when the **NDEBUG** macro is not defined), so they can be made "free" in release builds. Be generous with what you check. Never write expressions with side effects in **assert** statements. In release mode, when the **NDEBUG** macro is defined, **assert**s don't generate any code at all:

```
assert( ++i < limit );              // bad: i is incremented in debug mode only
```

According to information theory, the quantity of information in an event is inversely proportional to the likelihood of that event happening. Thus, the less likely some **assert** is to fire, the more information it will bring to you when it does fire.

Avoid **assert(false)**, and prefer **assert(!"informational message")**. Most compilers will helpfully emit the string in their error output. Also consider adding **&& "informational message"** to more complex assertions, especially instead of a comment.

Consider defining your own **assert**. The standard **assert** macro unceremoniously aborts the program with a message to the standard output. Your environment likely offers enhanced debugging capabilities; for example, it might allow starting an interactive debugger automatically. If so, you may want to define your own **MYASSERT** macro and use it. It can also be useful to retain most assertions even in release builds (prefer not to disable checks for performance reasons unless there's a proven need; see Item 8), and there is real benefit to having an assertion facility that can distinguish between "levels" of assertions, some of which stay on in release mode.

Assertions often check conditions that could be verified at compile time if the language were expressive enough. For example, your whole design might rely on every **Employee** having a nonzero **id_**. Ideally, the compiler would analyze **Employee**'s constructor and members and prove by static analysis that, indeed, that condition is always true. Absent such omniscience, you can issue an **assert(id_ != 0)** inside the implementation of **Employee** whenever you need to make sure an **Employee** is sane:

```
unsigned int Employee::GetID() {
    assert( id_ != 0 && "Employee ID is invalid (must be nonzero)" );
    return id_;
}
```

Don't use assertions to report run-time errors (see Items 70 and 72). For example, don't use **assert** to make sure that **malloc** worked, that a window creation succeeded, or that a thread was started. You can, however, use **assert** to make sure that APIs work as documented. For example, if you call some API function that is documented to always return a positive value, but you suspect it might have a bug, plant an **assert** after the call to validate its postcondition.

It is not recommended to throw an exception instead of asserting, even though the standard **std::logic_error** exception class was originally designed for this purpose. The primary disadvantage of using an exception to report a programming error is that you don't really want stack unwinding to occur—you want the debugger to launch on the exact line where the violation was detected, with the line's state intact.

In sum: There are errors that you know might happen (see Items 69 to 75). For everything else that shouldn't, and it's the programmer's fault if it does, there is **assert**.

Examples

*Example: Do **assert** on basic assumptions.* We all have war stories about assertions that "couldn't possibly fire," but did. Time and again, it's: "This value is certainly positive!" "That pointer is obviously not null!" Do recheck tautologies: Software development is complex, change is the norm, and anything can happen in a program that is changing. Assertions verify that what you believe is "obviously true" today actually stays true. Do **assert** on tautologies that the type system cannot enforce:

```
string Date::DayOfWeek() const {
    assert( day_ > 0 && day_ <= 31 );              // invariant checks
    assert( month_ > 0 && month_ <= 12 );
    // ...
}
```

References

[Abrahams01b] • *[Alexandrescu03b]* • *[Alexandrescu03c]* • *[Allison98]* §13 • *[Cargill92]* pp. 34-35 • *[Cline99]* §10.01-10 • *[Dewhurst03]* 28 • *[Keffer95]* pp. 24-25 • *[Lakos96]* §2.6, §10.2.1 • *[McConnell93]* §5.6 • *[Stroustrup00]* §24.3.7, §E.2, §E.3.5, §E.6 • *[Sutter00]* §47

69. Establish a rational error handling policy, and follow it strictly.

Summary

Consciously specify, and conscientiously apply, what so many projects leave to ad-hoc (mis)judgment: Develop a practical, consistent, and rational error handling policy early in design, and then stick to it. Ensure that it includes:

- *Identification:* What conditions are errors.
- *Severity:* How important or urgent each error is.
- *Detection:* Which code is responsible for detecting the error.
- *Propagation:* What mechanisms are used to report and propagate error notifications in each module.
- *Handling:* What code is responsible for doing something about the error.
- *Reporting:* How the error will be logged or users notified.

Change error handling mechanisms only on module boundaries.

Discussion

From this Item onward, this section focuses on dealing with run-time errors that are not due to faulty coding internal to a module or subsystem. (As Item 68 covers separately, prefer to use assertions to flag internal programming errors, ones that are just outright coding errors on some programmer's part.)

Determine an overall error reporting and handling policy for your application and for each module or subsystem, and stick to it. Include a policy for at least each of the following points.

Universally:

- *Error identification:* For each entity (e.g., each function, each class, each module), document the entity's internal and external invariants.

For each function:

- *Error identification:* For each function, document its preconditions and postconditions, the invariants it shares responsibility for maintaining, and the error-safety guarantee it supports. (See Items 70 and 71.) Note that destructors and deallocation functions in particular must always be written to support the no-fail guarantee, because otherwise it's often impossible to reliably and safely perform cleanup (see Item 51).

For each error (see the definition of "error" in Item 70):

- *Error severity and categorization:* For each error, identify a severity level. Preferably provide a way to fine-tune diagnostics for particular error categories and levels to facilitate remote user assistance.
- *Error detection:* For each error, document which code is responsible for detecting which error, following the advice of Item 70.
- *Error handling:* For each error, identify the code that is responsible for handling the error, following the advice in Item 74.
- *Error reporting:* For each error, identify appropriate reporting method(s). These commonly include recording the error in disk file logs, printed logs, electronic dump transmissions, or possibly inconvenient and annoying pager calls in the case of severe errors.

For each module:

- *Error propagation:* For each module (note: each module, not each error), identify which coding mechanism will be used to propagate errors (e.g., C++ exceptions, COM exceptions, CORBA exceptions, return codes).

We emphasize that error handling strategies should change only on module boundaries (see Items 62 and 63). Each module should consistently use a single error handling strategy and mechanism internally (e.g., modules written in C++ should use exceptions internally; see Item 72) and consistently use a single, possibly different, error handling strategy and mechanism in its interface (e.g., the module might present a flat C API to accommodate callers that could be written in various languages, or a COM wrapper that presents COM exceptions).

All functions that are entry points into the module are directly responsible for translating from the internal to the external strategy if they are different. For example, in a module that uses C++ exceptions internally but presents a C API boundary, all C APIs must **catch(...)** all exceptions and translate them to error codes.

Note in particular that callback functions and thread mainlines by definition are (or can be) on a module boundary. Each callback function body and thread mainline body should translate its internal error mechanism to the appropriate interface error strategy (see Item 62).

References

[Abrahams01b] • *[Allison98]* §13 • *[McConnell93]* §5.6 • *[Stroustrup94]* §16.2, §E.2 • *[Stroustrup00]* §14.9, §19.3.1 • *[Sutter04b]*

70. Distinguish between errors and non-errors.

Summary

A breach of contract is an error: A function is a unit of work. Thus, failures should be viewed as errors or otherwise based on their impact on functions. Within a function **f**, a failure is an error if and only if it violates one of **f**'s preconditions or prevents **f** from meeting any of its callees' preconditions, achieving any of **f**'s own postconditions, or reestablishing any invariant that **f** shares responsibility for maintaining.

In particular, here we exclude internal programming errors (i.e., where the caller and callee are the responsibility of the same person or team, such as inside a module), which are a separate category normally dealt with using assertions (see Item 68).

Discussion

It is crucial to crisply distinguish between errors and non-errors in terms of their effects on functions, especially for the purpose of defining safety guarantees (see Item 71). The key words in this Item are *precondition*, *postcondition*, and *invariant*.

The function is the basic unit of work, no matter whether you are programming C++ in a structured style, an OO style, or a generic style. A function makes assumptions about its starting state (documented as its preconditions, which the caller is responsible for fulfilling and the callee is responsible for validating) and performs one or more actions (documented as its results or postconditions, which the function as callee is responsible for fulfilling). A function may share responsibility for maintaining one or more invariants. In particular, a nonprivate mutating member function is by definition a unit of work on its object, and must take the object from one valid invariant-preserving state to another; during the body of the member function, the object's invariants can be (and nearly always must be) broken, and that is fine and normal as long as they are reestablished by the end of the member function. Higher-level functions compose lower-level functions into larger units of work.

An error is any failure that prevents a function from succeeding. There are three kinds:

- *Violation of, or failure to achieve, a precondition:* The function detects a violation of one its own preconditions (e.g., a parameter or state restriction), or encounters a condition that prevents it from meeting a precondition of another essential function that must be called.

- *Failure to achieve a postcondition:* The function encounters a condition that prevents it from establishing one of its own postconditions. If the function has a return value, producing a valid return value object is a postcondition.

- *Failure to reestablish an invariant:* The function encounters a condition that prevents it from reestablishing an invariant that it is responsible for maintaining.

This is a special kind of postcondition that applies particularly to member functions; an essential postcondition of every nonprivate member function is that it must reestablish its class's invariants. (See [Stroustrup00] §E.2.)

Any other condition is not an error and therefore should not be reported as an error. (See Examples.)

The code that could cause an error is responsible for detecting and reporting the error. In particular, the caller should detect and report when it cannot meet a to-be-called function's preconditions (especially ones the callee documents that it will not check, such as **vector::operator[]** which does not promise to range-check its argument). Because the called function cannot rely on callers to be well-behaved, however, the called function ought still to validate its preconditions and to report violations by emitting an error—or, if the function is internal to (only callable from within) the module, so that any precondition violation is by definition an error in the module's programming, by asserting (see Item 68). This is defensive programming.

A word of caution about specifying a function's preconditions: A condition should be a precondition of a function **f** if and only if it is reasonable to expect all callers to check and verify the condition's validity before calling **f**. For example, it is wrong for a function to state a precondition that can only be checked by doing some of the function's own substantial work, or by accessing private information; that work should stay in the function and not be duplicated in the caller.

For example, a function that takes a **string** containing a file name would not normally make the file's existence a precondition, because callers cannot reliably guarantee that the file exists without taking a lock on the file (if they only check for the file's existence without a lock, another user or process could delete or rename the file between the caller's check and the callee's attempt to open). One correct way to make the file's existence a precondition is to require the caller to open the file and make the function's parameter an **ifstream** or equivalent (which is also safer, because it works at a higher level of abstraction; see Item 63) instead of passing a bald file name as a raw **string**. Many preconditions can thus be replaced by stronger typing, which turns run-time errors into compile-time errors (see Item 14).

Examples

*Example 1: **std::string::insert** (precondition error).* When trying to insert a new character into a **string** at a specific position **pos**, a caller should check for invalid values of **pos** that would violate a documented parameter requirement; for example, **pos > size()**. The **insert** function can't perform its work successfully if it doesn't have a valid starting point.

*Example 2: **std::string::append** (postcondition error).* When appending a character to a **string**, failure to allocate a new buffer if the existing one is full prevents the operation from performing its documented function and achieving its documented post-conditions, and is therefore an error.

Example 3: Inability to produce a return value (postcondition error). For a value-returning function, producing a valid return object is a postcondition. If the return value can't be correctly created (e.g., if the function returns a **double**, but there exists no **double** value with the mathematical properties requested of a result), that is an error.

Example 4: **std::string::find_first_of** *(not an error in the context of* **string***).* When searching for a character in a **string**, failure to find the character is a legitimate outcome and not an error. At least, it is not an error as far the general-purpose **string** class is concerned; if the owner of the given **string** assumed the character would be present and its absence is thus an error according to a higher-level invariant, that higher-level calling code would then appropriately report an error with respect to its invariant.

Example 5: Different error conditions in the same function. In spite of the increased reliability of disks nowadays, writing to disk has traditionally remained subject to expected errors. If you design a **File** class, in the same function **File::Write(const char* buffer, size_t size)**, which requires that **buffer** is non-null and that the file be opened for writing, you might decide to do the following:

- *If **buffer** is **NULL***: Report an error on the precondition violation.

- *If the **File** is read-only:* Report an error on the precondition violation.

- *If the write does not succeed:* Report an error on the postcondition violation, because the function cannot do the work it promises to do.

Example 6: Different status for the same condition. The same condition can be a valid precondition for one function and not for another; the choice depends on the function's author, who is specifying his interface's semantics. In particular, **std::vector** provides two ways to perform indexed access: **operator[]**, which is not bounds-checked, and **at**, which is. Both require a precondition that the argument is not out of range. Because **operator[]** is not required to validate its argument or to be safe to call with an invalid argument, it must document that the caller has sole responsibility for ensuring that the argument is in the valid range; this function is inherently less safe. On the other hand, **at** is documented to behave safely even in the presence of an invalid argument, and to report an error (by throwing **std::out_of_range**) if the argument is found to be out of range.

References

[Abrahams01b] • *[Meyer00]* • *[Stroustrup00]* §8.3.3, §14.1, §14.5 • *[Sutter04b]*

71. Design and write error-safe code.

Summary

Promise, but don't punish: In each function, give the strongest safety guarantee that won't penalize callers who don't need it. Always give at least the basic guarantee.

Ensure that errors always leave your program in a valid state. This is the basic guarantee. Beware of invariant-destroying errors (including but not limited to leaks), which are just plain bugs.

Prefer to additionally guarantee that the final state is either the original state (if there was an error the operation was rolled back) or the intended target state (if there was no error the operation was committed). This is the strong guarantee.

Prefer to additionally guarantee that the operation can never fail at all. Although this is not possible for most functions, it is required for functions like destructors and deallocation functions. This is the no-fail guarantee.

Discussion

The basic, strong, and no-fail (then known as nothrow) guarantees were originally described in [Abrahams96] and publicized in [GotW], [Stroustrup00] §E.2, and [Sutter00] with respect to exception safety. They apply to all error handling regardless of the specific method used, and so we will use them to describe error handling safety in general. The no-fail guarantee is a strict superset of the strong guarantee, and the strong guarantee is a strict superset of the basic guarantee.

In general, every function should provide the strongest guarantee that it can provide without needlessly penalizing calling code that doesn't need the guarantee. Where possible, it should additionally provide enough functionality to allow calling code that needs a still stronger guarantee to achieve that (see the **vector::insert** case in the Examples).

Ideally, we write functions that always succeed and therefore can provide the no-fail guarantee. Certain functions must always provide the no-fail guarantee, notably destructors, deallocation functions, and swap functions (see Item 51).

Most functions, however, can fail. When errors are possible, the safest approach is to ensure that a function supports a transactional behavior: Either it totally succeeds and takes the program from the original valid state to the desired target valid state, or it fails and leaves the program in the state it was before the call—any object's visible state before the failed call is the same after the failed call (e.g., a global **int**'s value won't be changed from **42** to **43**) and any action that the calling code would have been able to take before the failed call is still possible with the same meaning after the failed call (e.g., no iterators into containers have been invalidated, performing **++** on the aforementioned global **int** will yield **43** not **44**). This is the strong guarantee.

Finally, if providing the strong guarantee is difficult or needlessly expensive, provide the basic guarantee: Either the function totally succeeds and reaches the intended target state, or it does not completely succeed and leaves the program in a state that is valid (preserves the invariants that the function knows about and is responsible for preserving) but not predictable (it might or might not be the original state, and none, some, or all of the postconditions could be met; but note that all invariants must still be reestablished). The design of your application must prepare for handling that state appropriately.

That's it; there is no lower level. A failure to meet at least the basic guarantee is always a program bug. Correct programs meet at least the basic guarantee for all functions; even those few correct programs that deliberately leak resources by design, particularly in situations where the program immediately aborts, do so knowing that they will be reclaimed by the operating system. Always structure code so that resources are correctly freed and data is in a consistent state even in the presence of errors, unless the error is so severe that graceful or ungraceful termination is the only option.

When deciding which guarantee to support, consider also versioning: It's always easy to strengthen the guarantee in a later release, whereas loosening a guarantee later will break calling code that has come to rely on the stronger guarantee.

Remember that "error-unsafe" and "poor design" go hand in hand: If it is difficult to make a piece of code satisfy even the basic guarantee, that almost always is a signal of its poor design. For example, a function having multiple unrelated responsibilities is difficult to make error-safe (see Item 5).

Beware if a copy assignment operator *relies* on a check for self-assignment in order to function correctly. An error-safe copy assignment operator is automatically safe for self-assignment. It's all right use a self-assignment check as an optimization to avoid needless work. (See Item 55.)

Examples

Example 1: Retry after failure. If your program includes a command for saving data to a file and the write fails, make sure you revert to a state where the caller can retry the operation. In particular, don't release any data structure before data has been safely flushed to disk. For example, one text editor we know of didn't allow changing the file name to save to after a write error, which is a suboptimal state for further recovery.

Example 2: Skins. If you write a skinnable application, don't destroy the existing skin before attempting to load a new one. If loading the new skin fails, your application might end up in an unusable state.

*Example 3: **std::vector::insert**.* Because a **vector<T>**'s internal storage is contiguous, inserting an element into the middle requires shuffling some existing values over by one position to make room for the new element. The shuffling is done using **T::T(const T&)** and **T::operator=**, and if either of those two operations can fail (by throwing an exception), the only way to make **insert** provide the strong guarantee is to make a complete copy of the container, perform the operation on the copy, and, if successful, swap the original's and copy's state using the no-fail **vector<T>::swap**.

But if that were done every time by **insert** itself, every caller of **vector::insert** would always incur the space and performance penalty of making a complete copy of the container, whether it needed the strong guarantee or not. That is needlessly expensive. Instead, those callers who do want the strong guarantee can do the work themselves, and are given sufficient tools for doing so. (In the best case: Arrange for the contained type to not throw from its copy constructor or copy assignment operators. In the worst case: Take a copy, **insert** into the copy, and **swap** the copy with the original when successful.)

Example 4: Unlaunching a satellite. Consider a function **f** that as part of its work launches a satellite, and the **LaunchSatellite** function it uses provides the strong or no-fail guarantee. If **f** can perform all of its work that could fail before launching the satellite, **f** can be coded to provide the strong guarantee. But if **f** must perform other operations that might fail after having already performed the launch, it cannot provide the strong guarantee because it cannot bring the satellite back. (At any rate, such an **f** probably ought to be split into two functions, because a single function should probably not be trying to do multiple pieces of work of such significance; see Item 5.)

References

[Abrahams96] • *[Abrahams01b]* • *[Alexandrescu03d]* • *[Josuttis99]* §5.11.2 • *[Stroustrup00]* §14.4.3, §E.2-4, §E.6 • *[Sutter00]* §8-19, §40-41, §47 • *[Sutter02]* §17-23 • *[Sutter04]* §11-13 • *[Sutter04b]*

72. Prefer to use exceptions to report errors.

Summary

When harmed, take exception: Prefer using exceptions over error codes to report errors. Use status codes (e.g., return codes, **errno**) for errors when exceptions cannot be used (see Item 62), and for conditions that are not errors. Use other methods, such as graceful or ungraceful termination, when recovery is impossible or not required.

Discussion

It's no coincidence that most modern languages created in the past 20 years use exceptions as their primary error reporting mechanism. Almost by definition, exceptions are for reporting *exceptions* to normal processing—also known as "errors," defined in Item 70 as violations of preconditions, postconditions, and invariants. Like all error reporting, exceptions should not arise during normal successful operation.

We will use the term "status codes" to cover all forms of reporting status via codes (including return codes, **errno**, a **GetLastError** function, and other strategies to return or retrieve codes), and "error codes" specifically for status codes that signify errors. In C++, reporting errors via exceptions has clear advantages over reporting them via error codes, all of which make your code more robust:

- *Exceptions can't be silently ignored:* The most terrible weakness of error codes is that they are ignored by default; to pay the slightest attention to an error code, you have to explicitly write code to accept the error and respond to it. It is common for programmers to accidentally (or lazily) fail to pay attention to error codes. This makes code reviews harder. Exceptions can't be silently ignored; to ignore an exception, you must explicitly **catch** it (even if only with **catch(...)**) and choose not to act on it.

- *Exceptions propagate automatically:* Error codes are not propagated across scopes by default; to inform a higher-level calling function of a lower-level error code, a programmer writing the intervening code has to explicitly hand-write code to propagate the error. Exceptions propagate across scopes automatically exactly until they are handled. ("It is not a good idea to try to make every function a fire-wall." —[Stroustrup94, §16.8])

- *Exception handling removes error handling and recovery from the main line of control flow:* Error code detection and handling, when it is written at all, is necessarily interspersed with (and therefore obfuscates) the main line of control flow. This makes both the main control flow and the error handling code harder to understand and maintain. Exception handling naturally moves error detection and recovery into distinct **catch** blocks; that is, it makes error handling distinctly modular instead of inline spaghetti. This makes the main line of control more understandable and maintainable, and it's more than just of aesthetic benefit to distinguish clearly between correct operation and error detection and recovery.

- *Exception handling is better than the alternatives for reporting errors from constructors and operators:* The copy constructors and the operators have predefined signatures that leave no room for return codes. In particular, constructors have no return type at all (not even **void**), and for example every **operator+** must take exactly two parameters and return one object (of a prescribed type; see Item 26). For operators, using error codes is at least possible if not desirable; it would require **errno**-like approaches, or inferior solutions like packaging status with an object. For constructors, using error codes is not feasible because the C++ language tightly binds together constructor exceptions and constructor failures so that the two have to be synonymous; if instead we used an **errno**-like approach such as

```
SomeType anObject;                         // construct an object
if( SomeType::ConstructionWasOk() ) {      // test whether construction worked
    // ...
```

then not only is the result ugly and error-prone, but it leads to misbegotten objects that don't really satisfy their type's invariants—never mind the race conditions inherent in calls to **SomeType::ConstructionWasOk** in multithreaded applications. (See [Stroustrup00] §E.3.5.)

The main potential drawback of exception handling is that it requires programmers to be familiar with a few recurring idioms that arise from exceptions' out-of-band control flow. For example, destructors and deallocation functions must not fail (see Item 51), and intervening code must be correct in the face of exceptions (see Item 71 and References); to achieve the latter, a common coding idiom is to perform all the work that might emit an exception safely off to the side and only then, when you know that the real work has succeeded, you commit and modify the program state using only operations that provide the no-fail guarantee (see Item 51 and [Sutter00] §9-10, §13). But then using error codes also has its own idioms; those have just been around longer and so more people already know them—but, unfortunately, also commonly and routinely ignore them. *Caveat emptor.*

Performance is not normally a drawback of exception handling. First, note that you should always turn on exception handling in your compiler even if it is off by default, otherwise you won't get standard behavior and error reporting from the C++ language operations such as **operator new** and standard library operations such as STL container insertions (see Exceptions).

[Aside: Turning on exception handling can be implemented so that it increases the size of your executable image (this part is unavoidable) but incurs zero or near-zero performance overhead in the case where no exception is thrown, and some compilers do so. Other compilers do incur overhead, especially when providing secure modes to prevent malicious code from attacking the exception handling mechanism via buffer overruns. Whether there is overhead or not, at minimum do always at least turn on your compiler's support for exception handling, because otherwise the language and standard library won't report errors correctly. We mention this because we know of projects that turn off exception handling, which is a far-reaching fundamental decision and should never be done except as a last resort and with extreme care (see Exceptions).]

Once your compiler's support for exception handling is turned on, the performance difference between throwing an exception and returning an error code is typically negligible in normal processing (the case where no error occurs). You may notice a performance difference in the case where an error does occur, but if you're throwing so frequently that the exception throwing/catching handling performance overhead is actually noticeable, you're almost certainly using exceptions for conditions that are not true errors and therefore not correctly distinguishing between errors and non-errors (see Item 70). If they're really errors that truly violate pre- and postconditions and invariants, and if they're really happening *that* frequently, the application has far more serious problems.

One symptom of error code overuse is when application code needs to check relentlessly for trivially true conditions, or (worse) fails to check error codes that it should check.

One symptom of exception overuse is when application code throws and catches exceptions so frequently that a **try** block's success count and failure count are within the same order of magnitude. Such a **catch** block is either not really handling a true error (one that violates preconditions, postconditions, or invariants), or the program is in serious trouble.

Examples

Example 1: Constructors (invariant error). If a constructor cannot successfully create an object of its type, which is the same as saying that it cannot establish all of the new object's invariants, it should throw an exception. Conversely, an exception thrown from a constructor always means that the object's construction failed and the object's lifetime never began; the language enforces this.

Example 2: Successful recursive tree search. When searching a tree using a recursive algorithm, it can be tempting to return the result—and conveniently unwind the search stack—by throwing the result as an exception. But don't do it: An exception means an error, and finding the result is not an error (see [Stroustrup00]). (Note that, of course, failing to find the result is also not an error in the context of the search function; see the **find_first_of** example in Item 70.)

See also Item 70's examples, replacing "report an error" with "throw an exception."

Exceptions

In rare cases, consider using an error code if you are certain that both of the following are true:

- *The benefits of exceptions don't apply:* For example, you know that nearly always the immediate caller must directly handle the error and so propagation should happen either never or nearly never. This is very rare because usually the callee does not have this much information about the characteristics of all of its callers).

- *The actual measured performance of throwing an exception over using an error code matters:* That is, the performance difference is measured empirically, so you're probably in an inner loop and throwing often; the latter is rare because it usually means the condition is not really an error after all, but let's assume that somehow it is.

In very rare cases, some hard real-time projects may find themselves under pressure to consider turning off exception handling altogether because their compiler's exception handling mechanism has worst-case time guarantees that make it difficult or impossible for key operations to meet deadline schedules. Of course, turning off exception handling means that the language and standard library will not report errors in a standard way (or in some cases at all; see your compiler's documentation) and the project's own error reporting mechanisms would have to be based on codes instead. It is difficult to exaggerate just how undesirable and how much of a last resort this should be; before making this choice, analyze in detail how you will report errors from constructors and operators and how that scheme will actually work on the compiler(s) you are using. If after serious and deep analysis you still feel that you are really forced to turn off exception handling, still don't do it project-wide: Do so in as few modules as possible, and facilitate this by trying to group such deadline-sensitive operations together into the same module as much as possible.

References

[Alexandrescu03d] • *[Allison98]* §13 • *[Stroustrup94]* §16 • *[Stroustrup00]* §8.3.3, §14.1, §14.4-5, §14.9, §E.3.5 • *[Sutter00]* §8-19, §40-41, §47 • *[Sutter02]* §17-23 • *[Sutter04]* §11-16 • *[Sutter04b]*

73. Throw by value, catch by reference.

Summary

Learn to **catch** properly: Throw exceptions by value (not pointer) and catch them by reference (usually to **const**). This is the combination that meshes best with exception semantics. When rethrowing the same exception, prefer just **throw;** to **throw e;**.

Discussion

When throwing an exception, throw an object by value. Avoid throwing a pointer, because if you throw a pointer, you need to deal with memory management issues: You can't throw a pointer to a stack-allocated value because the stack will be unwound before the pointer reaches the call site. You could throw a pointer to dynamically allocated memory (if the error you're reporting isn't "out of memory" to begin with), but you've put the burden on the catch site to deallocate the memory. If you feel you really must throw a pointer, consider throwing a value-like smart pointer such as a **shared_ptr<T>** instead of a plain **T***.

Throwing by value enjoys the best of all worlds because the compiler itself takes responsibility for the intricate process of managing memory for the exception object. All you need to take care of is ensuring that you implement a non-throwing copy constructor for your exception classes (see Item 32).

Unless you are throwing a smart pointer, which already adds an indirection that preserves polymorphism, catching by reference is the only good way to go. Catching a plain value by value results in slicing at the catch site (see Item 54), which violently strips away the normally-vital polymorphic qualities of the exception object. Catching by reference preserves the polymorphism of the exception object.

When rethrowing an exception **e**, prefer writing just **throw;** instead of **throw e;** because the first form always preserves polymorphism of the rethrown object.

Examples

Example: Rethrowing a modified exception. Prefer to rethrow using **throw;**:

```
catch( MyException& e ) {                    // catch by reference to non-const
    e.AppendContext("Passed through here");  // modify
    throw;                                   // rethrow modified object
}
```

References

[Dewhurst03] §64-65 • [Meyers96] §13 • [Stroustrup00] §14.3 • [Vandevoorde03] §20

74. Report, handle, and translate errors appropriately.

Summary

Know when to say when: Report errors at the point they are detected and identified as errors. Handle or translate each error at the nearest level that can do it correctly.

Discussion

Report an error (e.g., write **throw**) wherever a function detects an error that it cannot resolve itself and that makes it impossible for the function to continue execution. (See Item 70.)

Handle an error (e.g., write a **catch** that doesn't rethrow the same or another exception or emit another kind of error code) in the places that have sufficient knowledge to handle the error, including to enforce boundaries defined in the error policy (e.g., on **main** and thread mainlines; see Item 62) and to absorb errors in the bodies of destructors and deallocation operations.

Translate an error (e.g., write a **catch** that does rethrow a different exception or emits another kind of error code) in these circumstances:

- *To add higher-level semantic meaning:* For example, in a word processing application, **Document::Open** could accept a low-level unexpected-end-of-file error and translate it to a document-invalid-or-corrupt error, adding semantic information.
- *To change the error handling mechanism:* For example, in a module that uses exceptions internally but whose C API public boundary reports error codes, a boundary API would catch an exception and emit a corresponding error code that fulfills the module's contract and that the caller can understand.

Code should not accept an error if it doesn't have the context to do something useful about that error. If a function isn't going to handle (or translate, or deliberately absorb) an error itself, it should allow or enable the error to propagate up to a caller who can handle it.

Exceptions

It can occasionally be useful to accept and re-emit (e.g., **catch** and rethrow) the same error in order to add instrumentation, even though the error is not actually being handled.

References

[Stroustrup00] §3.7.2, §14.7, §14.9 • [Sutter00] §8 • [Sutter04] §11 • [Sutter04b]

75. Avoid exception specifications.

Summary

Take exception to these specifications: Don't write exception specifications on your functions unless you're forced to (because other code you can't change has already introduced them; see Exceptions).

Discussion

In brief, don't bother with exception specifications. Even experts don't bother. The main problems with exception specifications are that they're only "sort of" part of the type system, they don't do what most people think, and you almost always don't want what they actually do.

Exception specifications aren't part of a function's type, except when they are. They form a shadow type system whereby writing an exception specification is variously:

- *Illegal:* In a typedef for a pointer to function.
- *Allowed:* In the identical code without the typedef.
- *Required:* In the declaration of a virtual function that overrides a base class virtual function that has an exception specification.
- *Implicit and automatic:* In the declaration of the constructors, assignment operators, and destructors when they are implicitly generated by the compiler.

A common but nevertheless incorrect belief is that exception specifications statically guarantee that functions will throw only listed exceptions (possibly none), and enable compiler optimizations based on that knowledge.

In fact, exception specifications actually do something slightly but fundamentally different: They cause the compiler to inject additional run-time overhead in the form of implicit **try**/**catch** blocks around the function body to enforce via run-time checking that the function does in fact emit only listed exceptions (possibly none), unless the compiler can statically prove that the exception specification can never be violated in which case it is free to optimize the checking away. And exception specifications can both enable and prevent further compiler optimizations (besides the inherent overhead already described); for example, some compilers refuse to inline functions that have exception specifications.

Worst of all, however, is that exception specifications are a blunt instrument: When violated, by default they immediately terminate your program. You can register an **unexpected_handler**, but it's highly unlikely to help you much because you get exactly one global handler and the only way the handler could avoid immediately calling **terminate** would be to rethrow an exception that is permissible—but because you have only one handler for your whole application, it's hard to see how it could do useful recovery or usefully know what exceptions might be legal without trivializing exception specifications altogether (e.g., following the discipline of having all exception specifications allow some general **UnknownException** eliminates any advantage that having an exception specification might have had in the first place).

You generally can't write useful exception specifications for function templates anyway, because you generally can't tell what exceptions the types they operate on might throw.

Paying a performance overhead in exchange for enforcements that are nearly always useless because they are fatal if they ever fire is an excellent example of a premature pessimization (see Item 9).

These is no easy fix for the problems described in this Item. In particular, the problems are not easily solved by switching to static checking. People often suggest switching from dynamically checked exception specifications to statically checked ones, as provided in Java and other languages. In short, that just trades one set of problems for another; users of languages with statically checked exception specifications seem to equally often suggest switching to dynamically checked ones.

Exceptions

If you have to override a base class virtual function that already has an exception specification (e.g., ahem, **std::exception::what**), and you don't have the ability to change the class to remove the exception specifications (or to convince the class's maintainer to remove them), you will have to write a compatible exception specification on your overriding function, and you should prefer to make it no less restrictive than the base version so as to minimize the frequency with which it might be violated:

```
class Base { // ...                 // in a class written by someone else
  virtual f() throw( X, Y, Z );     // the author used an exception specification,
};                                  // and if you can't get him to remove it...

class MyDerived : public Base { // ...  // ...then in your own class your override
  virtual f() throw( X, Y, Z );     // must have a compatible (and preferably
};                                  // the identical) exception specification
```

[BoostLRG]'s experience is that a throws-nothing exception specification (i.e., **throw()**) on a non-inline function "may have some benefit with some compilers." Not a stunning endorsement from one of the most highly regarded and expertly designed C++ library projects in the world.

References

[BoostLRG] • *[Stroustrup00] §14.1, §14.6* • *[Sutter04] §13*

STL: Containers

*By default, use **vector** when you need a container.*

—Bjarne Stroustrup,
[Stroustrup00] §17.7

We know that you already prefer to use standard containers instead of handcrafted ones. But which container should you use? What should (and shouldn't) you store in containers, and why? How should you populate them? What are the essential idioms to know?

This section covers the answers to these questions and more. And it's no accident that the first three Items of the section all begin with the words: "Use **vector**…".

Our vote for the most valuable Item in this section goes to Item 79: Store only values and smart pointers in containers. To this we add: If you use [Boost] and [C++TR104] for nothing else, use them for **shared_ptr**.

76. Use vector by default. Otherwise, choose an appropriate container.

Summary

Using the "right container" is great: If you have a good reason to use a specific container type, use that container type knowing that you did the right thing.

So is using **vector**: Otherwise, write **vector** and keep going without breaking stride, also knowing you did the right thing.

Discussion

Here are three fundamental issues and related questions for programming in general, and for choosing a container in particular:

- *Write for correctness, simplicity, and clarity first (see Item 6):* Prefer to choose the container that will let you write the clearest code. Examples: If you need to insert at a specific position, use a sequence container (e.g., **vector**, **list**). If you need random-access iterators, use **vector**, **deque**, or **string**. If you need dictionary-like lookups like **c[0] = 42;**, use an associative container (e.g., **set**, **map**)—but if you need an *ordered* associative collection, you can't use hash-based (nonstandard **hash_**... or standard **unordered_**...) containers.

- *Write for efficiency only when and where necessary (see Item 8):* If lookup speed is a proven critical consideration, based on actual performance data, prefer a hash-based (nonstandard **hash_**... or standard **unordered_**...) containers, then a sorted **vector**, then a **set** or **map**, usually in that order. Even then, big-Oh differences (e.g., linear-time vs. logarithmic-time; see Item 7) only matter if the containers are big enough to swamp the constant factor, which for containers of small objects like **double**s frequently doesn't happen until after container sizes exceed several thousand elements.

- *Prefer to write transactional, strongly error-safe code where reasonably possible (see Item 71), and don't use invalid objects (see Item 99):* If you need transactional semantics for inserting and erasing elements, or need to minimize iterator invalidations, prefer a node-based container (e.g., **list**, **set**, **map**).

Otherwise, follow the Standard's advice: "**vector** is the type of sequence that should be used by default." ([C++03] §23.1.1)

If you doubt this advice, ask yourself if you really have a compelling reason *not* to use the only standard container that guarantees all of the following properties. **vector** alone is:

- Guaranteed to have the lowest space overhead of any container (zero bytes per object).

- Guaranteed to have the fastest access speed to contained elements of any container.

- Guaranteed to have inherent locality of reference, meaning that objects near each other in the container are guaranteed to be near each other in memory, which is not guaranteed by any other standard container.

- Guaranteed to be layout-compatible with C, unlike any other standard container. (See Items 77 and 78.)

- Guaranteed to have the most flexible iterators (random access iterators) of any container.

- Almost certain to have the fastest iterators (pointers, or classes with comparable performance that often compile away to the same speed as pointers when not in debug mode), faster than those of all other containers.

Do you have a reason not to use that container by default? If you do have a reason, because of your answers to the first three bulleted questions in this Item, that's just great and perfectly fine—use the other container knowing you did the right thing. If you don't, write **vector** and keep going without breaking stride, again knowing you did the right thing.

Finally, prefer to use standard library containers and algorithms over vendor-specific or handcrafted code.

Examples

*Example: **vector** for small lists.* Is it a common fallacy to use **list** just because "**list** is obviously the right type for list operations," such as insertion into the middle of a sequence. Using a **vector** for small lists is almost always superior to using **list**. Even though insertion in the middle of the sequence is a linear-time operation for **vector** and a constant-time operation for **list**, **vector** usually outperforms **list** when containers are relatively small because of its better constant factor, and **list**'s Big-Oh advantage doesn't kick in until data sizes get larger.

Here, use **vector** unless the data sizes warrant a different choice (see Item 7), or because the strong safety guarantee is essential and the contained type's copy constructor or copy assignment operator might fail (in which case, it can be important that **list** provides the strong guarantee for **insert** operations for collections of such types).

References

[Austern99] §5.4.1 • [C++03] §23.1.1 • [Josuttis99] §6.9 • [Meyers01] §1-2, §13, §16, §23, §25 • [Musser01] §6.1 • [Stroustrup00] §17.1, §17.6 • [Sutter00] §7, §20 • [Sutter02] §7

77. Use vector and string instead of arrays.

Summary

Why juggle Ming vases? Avoid implementing array abstractions with C-style arrays, pointer arithmetic, and memory management primitives. Using **vector** or **string** not only makes your life easier, but also helps you write safer and more scalable software.

Discussion

Buffer overruns and security flaws are, hands down, a front-running scourge of today's software. Silly limitations due to fixed-length arrays are a major annoyance even when within the limits of correctness. Most of these are caused by using bare C-level facilities—such as built-in arrays, pointers and pointer arithmetic, and manual memory management—as a substitute for higher-level concepts such as buffers, vectors, or strings.

Here are some reasons to prefer the standard facilities over C-style arrays:

- *They manage their own memory automatically:* No more need for fixed buffers of "longer than any reasonable length" ("time bombs" is a more accurate description), or for frantic **realloc**'ing and pointer adjustment.
- *They have a rich interface:* You can implement complex functionality easily and expressively.
- *They are compatible with C's memory model:* **vector** and **string::c_str** can be passed to C APIs—in both read and write modes, of course. In particular, **vector** is C++'s gateway to C and other languages. (See Items 76 and 78.)
- *They offer extended checking:* The standard facilities can implement (in debug mode) iterators and indexing operators that expose a large category of memory errors. Many of today's standard library implementations offer such debugging facilities—use them! (Run, don't walk, to Item 83.)
- *They don't waste much efficiency for all that:* Truth be told, in release mode **vector** and **string** favor efficiency over safety when the two are in tension. Still, all in all, the standard facilities offer a much better platform for creating safe components than do bare arrays and pointers.
- *They foster optimizations:* Modern standard library implementations include optimizations that many of us mere mortals have never thought of.

An array can be acceptable when its size really is fixed at compile time (e.g., **float[3]** for a three-dimensional point; switching to four dimensions would be a redesign anyway).

References

[Alexandrescu01a] • *[Dewhurst03] §13, §60, §68* • *[Meyers01] §13, §16* • *[Stroustrup00] §3.5-7, §5.3, §20.4.1, §C.7* • *[Sutter00] §36*

78. Use vector (and string::c_str) to exchange data with non-C++ APIs.

Summary

vector isn't lost in translation: **vector** and **string::c_str** are your gateway to communicate with non-C++ APIs. But don't assume iterators are pointers; to get the address of the element referred to by a **vector<T>::iterator iter**, use **&*iter**.

Discussion

vector (primarily) and **string::c_str** and **string::data** (secondarily) are the best way to communicate data with non-C++ APIs in general, and C libraries in particular.

vector's storage is always contiguous, so accessing the address of its first element returns a pointer to its contents. Use **&*v.begin()**, **&v[0]**, or **&v.front()** to get a pointer to **v**'s first element. To get a pointer to a **vector**'s n-th element, prefer to do the arithmetic first and take the address later (e.g., **&v.begin()[n]** or **&v[n]**) instead of fetching a pointer to **front** and then doing pointer arithmetic (e.g., **(&v.front())[n]**). This is because in the former case you are giving a checked implementation a crack at verifying that you don't access an element outside **v**'s bounds (see Item 83).

Do not assume that **v.begin()** returns a pointer to the first element, or in general that **vector** iterators are pointers. Although some STL implementations do define **vector<T>::iterator**s as bare **T*** pointers, iterators can be, and increasingly are, full-blown types (see again Item 83).

Although most implementations use contiguous memory for **string**, that's not guaranteed, so never take the address of a character in a **string** and assume it points to contiguous memory. The good news is that **string::c_str** always returns a null-terminated C-style string. (**string::data** also returns a pointer to contiguous memory, except that it's not guaranteed to be zero-terminated.)

When you pass pointers into a **vector v**'s data, C code can both read from and write to **v**'s elements but must stay within **size**'s bounds. A well-designed C API takes a maximum number of objects (up to **v.size()**) or a past-the-end pointer (**&*v.begin()+v.size()**).

If you have a container of **T** objects other than **vector** or **string** and want to pass its contents to (or populate it from) a non-C++ API that expects a pointer to an array of **T** objects, copy the container's contents to (or from) a **vector<T>** that can directly communicate with the non-C++ API.

References

[Josuttis99] §6.2.3, §11.2.4 • [Meyers01] §16 • [Musser01] §B • [Stroustrup00] §16.3.1

79. Store only values and smart pointers in containers.

Summary

Store objects of value in containers: Containers assume they contain value-like types, including value types (held directly), smart pointers, and iterators.

Discussion

The most common use of containers is to store values held directly (e.g., **vector<int>**, **set<string>**). For containers of pointers: If the container owns the pointed-to objects, prefer a container of reference-counted smart pointers (e.g., **list<shared_ptr<Widget> >**); otherwise, a container of raw pointers (e.g., **list<Widget*>**) or of other pointer-like values such as iterators (e.g., **list< vector<Widget>::iterator >**) is fine.

Examples

*Example 1: **auto_ptr**.* Objects of **auto_ptr<T>** are not value-like because of their transfer-of-ownership copy semantics. Using a container of **auto_ptr**s (e.g., a **vector< auto_ptr<int> >**) should fail to compile. Even if it does compile, *never* write that; if you want to write it, you almost certainly want a container of **shared_ptr**s instead.

Example 2: Heterogeneous containers. To have a container store and own objects of different but related types, such as types derived from a common **Base** class, prefer **container< shared_ptr<Base> >**. An alternative is to store proxy objects whose non-virtual functions pass through to corresponding virtual functions of the actual object.

Example 3: Containers of non-value types. To contain objects even though they are not copyable or otherwise not value-like (e.g., **DatabaseLock**s and **TcpConnection**s), prefer containing them indirectly via smart pointers (e.g., **container< shared_ptr<DatabaseLock> >** and **container< shared_ptr<TcpConnection> >**).

Example 4: Optional values. When you want a **map<Thing, Widget>**, but some **Thing**s have no associated **Widget**, prefer **map<Thing, shared_ptr<Widget> >**.

Example 5: Index containers. To have a main container hold the objects and access them using different sort orders without resorting the main container, you can set up secondary containers that "point into" the main one and sort the secondary containers in different ways using dereferenced compare predicates. But prefer a container of **MainContainer::iterator**s (which are value-like) instead of a container of pointers.

References

[Allison98] §14 • *[Austern99] §6* • *[Dewhurst03] §68* • *[Josuttis99] §5.10.2* • *[Koenig97] §5* • *[Meyers01] §3, §7-8* • *[SuttHysl04b]*

80. Prefer push_back to other ways of expanding a sequence.

Summary

push_back all you can: If you don't need to care about the insert position, prefer using **push_back** to add an element to sequence. Other means can be both vastly slower and less clear.

Discussion

You can insert elements into sequences at different points using **insert**, and you can append elements to sequences in various ways including:

```
vector<int> vec;                  // vec is empty
vec.resize(vec.size() + 1, 1);    // vec contains { 1 }
vec.insert(vec.end(), 2);         // vec contains { 1, 2 }
vec.push_back(3);                 // vec contains { 1, 2, 3 }
```

Of all forms, **push_back** alone takes *amortized constant time*. The other forms' performance can be as bad as quadratic. Needless to say, beyond small data volumes that makes those alternatives potential scalability barriers. (See Item 7.)

push_back's magic is simple: It expands capacity exponentially, not by a fixed increment. Hence the number of reallocations and copies decreases rapidly with size. For a container populated using only **push_back** calls, on average each element has been copied only once—regardless of the final size of the container.

Of course, **resize** and **insert** could employ the same strategy, but that is dependent on the implementation; only **push_back** offers the guarantee.

Algorithms can't call **push_back** directly because they don't have access to the container. You can ask algorithms to use **push_back** anyway by using a **back_inserter**.

Exceptions

If you know you're adding a range, even at the end of a container, prefer to use a range insertion function (see Item 81).

Exponential growth is generous with memory allocation. To fine-tune growth, call **reserve** explicitly—**push_back**, **resize**, and the like never trigger reallocation if they have enough space. To "right-size" a **vector**, use the shrink-to-fit idiom (see Item 82).

References

[Stroustrup00] §3.7-8, §16.3.5, §17.1.4.1

81. Prefer range operations to single-element operations.

Summary

Don't use oars when the wind is fair (based on a Latin proverb): When adding elements to sequence containers, prefer to use range operations (e.g., the form of **insert** that takes a pair of iterators) instead of a series of calls to the single-element form of the operation. Calling the range operation is generally easier to write, easier to read, and more efficient than an explicit loop. (See also Item 84.)

Discussion

The more context you can give a function, the better the chances that it can do something useful with the information. In particular, when you call a single function and pass it a pair of iterators **first** and **last** that delimit a range, it can perform optimizations based on knowing the number of objects that are going to be added, which it obtains by computing **distance(first,last)**.

The same applies to "repeat *n* times" operations, such as the **vector** constructor that takes a repeat count and a value.

Examples

*Example 1: **vector::insert**.* Let's say you want to add **n** elements into a **vector v**. Calling **v.insert(position,x)** repeatedly can cause multiple reallocations as **v** grows its storage to accommodate each new element. Worse, each single-element **insert** is a linear operation because it has to shuffle over enough elements to make room, and this makes inserting **n** elements with repeated calls to the single-element **insert** actually a quadratic operation! Of course, you could get around the multiple-reallocation problem by calling **reserve**, but that doesn't reduce the shuffling and the quadratic nature of the operation. It's faster and simpler to just say what you're doing: **v.insert(position,first,last)**, where **first** and **last** are iterators delimiting the range of elements to be added into **v**. (If **first** and **last** are input iterators, there's no way to determine the size of the range before actually traversing it, and therefore **v** might still need to perform multiple reallocations; but the range version is still likely to perform better than inserting elements individually.)

Example 2: Range construction and assignment. Calling a constructor (or **assign** function) that takes an iterator range typically performs better than calling the default constructor (or **clear**) followed by individual insertions into the container.

References

[Meyers01] §5 • [Stroustrup00] §16.3.8

82. Use the accepted idioms to really shrink capacity and really erase elements.

Summary

Use a diet that works: To really shed excess capacity from a container, use the "swap trick." To really erase elements from a container, use the erase-remove idiom.

Discussion

Some containers (e.g., **vector**, **string**, **deque**) can end up carrying around extra capacity that's no longer needed. Although the C++ standard library containers provide no guaranteed way to trim excess capacity, the following "swap trick" idiom works in practice to get rid of excess capacity for such a **c** of type **container**:

> container<T>(c).swap(c);   *// the shrink-to-fit idiom to shed excess capacity*

Or, to empty **c** out completely, clearing all contained elements and shedding all possible capacity, the idiom is:

> container<T>().swap(c);   *// the idiom to shed all contents and capacity*

In related news, a common surprise for new STL programmers is that the **remove** algorithm doesn't really remove elements from a container. Of course, it can't; an algorithm just works on an iterator range, and you can't actually remove something from a container without calling a container member function, usually **erase**. All **remove** does is to shuffle values around so that the elements that shouldn't be "removed" get shuffled up toward the beginning of the range, and return an iterator to one past the end of the unremoved elements. To really get rid of them, the call to **remove** needs to be followed by a call to **erase**—hence the "erase-remove" idiom. For example, to erase all elements equal to **value** from a container **c**, you can write:

> c.**erase**(**remove**(c.begin(), c.end(), value), c.end());

Prefer to use a member version of **remove** or **remove_if** on a container that has it.

Exceptions

The usual shrink-to-fit idiom won't work on copy-on-write implementations of **std::string**. What usually does work is to call **s.reserve(0)** or to fake the **string** out by writing **string(s.begin(), s.end()).swap(s);** to use the iterator range constructor. In practice, these work to shed excess capacity. (Better still, **std::string** implementations are abandoning copy-on-write, which is an outdated optimization; see [Sutter02].)

References

[Josuttis99] §6.2.1 • [Meyers01] §17, §32, §44 • [Sutter00] §7 • [Sutter02] §7, §16

STL: Algorithms

Prefer algorithms to loops.

—Bjarne Stroustrup,
[Stroustrup00] §18.12

Algorithms are loops—only better. Algorithms are the "patterns" of loops, adding far more semantic content and richness than a naked **for** would **do** alone. Of course, the moment you start using algorithms you'll also start using function objects and predicates; write them correctly, and use them well.

Our vote for the most valuable Item in this section goes to Item 83: Use a checked STL implementation.

83. Use a checked STL implementation.

Summary

Safety first (see Item 6): Use a checked STL implementation, even if it's only available for one of your compiler platforms, and even if it's only used during pre-release testing.

Discussion

Just like pointer mistakes, iterator mistakes are far too easy to make and will usually silently compile but then crash (at best) or appear to work (at worst). Even though your compiler doesn't catch the mistakes, you don't have to rely on "correction by visual inspection," and shouldn't: Tools exist. Use them.

Some STL mistakes are distressingly common even for experienced programmers:

- *Using an invalidated or uninitialized iterator:* The former in particular is easy to do.
- *Passing an out-of-bounds index:* For example, accessing element 113 of a 100-element container.
- *Using an iterator "range" that isn't really a range:* Passing two iterators where the first doesn't precede the second, or that don't both refer into the same container.
- *Passing an invalid iterator position:* Calling a container member function that takes an iterator position, such as the position passed to **insert**, but passing an iterator that refers into a different container.
- *Using an invalid ordering:* Providing an invalid ordering rule for ordering an associative container or as a comparison criterion with the sorting algorithms. (See [Meyers01] §21 for examples.) Without a checked STL, these would typically manifest at run time as erratic behavior or infinite loops, not as hard errors.

Most checked STL implementations detect these errors automatically, by adding extra debugging and housekeeping information to containers and iterators. For example, an iterator can remember the container it refers into, and a container can remember all outstanding iterators into itself so that it can mark the appropriate iterators as invalid as they become invalidated. Of course, this makes for fatter iterators, containers with extra state, and some extra work every time you modify the container. But it's worth it—at least during testing, and perhaps even during release (remember Item 8; don't disable valuable checks for performance reasons unless and until you know performance is an issue in the affected cases).

Even if you don't ship with checking turned on, and even if you only have a checked STL on one of your target platforms, at minimum ensure that you routinely run your full complement of tests against a version of your application built with a checked STL. You'll be glad you did.

Examples

Example 1: Using an invalid iterator. It's easy to forget when iterators are invalidated and use an invalid iterator (see Item 99). Consider this example adapted from [Meyers01] that inserts elements at the front of a **deque**:

```
deque<double>::iterator current = d.begin();

for( size_t i = 0; i < max; ++i )
    d.insert( current++, data[i] + 41 );          // do you see the bug?
```

Quick: Do you see the bug? You have three seconds.—Ding! If you didn't get it in time, don't worry; it's a subtle and understandable mistake. A checked STL implementation will detect this error for you on the second loop iteration so that you don't need to rely on your unaided visual acuity. (For a fixed version of this code, and superior alternatives to such a naked loop, see Item 84.)

Example 2: Using an iterator range that isn't really a range. An iterator range is a pair of iterators **first** and **last** that refer to the first element and the one-past-the-end-th element of the range, respectively. It is required that **last** be reachable from **first** by repeated increments of **first**. There are two common ways to accidentally try to use an iterator range that isn't actually a range: The first way arises when the two iterators that delimit the range point into the same container, but the first iterator doesn't actually precede the second:

```
for_each( c.end(), c.begin(), Something );     // not always this obvious
```

On each iteration of its internal loop, **for_each** will compare the first iterator with the second for equality, and as long as they are not equal it will continue to increment the first iterator. Of course, no matter how many times you increment the first iterator, it will never equal the second, so the loop is essentially endless. In practice, this will, at best, fall off the end of the container **c** and crash immediately with a memory protection fault. At worst, it will just fall off the end into uncharted memory and possibly read or change values that aren't part of the container. It's not that much different in principle from our infamous and eminently attackable friend the buffer overrun.

The second common case arises when the iterators point into different containers:

```
for_each( c.begin(), d.end(), Something );     // not always this obvious
```

The results are similar. Because checked STL iterators remember the containers that they refer into, they can detect such run-time errors.

References

[Dinkumware-Safe] • *[Horstmann95]* • *[Josuttis99] §5.11.1* • *[Metrowerks]* • *[Meyers01] §21, §50* • *[STLport-Debug]* • *[Stroustrup00] §18.3.1, §19.3.1*

84. Prefer algorithm calls to handwritten loops.

Summary

Use function objects judiciously: For very simple loops, handwritten loops can be the simplest and most efficient solution. But writing algorithm calls instead of handwritten loops can be more expressive and maintainable, less error-prone, and as efficient.

When calling algorithms, consider writing your own custom function object that encapsulates the logic you need. Avoid cobbling together parameter-binders and simple function objects (e.g., **bind2nd**, **plus**), which usually degrade clarity. Consider trying the [Boost] Lambda library, which automates the task of writing function objects.

Discussion

Programs that use the STL tend to have fewer explicit loops than non-STL programs, replacing low-level semantics-free loops with higher-level and better-defined abstract operations that convey greater semantic information. Prefer a "process this range" algorithmic mindset over "process each element" loopy thinking.

A primary benefit that algorithms and design patterns have in common is that they let us speak at a higher level of abstraction with a known vocabulary. These days, we don't say "let many objects watch one object and get automatic notifications when its state changes;" rather, we say just "Observer." Similarly, we say "Bridge," "Factory," and "Visitor." Our shared pattern vocabulary raises the level, effectiveness, and correctness of our discussion. With algorithms, we likewise don't say "perform an action on each element in a range and write the results somewhere;" rather, we say **transform**. Similarly, we say **for_each**, **replace_if**, and **partition**. Algorithms, like design patterns, are self-documenting. Naked **for** and **while** loops just don't **do** when it comes to imparting any inherent semantic information about the purpose of the loop; they force readers to inspect their loop bodies to decipher what's going on.

Algorithms are also more likely to be correct than loops. Handwritten loops easily make mistakes such as using invalidated iterators (see Items 83 and 99); algorithms come already debugged for iterator invalidation and other common errors.

Finally, algorithms are also often more efficient than naked loops (see [Sutter00] and [Meyers01]). They avoid needless minor inefficiencies, such as repeated evaluations of **container.end()**. Slightly more importantly, the standard algorithms you're using were implemented by the same people who implemented the standard containers you're using, and by dint of their inside knowledge those people can write algorithms that are more efficient than any version you would write. Most important of all, however, is that many algorithms have highly sophisticated implementations that we in-the-trenches programmers are unlikely ever to match in handwritten code (unless we don't need the full generality of everything a given algorithm does).

In general, the more widely used a library is, the better debugged and more efficient it will be simply because it has so many users. You are unlikely to be using any other library that is as widely used as your standard library implementation. Use it and benefit. STL's algorithms are already written; why write them again?

Consider trying [Boost] lambda functions. Lambda functions are an important tool that solves the biggest drawback of algorithms, namely readability: They write the function objects for you, leaving the actual code in place at the call point. Without lambda functions, your choices are to either use function objects (but then even simple loop bodies live in a separate place away from the call point) or else use the standard binders and function objects such as **bind2nd** and **plus** (these are tedious and confusing to use, and hard to combine because fundamental operations like **compose** are not part of the standard; but do consider the [C++TR104] bind library).

Examples

Here are two examples adapted from [Meyers01]:

*Example 1: Transforming a **deque**.* After working through several incorrect iterations that ran afoul of iterator invalidation issues (e.g., see Item 83), we finally come up with the following correct handwritten loop for adding **41** to every element of **data**, an array of **double**s, and placing the result at the beginning of **d**, a **deque<double>**:

```
deque<double>::iterator current = d.begin();

for( size_t i = 0; i < max; ++i ) {
  current = d.insert( current, data[i] + 41 );   // be careful to keep current valid...
  ++current;                                      // ... then increment it when it's safe
}
```

An algorithm call would have bypassed the correctness pitfalls straight away:

```
transform( data.begin(), data.end(),          // copy elements from data
          inserter(d, d.begin()),             // to the front of d
          bind2nd(plus<double>(), 41) );      // adding 41 to each
```

Granted, **bind2nd** and **plus** are awkward. Frankly, nobody really uses them much, and that's just as well because they hurt readability (see Item 6).

But lambda functions, which generate the function object for us, let us write simply:

```
transform( data, data + max, inserter( d, d.begin() ), _1 + 41 );
```

*Example 2: Find the first element between **x** and **y**.* Consider this naked loop that searches a **vector<int> v** for the first value between **x** and **y**, by calculating an iterator that points to the found element or to **v.end()**:

```
vector<int>::iterator i = v.begin();
for( ; i != v.end(); ++i )
  if( *i > x && *i < y ) break;
```

An algorithm call is problematic. Absent lambdas, the two options are to write a custom function object or to use the standard binders. Alas, with the binders option we can't use the standard binders alone but need to use the nonstandard (although widely-available) **compose2** adapter, and even at that the code is just impenetrable, and nobody would ever really write it:

```
vector<int>::iterator i = find_if( v.begin(), v.end(),
                       compose2( logical_and<bool>(),
                                 bind2nd(gr
                                 bind2nd(less<int>(), y) ) );
```

The other option, namely writing a custom function object, is viable. It looks good at the call point, and its main drawback is that it requires writing a **BetweenValues** function object that moves the body's logic visually away from the call point:

```
template<typename T>
class BetweenValues : public unary_function<T, bool> {
public:
  BetweenValues( const T& low, const T& high ) : low_(low), high_(high) { }
  bool operator()( const T& val ) const { return val > low_ && val < high_; }

private:                                    // far away from the point of use
  T low_, high_;
};
```

```
vector<int>::iterator i = find_if( v.begin(), v.end(), BetweenValues<int>(x, y) );
```

Lambda functions, which generate the function object for us, let us write simply:

```
vector<int>::iterator i = find_if( v.begin(), v.end(), _1 > x && _1 < y );
```

Exceptions

When used with function objects, algorithm calls place the body of the loop away from the call site, which can make the loop harder to read. (Cobbling together simple objects with the standard and nonstandard binders isn't a realistic option.)

[Boost] lambda functions solve these two problems and work reliably on modern compilers, but they don't work on older compilers and they can generate dense error messages when they're coded incorrectly. Calling named functions, including member functions, still requires binder-like syntax.

References

[Allison98] §15 • *[Austern99]* §11-13 • *[Boost]* Lambda library • *[McConnell93]* §15 • *[Meyers01]* §43 • *[Musser01]* §11 • *[Stroustrup00]* §6.1.8, §18.5.1 • *[Sutter00]* §7

85. Use the right STL search algorithm.

Summary

Search "just enough"—the right search may be STL (slower than light), but it'll still be pretty fast: This Item applies to searching for a particular value in a range, or for the location where it would be if it were in the range. To search an unsorted range, use **find/find_if** or **count/count_if**. To search a sorted range, use **lower_bound**, **upper_bound**, **equal_range**, or (rarely) **binary_search**. (Despite its common name, **binary_search** is usually not the right choice.)

Discussion

For unsorted ranges, **find/find_if** and **count/count_if** can tell you in linear time whether and where, respectively, an element exists in a range. Note that **find/find_if** is typically more efficient because it can stop searching when a match is found.

For sorted ranges, prefer the four binary search algorithms, **binary_search**, **lower_bound**, **upper_bound**, and **equal_range**, which work in logarithmic time. Alas, despite its nice name, **binary_search** is nearly always useless because it only returns a **bool** indicating whether a match was found or not. Usually, you want **lower_bound** or **upper_bound**—or **equal_range**, which gives you the results of both **lower_bound** and **upper_bound** (but not at twice the cost).

lower_bound returns an iterator pointing to the first match (if there is one) or the location where it would be (if there is not); the latter is useful to find the right place to insert new values into a sorted sequence. **upper_bound** returns an iterator pointing to one past the last match (if there is one), which is the location where the next equivalent element can be added; this is useful to find the right place to insert new values into a sorted sequence while keeping equivalent elements in the order in which they were inserted.

Prefer **p = equal_range(first, last, value); distance(p.first, p.second);** as a faster version of **count(first, last, value);** for sorted ranges.

If you are searching an associative container, prefer using the member functions with the same names instead of the nonmember algorithms. The member versions are usually more efficient, including that the member version of **count** runs in logarithmic time (and so there's no motivation to replace a call to the member **count** with a call to **equal_range** followed by **distance**, as there is with the nonmember **count**).

References

[Austern99] §13.2-3 • [Bentley00] §13 • [Meyers01] §34, §45 • [Musser01] §22.2 • [Stroustrup00] §17.1.4.1, §18.7.2

86. Use the right STL sort algorithm.

Summary

Sort "just enough:" Understand what each of the sorting algorithms does, and use the cheapest algorithm that does what you need.

Discussion

You don't always need a full **sort**; you usually need less, and rarely you need more. In general order from cheapest to most expensive, your standard sorting algorithm options are: **partition, stable_partition, nth_element, partial_sort** (with its variant **partial_sort_copy**), **sort**, and **stable_sort**. Use the least expensive one that does the work you actually need; using a more powerful one is wasteful.

partition, stable_partition, and **nth_element** run in linear time, which is nice.

nth_element, partial_sort, sort, and **stable_sort** require random-access iterators. You can't use them if you have only bidirectional iterators (e.g., **list<T>::iterator**s). If you need these algorithms but you don't have random-access iterators, consider using the index container idiom: Create a container that does support random-access iterators (e.g., a **vector**) of iterators into the range you have, and then use the more powerful algorithm on that using a dereferencing version of your predicate (one that dereferences the iterators before doing its usual comparison).

Use the **stable_...** versions only if you need to preserve the relative ordering of equal elements. Note that **partial_sort** and **nth_element** aren't stable (meaning that they don't keep equivalent elements in the same relative order they were in before the sort), and they have no standardized stable versions. If you otherwise want these algorithms but need stability, you probably want **stable_sort**.

Of course, don't use any sorting algorithm at all if you don't have to: If you are using a standard associative container (**set/multiset** or **map/multimap**) or the **priority_queue** adapter, and only need one sort order, the elements in the container stay sorted all the time.

Examples

Example 1: partition. Use **partition** to just divide the range into two groups: all elements that satisfy the predicate, followed by all elements that don't. This is all you need to answer questions like these:

- "Who are all the students with a grade of B+ or better?" For example, **partition(students.begin(), students.end(), GradeAtLeast("B+"));** does the work and returns an iterator to the first student whose grade is not at least B+.

- "What are all the products with weight less than 10kg?" For example, **partition(products.begin(), products.end(), WeightUnder(10));** does the work and returns an iterator to the first product whose weight is 10kg or more.

Example 2: nth_element. Use **nth_element** to put a single element in the correct **n**-th position it would occupy if the range were completely sorted, and with all other elements correctly preceding or following that **n**-th element. This is all you need to answer questions like these:

- "Who are my top 20 salespeople?" For example, **nth_element(s.begin(), s.begin()+19, s.end(), SalesRating);** puts the 20 best elements at the front.

- "What is the item with the median level of quality in this production run?" That element would be in the middle position of a sorted range. To find it, do **nth_element(run.begin(), run.begin()+run.size()/2, run.end(), ItemQuality);.**

- "What is the item whose quality is at the 75th percentile?" That item would be 25% of the way through the sorted range. To find it, do **nth_element(run.begin(), run.begin()+run.size()*.25, run.end(), ItemQuality);.**

Example 3: partial_sort. **partial_sort** does the work of **nth_element**, plus the elements preceding the **n**-th are all in their correct sorted positions. Use **partial_sort** to answer questions similar to those nth_element answers, but where you need the elements that match to be sorted (and those that don't match don't need to be sorted). This is all you need to answer questions like, "Who are the first-, second-, and third-place winners?" For example, **partial_sort(contestants.begin(), contestants.begin()+3, contestants.end(), ScoreCompare);** puts the top three contestants, in order, at the front of the container—and no more.

Exceptions

Although **partial_sort** is usually faster than a full **sort** because it has to do less work, if you are going to be sorting most (or all) of the range, it can be slower than a full **sort**.

References

[Austern99] §13.1 • [Bentley00] §11 • [Josuttis99] §9.2.2 • [Meyers01] §31 • [Musser01] §5.4, §22.26 • [Stroustrup00] §17.1.4.1, §18.7

87. Make predicates pure functions.

Summary

Predicate purity: A predicate is a function object that returns a yes/no answer, typically as a **bool** value. A function is pure in the mathematical sense if its result depends only on its arguments (note that this use of "pure" has nothing to do with pure virtual functions).

Don't allow predicates to hold or access state that affects the result of their **operator()**, including both member and global state. Prefer to make **operator()** a **const** member function for predicates (see Item 15).

Discussion

Algorithms make an unknowable number of copies of their predicates at unknowable times in an unknowable order, and then go on to pass those copies around while casually assuming that the copies are all equivalent.

That is why it's your responsibility to make sure that copies of predicates are indeed all equivalent, and that means that they must be pure functions: functions whose result is not affected by anything other than the arguments passed to **operator()**. Additionally, predicates must also consistently return the same result for the same set of arguments they are asked to evaluate.

Stateful predicates may seem useful, but they are explicitly *not* very useful with the C++ standard library and its algorithms, and that is intentional. In particular, stateful predicates can only be useful if:

- *The predicate is not copied:* The standard algorithms make no such guarantee, and in fact assume that predicates are safely copyable.
- *The predicate is applied in a documented deterministic order:* The standard algorithms generally make no guarantee about the order in which the predicate will be applied to the elements in the range. In the absence of guarantees about the order in which objects will be visited, operations like "flag the third element" (see Examples) make little sense, because which element will be visited "third" is not well-defined.

It is possible to work around the first point by writing a lightweight predicate that uses reference-counting techniques to share its deep state. That solves the predicate-copying problem too because the predicate can be safely copied without changing its semantics when it is applied to objects. (See [Sutter02].) It is not possible, however, to work around the second point.

Always declare a predicate type's **operator()** as a const member function so that the compiler can help you avoid this mistake by emitting an error if you try to change any data members that the predicate type may have. This won't prevent all abuses—for example, it won't flag accesses to global data—but it will help the compiler to help you avoid at least the most common mistakes.

Examples

*Example: **FlagNth**.* Here is the classic example from [Sutter02], which is intended to remove the third element from a container **v**:

```
class FlagNth {
public:
  FlagNth( size_t n ) : current_(0), n_(n) { }

  // evaluate to true if and only if this is the n-th invocation
  template<typename T>
  bool operator()( const T& ) { return ++current_ == n_; }      // bad: non-const

private:
  size_t current_, n_;
};

// ... later ...

v.erase( remove_if( v.begin(), v.end(), FlagNth(3) ) );
```

This is not guaranteed to remove the third element, even though that was intended. In most real-world STL implementations, it erases both the third and the sixth elements. Why? Because **remove_if** is commonly implemented in terms of **find_if** and **remove_copy_if**, and it passes along a copy of the predicate to each of those functions, possibly after it has already itself done some work that affects the predicate's state.

Conceptually, this example is perverse because **remove_if** only guarantees that it will remove all elements satisfying some criterion. It does not document the order in which elements in the range will be visited or removed, so the code is relying on an assumed, but undocumented and unsatisfied, assumption.

The correct way to remove a particular element is to iterate to it and then call **erase**.

References

[Austern99] §4.2.2 • [Josuttis99] §5.8.2, §8.1.4 • [Meyers01] §39 • [Stroustrup00] §10.2.6 • [Sutter02] §2-3

88. Prefer function objects over functions as algorithm and comparer arguments.

Summary

Objects plug in better than functions: Prefer passing function objects, not functions, to algorithms. Comparers for associative containers must be function objects. Function objects are adaptable and, counterintuitively, they typically produce faster code than functions.

Discussion

First, function objects are easy to make adaptable, and always should be (see Item 89). Even if you already have a function, sometimes you have to wrap it in **ptr_fun** or **mem_fun** anyway to add adaptability. For example, you have to do this in order to build up more complex expressions using binders (see also Item 84):

```
inline bool IsHeavy( const Thing& ) { /*...*/ }

find_if( v.begin(), v.end(), not1( IsHeavy ) );          // error: isn't adaptable
```

The usual workaround is to insert **ptr_fun** (or, for a member function, **mem_fun** or **mem_fun_ref**), which unfortunately doesn't work in this particular case:

```
inline bool IsHeavy( const Thing& ) { /*...*/ }

find_if( v.begin(), v.end(), not1( ptr_fun( IsHeavy ) ) );  // a valiant attempt
```

It's a pain that this wouldn't work even if you explicitly specified **ptr_fun**'s template arguments. Briefly, the problem is that **ptr_fun** deduces the argument and return types exactly (in particular, the parameter type is deduced as **const Thing&**) and goes on to create internal machinery which, along the way, in turn helpfully tries to add another **&**, and references to references are not currently allowed by ISO C++. There are ways in which the standard language and/or library could, and probably should, be fixed so as to make this work correctly (e.g., by allowing references to references to collapse to a single reference; or see also Item 89), but it doesn't do that today.

You don't have to remember this stuff if you're using a correctly-written function object (see Item 89), which is adaptable from the get-go without special syntax:

```
struct IsHeavy : unary_function<Thing, bool> {
  bool operator()( const Thing& ) const { /*...*/ }
};

find_if( v.begin(), v.end(), not1( IsHeavy() ) );          // ok: adaptable
```

More importantly, you need a function object, not a function, to specify comparers for associative containers. This is because it's illegal to instantiate a template type parameter with a function directly:

```
bool CompareThings( const Thing&, const Thing& );

set<Thing, CompareThings> s;                          // error
```

Instead, you need:

```
struct CompareThings : public binary_function<Thing,Thing,bool> {
  bool operator()( const Thing&, const Thing& ) const;
};

set<Thing, CompareThings> s;                          // ok
```

Finally, there is also an efficiency benefit. Consider this familiar algorithm:

```
template<typename Iter, typename Compare>
Iter find_if( Iter first, Iter last, Compare comp );
```

If we pass a function as the comparer to **find_if**

```
inline bool Function( const Thing& ) { /*...*/ }

find_if( v.begin(), v.end(), Function );
```

we're actually passing a reference to **Function**. Compilers rarely inline such function calls (except as part of whole-program analysis, which is still a relatively recent feature on popular compilers), even when as above the function is declared **inline** and is visible while compiling the **find_if** call. And, as noted, functions aren't adaptable.

If we pass a function object as the comparer to **find_if**

```
struct FunctionObject : unary_function<Thing, bool> {
  bool operator()( const Thing& ) const { /*...*/ }
};

find_if( v.begin(), v.end(), FunctionObject() );
```

we're passing an object that typically has an (implicitly or explicitly) inline **operator()** function. Compilers have routinely inlined such calls since C++'s Bronze Age.

Note: This is not to encourage premature optimization (see Item 8), but to discourage premature pessimization (see Item 9). If you already have a function, go ahead and pass a pointer to the function (unless you have to wrap it with **ptr_fun** or **mem_fun** anyway). But if you're writing a new piece of code for use as an argument to an algorithm, prefer writing the extra boilerplate to make it a function object.

References

[Austern99] §4, §8, §15 • [Josuttis99] §5.9 • [Meyers01] §46 • [Musser01] §8 • [Sutter04] §25

89. Write function objects correctly.

Summary

Be cheap, be adaptable: Design function objects to be values that are cheap to copy. Where possible, make them adaptable by inheriting from **unary_-** or **binary_function**.

Discussion

Function objects are modeled on function pointers. Like function pointers, the convention is to pass them by value. All of the standard algorithms pass objects by value, and your algorithms should too. For example:

```
template<class InputIter, class Func>
Function for_each( InputIter first, InputIter last, Function f );
```

Therefore, function objects must be cheap to copy and monomorphic (immune to slicing, so avoid virtual functions; see Item 54). But large and/or polymorphic objects are useful, and using them is okay; just hide the size and richness using the Pimpl idiom (see Item 43), which leaves the outer class as the required cheap-to-copy monomorphic type that still accesses rich state. The outer class should:

- *Be adaptable:* Inherit from **unary_function** or **binary_function**. (See below.)
- *Have a Pimpl:* Store a pointer (e.g., **shared_ptr**) to a large/rich implementation.
- *Have the function call operator(s):* Pass these through to the implementation object.

That should be all that's needed in the outer class, other than possibly providing non-default versions of construction, assignment, and/or destruction.

Function objects should be adaptable. The standard binders and adapters rely on certain typedefs, which are provided most conveniently when your function object derives from **unary_function** or **binary_function**. Instantiate **unary_function** or **binary_function** with the same types as your **operator()** takes and returns, except that for each non-pointer type strip off any top-level **const**s and **&**s from the type.

Avoid providing multiple **operator()** functions, because that makes adaptability difficult. It's usually impossible to provide the right adaptability typedefs because the same typedef would have different values for different **operator()** functions.

Not all function objects are predicates. Predicates are a subset of function objects. (See Item 87.)

References

[Allison98] §15, §C • [Austern99] §4, §8, §15 • [Gamma95] Bridge • [Josuttis99] §8.2.4 • [Koenig97] §21, §29 • [Meyers97] §34 • [Meyers01] §38, §40, §46 • [Musser01] §2.4, §8, §23 • [Sutter00] §26-30 • [Vandevoorde03] §22

Type Safety

Trying to outsmart a compiler defeats much of the purpose of using one.

—Brian Kernighan & P.J. Plauger

If you lie to the compiler, it will get its revenge.

—Henry Spencer

*There will always be things we wish to say in our programs
that in all known languages can only be said poorly.*

—Alan Perlis

Last, but certainly not least, we will consider type correctness—a very important property of a program that you should strive to preserve at all times. Theoretically, a type-correct function can never access untyped memory or return forged values. Practically, if your code maintains type soundness, it avoids a large category of nasty errors ranging from nonportability to corrupting memory to creating bogus values to exhibiting undefined behavior.

The basic idea underpinning how to maintain type soundness is to always read bits in the format in which they were written. Sometimes, C++ makes it easy to break this rule, and the following Items detail how to avoid such mistakes.

Our vote for the most valuable Item in this section goes to Item 91: Rely on types, not on representations. The type system is your friend and your staunchest ally; enlist its help, and try never to abuse its trust.

90. Avoid type switching; prefer polymorphism.

Summary

Switch off: Avoid switching on the type of an object to customize behavior. Use templates and virtual functions to let types (not their calling code) decide their behavior.

Discussion

Type switching to customize behavior is brittle, error-prone, unsafe, and a clear sign of attempting to write C or Fortran code in C++. It is a rigid technique that forces you to go back and do surgery on existing code whenever you want to add new features. It is also unsafe because the compiler will not tell you if you forget to modify all of the switches when you add a type.

Ideally, adding new features to a program equates to adding more new code (see Item 37). In reality, we know that that's not always true—oftentimes, in addition to writing new code, we need to go back and modify some existing code. Changing working code is undesirable and should be minimized, however, for two reasons: First, it might break existing functionality. Second, it doesn't scale well as the system grows and more features are added, because the number of "maintenance knots" that you need to go back and change increases as well. This observation led to the Open-Closed principle that states: An entity (e.g., class or module) should be open for extension but closed for modification. (See [Martin96c] and [Meyer00].)

How can we write code that can be easily extended without modifying it? Use polymorphism by writing code in terms of abstractions (see also Item 36) and then adding various implementations of those abstractions as you add functionality. Templates and virtual function calls form a dependency shield between the code using the abstractions and the code implementing them (see Item 64).

Of course, managing dependencies this way depends on finding the right abstractions. If the abstractions are imperfect, adding new functionality will require changing the interface (not just adding new implementations of the interface), which usually requires changes to existing code. But abstractions are called "abstractions" for a reason—they are supposed to be much more stable than the "details," that is, the abstractions' possible implementations.

Contrast that with code that uses few or no abstractions, but instead traffics directly in concrete types and their specific operations. That code is "detailed" already—in fact, it is swimming in a sea of details, a sea in which it is doomed soon to drown.

Examples

Example: Drawing shapes. The classic example is drawing objects. A typical C-style, **switch**-on-type solution would define an enumerated member variable **id_** for each shape that stores the type of that shape: rectangle, circle, and so on. Drawing code looks up the type and performs specific tasks:

```cpp
class Shape { // ...
  enum { RECTANGLE, TRIANGLE, CIRCLE } id_;

  void Draw() const {
    switch( id_ ) {                         // bad
    case RECTANGLE:
      // ... rectangle drawing code ...
      break;

    case TRIANGLE:
      // ... triangle drawing code ...
      break;

    case CIRCLE:
      // ... circle drawing code ...
      break;

    default:                                // bad
      assert( !"Oops, forgot to update this switch when adding a new Shape" );
      break;
    }
  }
};
```

Such code creaks under its own weight, fragility, rigidity, and complexity. In particular, it suffers from the dreaded transitive cyclic dependency mentioned in Item 22. The **default** branch is symptomatic of "don't know what to do with this type" syndrome. Contrast that with an implementation that you could pull from any OO text:

```cpp
class Shape { // ...
  virtual void Draw() const = 0;            // let each derived class implement it
};
```

Alternatively (or in addition), consider this implementation that follows the advice to make decisions at compile time where possible (see Item 64):

```cpp
template<class S>
void Draw( const S& shape ) {
  shape.Draw();                             // might or might not be virtual;
};                                          // see Item 64
```

Now the responsibility of drawing each geometric figure goes to the figure implementation itself—and there's no more "can't handle this type" syndrome anymore.

References

[Dewhurst03] §69, §96 • [Martin96c] • [Meyer00] • [Stroustrup00] §12.2.5 • [Sutter04] §36

91. **Rely on types, not on representations.**

Summary

Don't try to X-ray objects (see Item 96): Don't make assumptions about how objects are exactly represented in memory. Instead, let types decide how their objects are written to and read from memory.

Discussion

The C++ Standard makes few guarantees about how types are represented in memory:

- Base two is guaranteed for integral numbers.
- Two's complement is guaranteed for negative integral numbers.
- Plain Old Data (POD) types have C-compatible layout: Member variables are stored in their order of declaration.
- **int** holds at least 16 bits.

In particular, the following may be common but are *not* guaranteed on all current architectures, and in particular are liable to be broken on newer architectures:

- **int** is not exactly 32 bits, nor any particular fixed size.
- Pointers and **int**s don't always have the same size and can't always be freely cast to one another.
- Class layout does not always store bases and members in declaration order.
- There can be gaps between the members of a class (even a POD) for alignment.
- **offsetof** only works for PODs, not all classes (but compilers might not emit errors).
- A class might have hidden fields.
- Pointers might not look like integers at all. If two pointers are ordered, and you cast them to integral values, the resulting values might not be ordered the same way.
- You can't portably assume anything about the placement in memory of automatic variables, or about the direction in which the stack grows.
- Pointers to functions might have a different size than **void***, even though some APIs force you to assume that their sizes are the same.
- You can't always write just any object at just any memory address, even if you have enough space, due to alignment issues.

Just define types appropriately, then read and write data using those types instead of thinking bits and words and addresses. The C++ memory model ensures efficient execution without forcing you to rely on manipulating representation. So don't.

References

[Dewhurst03] §95

92. Avoid using reinterpret_cast.

Summary

Lies have short legs (German and Romanian proverb): Don't try to use **reinterpret_-cast** to force the compiler to reinterpret the bits of an object of one type as being the bits of an object of a different type. That's the opposite of maintaining type safety, and **reinterpret_cast** isn't even guaranteed to do that or anything else in particular.

Discussion

Recall: *If you lie to the compiler, it will get its revenge.* —Henry Spencer

reinterpret_cast reflects the strongest assumption a programmer can make about object representation, namely that the programmer knows better than the compiler—to the point of being determined to pick an argument with the compiler's carefully maintained type information. Compilers will shut up if you tell them to, but use of force should be a last resort. Avoid assuming how data is represented, because such assumptions dramatically affect the safety and reliability of your code.

Besides, the reality is that **reinterpret_cast**'s effects are worse than reinterpreting objects' bit patterns (which would be bad enough). Except that some conversions are guaranteed to be reversible, its effects are actually implementation-defined, so you don't know if it will do even that. It is unreliable and nonportable.

Exceptions

Some low-level system-specific programming might force you to use **reinterpret_cast** to stream bits in and out some port, or to transform integers in addresses. Use unsafe casting as rarely as you can and only in well-hidden functions that abstract it away, so as to make your code ready for porting with minimal changes. If you need to cast among unrelated pointer types, prefer casting via **void*** instead of using **reinterpret_cast** directly. That is, instead of

```
T1* p1 = ... ;
T2* p2 = reinterpret_cast<T2*>( p1 );
```

write

```
T1* p1 = ... ;
void* pV = p1;
T2* p2 = static_cast<T2*>( pV );
```

References

[C++03] §5.2.10(3) • [Dewhurst03] §39 • [Stroustrup00] §5.6

93. Avoid using static_cast on pointers.

Summary

Pointers to dynamic objects don't **static_cast**: Safe alternatives range from using **dynamic_cast** to refactoring to redesigning.

Discussion

Consider replacing uses of **static_cast** with its more powerful relative **dynamic_cast**, and then you won't have to remember when **static_cast** is safe and when it's dangerous. Although **dynamic_cast** can be slightly less efficient, it also detects illegal casting (and don't forget Item 8). Using **static_cast** instead of **dynamic_cast** is like eliminating the stairs night-light, risking a broken leg to save 90 cents a year.

Prefer to design away downcasting: Refactor or redesign your code so that it isn't needed. If you see that you are passing a **Base** to a function that really needs a **Derived** to do its work, examine the chain of calls to identify where the needed type information was lost; often, changing a couple of prototypes leads to an excellent solution that also clarifies the type information flow to you.

Excessive downcasts might indicate that the base class interface is too sparse. This can lead to designs that define more functionality in derived classes, and then downcast every time the extended interface is needed. The one good solution is to redesign the base interface to provide more functionality.

If, and only if, the overhead of the **dynamic_cast** actually matters (see Item 8), consider defining your own cast that uses **dynamic_cast** during debugging and **static_cast** in the "all speed no guarantees" mode (see [Stroustrup00]):

```
template<class To, class From> To checked_cast( From* from ) {
    assert( dynamic_cast<To>(from) == static_cast<To>(from) && "checked_cast failed" );
    return static_cast<To>( from );
}

template<class To, class From> To checked_cast( From& from ) {
    typedef tr1::remove_reference<To>::type* ToPtr;        // leverage [C++TR104]
    assert( dynamic_cast<ToPtr>(&from) == static_cast<ToPtr>(&from) && "checked_cast failed" );
    return static_cast<To>( from );
}
```

This little duo of functions (one each needed for pointers and references) simply tests whether the two casts agree. We leave it up to you to customize **checked_cast** for your needs, or to use one provided by a library.

References

[Dewhurst03] §29, §35, §41 • [Meyers97] §39 • [Stroustrup00] §13.6.2 • [Sutter00] §44

94. Avoid casting away const.

Summary

Some fibs are punishable: Casting away **const** sometimes results in undefined behavior, and it is a staple of poor programming style even when legal.

Discussion

Once you go **const**, you (should) never go back. If you cast away **const** on an object whose original definition really did define it to be **const**, all bets are off and you are in undefined behavior land. For example, compilers can (and do) put constant data into ROM or write-protected RAM pages. Casting away **const** from such a truly **const** object is a punishable lie, and often manifests as a memory fault.

Even when it doesn't crash your program, casting away **const** is a broken promise and doesn't do what many expect. For example, this doesn't allocate a variable-sized array:

```
void Foolish( unsigned int n ) {
  const unsigned int size = 1;
  const_cast<unsigned int&>(size) = n;     // bad: don't do this
  char buffer[size];                        // will always have size 1
  // ...
}
```

C++ has one implicit **const_cast**, the "conversion of death" from a string literal to **char***:

```
char* weird = "Trick or treat?";
```

The compiler performs a silent **const_cast** from **const char[16]** to **char***. This was allowed for compatibility with C APIs, but it's a hole in C++'s type system. String literals are ROM-able, and trying to modify the string is liable to cause a memory fault.

Exceptions

Casting away **const** can be necessary to call const-incorrect APIs (see Item 15). It is also useful when a function that must take and return the same kind of reference has **const** and non-**const** overloads, implemented by having one call the other:

```
const Object& f( const Object& );

Object& f( Object& obj ) {
  const Object& ref = obj;
  return const_cast<Object&>( f(ref) );    // have to const_cast the return type
}
```

References

[Dewhurst03] §32, §40 • [Sutter00] §44

95. Don't use C-style casts.

Summary

Age doesn't always imply wisdom: C-style casts have different (and often dangerous) semantics depending on context, all disguised behind a single syntax. Replacing C-style casts with C++-style casts helps guard against unexpected errors.

Discussion

One problem with C-style casts is that they provide one syntax to do subtly different things, depending on such vagaries as the files that you **#include**. The C++ casts, while retaining some of the dangers inherent in casts, avoid such ambiguities, clearly document their intent, are easy to search for, take longer to write (which makes one think twice)—and don't silently inject evil **reinterpret_cast**s (see Item 92).

Consider the following code, where **Derived** inherits from **Base**:

```
extern void Fun( Derived* );

void Gun( Base* pb ) {
  // let's assume Gun knows for sure pb actually points to a Derived
  // and wants to forward to Fun
  Derived* pd = (Derived*)pb;              // bad: C-style cast
  Fun( pd );
}
```

If **Gun** has access to the definition of **Derived** (say by including "derived.h"), the compiler will have the necessary object layout information to make any needed pointer adjustments when casting from **Base** to **Derived**. But say **Gun**'s author forgets to **#include** the appropriate definition file, and **Gun** only sees a forward declaration of **class Derived;**. In that case, the compiler will just assume that **Base** and **Derived** are unrelated types, and will reinterpret the bits that form **Base*** as a **Derived***, without making any necessary adjustments dictated by object layout!

In short, if you forget to **#include** the definition, your code crashes mysteriously, even though it compiles without errors. Avoid the problem this way:

```
extern void Fun( Derived* );

void Gun( Base* pb ) {
  // if we know for sure that pb actually points to a Derived, use:
  Derived* pd  = static_cast<Derived*>(pb);   // good: C++-style cast
  // otherwise:  = dynamic_cast<Derived*>(pb);  // good: C++-style cast
  Fun(pd);
}
```

Now, if the compiler doesn't have enough static information about the relationship between **Base** and **Derived**, it will issue an error instead of automatically performing a bitwise (and potentially lethal) **reinterpret_cast** (see Item 92).

The C++-style casts can protect the correctness of your code during system evolution as well. Say you have an **Employee**-rooted hierarchy and you need to define a unique employee ID for each **Employee**. You could define the ID to be a pointer to the **Employee** itself. Pointers uniquely identify the objects they point to and can be compared for equality, which is exactly what's needed. So you write:

```
typedef Employee* EmployeeID;

Employee& Fetch( EmployeeID id ) {
  return *id;
}
```

Say you code a fraction of the system with this design. Later on, it turns out that you need to save your records to a relational database. Clearly, saving pointers is not something that you'd want to do. So, you change the design such that each employee has a unique *integral* identifier. Then, the integral IDs can be persisted in the database, and a hash table maps the IDs to **Employee** objects. Now the **typedef** is:

```
typedef int EmployeeID;

Employee& Fetch( EmployeeID id ) {
  return employeeTable_.lookup(id);
}
```

That is a valid design, and you'd expect that all misuses of **EmployeeID** would be flagged as compile-time errors. And they will, except for this little obscure code:

```
void TooCoolToUseNewCasts( EmployeeID id ) {
  Secretary* pSecretary = (Secretary*)id;        // bad: C-style cast
  // ...
}
```

With the old **typedef**, the C-style cast performed a **static_cast**; with the new one, it performs a **reinterpret_cast** against some integer, firmly planting the code in the scary realm of undefined behavior (see Item 92).

C++-style casts are also easy to search for with automatic tools such as **grep**. (No **grep** regular expression can catch the C cast syntax.) Because casts are very dangerous (especially **static_cast** of pointers and **reinterpret_cast**; see Item 92), using automated tools to keep track of them is always a good idea.

References

[Dewhurst03] §40 • [Meyers96] §2 • [Stroustrup00] §15.4.5 • [Sutter00] §44

96. Don't memcpy or memcmp non-PODs.

Summary

Don't try to X-ray objects (see Item 91): Don't use **memcpy** and **memcmp** to copy or compare anything more structured than raw memory.

Discussion

memcpy and **memcmp** violate the type system. Using **memcpy** to copy objects is like making money using a photocopier. Using **memcmp** to compare objects is like comparing leopards by counting their spots. The tools and methods might appear to do the job, but they are too coarse to do it acceptably.

C++ objects are all about information hiding (arguably the most profitable principle in software engineering; see Item 11): Objects hide data (see Item 41) and devise precise abstractions for copying that data through constructors and assignment operators (see Items 52 through 55). Bulldozing over all that with **memcpy** is a serious violation of information hiding, and often leads to memory and resource leaks (at best), crashes (worse), or undefined behavior (worst). For example:

```
{
  shared_ptr<int> p1( new int ), p2( new int );   // create two ints on the heap
  memcpy( &p1, &p2, sizeof(p1) );                  // bad: a heinous crime
} // memory leak: p2's int is never deleted
  // memory corruption: p1's int is deleted twice
```

Abusing **memcpy** can affect aspects as fundamental as the type and the identity of an object. Compilers often embed hidden data inside polymorphic objects (the so-called virtual table pointer, or **vptr**) that give the object its run-time identity. In the case of multiple inheritance, several such **vptr**s can coexist at various offsets inside the object, and most implementations add yet more internal pointers when using virtual inheritance. During normal use, the compiler takes care of managing all of these hidden fields; **memcpy** can only wreak havoc.

Similarly, **memcmp** is an inappropriate tool for comparing anything more elaborate than bits. Sometimes, it does too little (e.g., comparing C-style strings is not the same as comparing the pointers with which the strings are implemented). And sometimes, paradoxically, **memcmp** does too much (e.g., **memcmp** will needlessly compare bytes that are not part of an object's state, such as padding inserted by the compiler for alignment purposes). In both cases, the comparison's result will be wrong.

References

[Dewhurst03] §50 • [Stroustrup94] §11.4.4

97. Don't use unions to reinterpret representation.

Summary

A deceit is still a lie: Unions can be abused into obtaining a "cast without a cast" by writing one member and reading another. This is more insidious and even less predictable than **reinterpret_cast** (see Item 92).

Discussion

Don't read a field of a **union** unless it was the field that was last written. Reading a different field of a **union** than the field that was last written has undefined behavior, and is even worse than doing a **reinterpret_cast** (see Item 92); at least with the latter the compiler has the fighting chance to warn and repel an "impossible reinterpretation" such as pointer to **char**. When abusing a **union**, no reinterpretation of bits will ever yield a compile-time error or a reliable result.

Consider this code that is intended to deposit a value of one type (**char***) and extract the bits of that value as a different type (**long**):

```
union {
  long intValue_;
  char* pointerValue_;
};

pointerValue_ = somePointer;
long int gotcha = intValue_;
```

This has two problems:

- *It assumes too much:* It assumes that **sizeof(long)** and **sizeof(char*)** are equal, and that the bit representations are identical. These things are not true on all implementations (see Item 91).
- *It obscures your intent for both human readers and compilers:* Playing **union** games makes it harder for compilers to catch genuine type errors, and for humans to spot logical errors, than even the infamous **reinterpret_cast** (see Item 92).

Exceptions

If two POD **struct**s are members of a **union** and start with the same field types, it is legal to write one such matching field and read another.

References

[Alexandrescu02b] • [Stroustrup00] §C.8.2 • [Sutter04] §36

98. Don't use varargs (ellipsis).

Summary

Ellipses cause collapses: The ellipsis is a dangerous carryover from C. Avoid varargs, and use higher-level C++ constructs and libraries instead.

Discussion

Functions taking a variable number of arguments are a nice commodity, but C-style varargs aren't the way to get them. Varargs have many serious shortcomings:

- *Lack of type safety:* Essentially, the ellipsis tells the compiler: "Turn all checking off. I'll take over from here and start **reinterpret_cast**ing." (See Item 92.)

- *Tight coupling and required manual cooperation between caller and callee:* The language's type checking has been disabled, so the call site must use alternate ways to communicate the types of the arguments being passed. Such protocols (e.g., **printf**'s format string) are notoriously error-prone and unsafe because they cannot be fully checked or enforced by either the caller or the callee. (See Item 99.)

- *Undefined behavior for objects of class type:* Passing anything but primitive and POD (plain old data) types via varargs has undefined behavior in C++. Unfortunately, most compilers don't give a warning when you do it.

- *Unknown number of arguments:* For even the simplest variable-arguments function (e.g., **min**) with a variable number of arguments of known type (e.g., **int**), you still need to have a protocol for figuring out the number of arguments. (Ironically, this is a good thing because it further discourages using varargs.)

Avoid using varargs in your functions' signatures. Avoid calling functions with varargs in their own signatures, including legacy functions and standard C library functions such as **sprintf**. Admittedly, calls to **sprintf** can often look more compact and easier to read than equivalent calls using **stringstream** formatting and **operator<<**— just like it's also admittedly easier to hop into a car without pesky safety belts and bumpers. The risks are just not worth it. **printf**-related vulnerabilities continue to be a serious security problem at the time of this writing (see [Cowan01]), and an entire subindustry of tools exists to help find such type errors (see [Tsai01]).

Prefer to use type-safe libraries that support variable arguments using other means. For example, the [Boost] **format** library uses advanced C++ features to combine safety with speed and convenience.

References

[Boost] • [Cowan01] • [Murray93] §2.6 • [Sutter04] §2-3 • [Tsai01]

99. Don't use invalid objects. Don't use unsafe functions.

Summary

Don't use expired medicines: Both invalid objects and historical but unsafe functions wreak havoc on your program's health.

Discussion

There are three major kinds of invalid objects:

- *Destroyed objects:* Typical examples are automatic objects that have gone out of scope and deleted heap-based objects. After you call an object's destructor, its lifetime is over and it is undefined and generally unsafe to do anything with it.

- *Semantically invalidated objects:* Typical examples include dangling pointers to deleted objects (e.g., a pointer **p** after a **delete p;**) and invalidated iterators (e.g., a **vector<T>::iterator i** after an insertion at the beginning of the container the iterator refers into). Note that dangling pointers and invalidated iterators are conceptually identical, and the latter often directly contain the former. It is generally undefined and unsafe to do anything except assign another valid value to an invalidated object (e.g., **p = new Object;** or **i = v.begin();**).

- *Objects that were never valid:* Examples include objects "obtained" by forging a pointer (using **reinterpret_cast**, see Item 92), or accessing past array boundaries.

Be aware of object lifetimes and validity. Never dereference an invalid iterator or pointer. Don't make assumptions about what **delete** does and doesn't do; freed memory is freed, and shouldn't be subsequently accessed under any circumstances. Don't try to play with object lifetime by calling the destructor manually (e.g., **obj.~T()**) and then calling placement **new**. (See Item 55.)

Don't use the unsafe C legacy: **strcpy**, **strncpy**, **sprintf**, or any other functions that do write to range-unchecked buffers, and/or do not check and correctly handle out-of-bounds errors. C's **strcpy** does not check limits, and [C99]'s **strncpy** checks limits but does not append a null if the limit is hit; both are crashes waiting to happen and security hazards. Use more modern, safer, and more flexible structures and functions, such as those found in the C++ standard library (see Item 77). They are not always perfectly safe (for the sake of efficiency), but they are much less prone to errors and can be better used to build safe code.

References

[C99] • *[Sutter00] §1* • *[Sutter04] §2-3*

100. Don't treat arrays polymorphically.

Summary

Arrays are ill-adjusted: Treating arrays polymorphically is a gross type error that your compiler will probably remain silent about. Don't fall into the trap.

Discussion

Pointers serve two purposes at the same time: that of monikers (small identifiers of objects), and that of array iterators (they can walk through arrays of objects using pointer arithmetic). As monikers, it makes a lot of sense to treat a pointer to **Derived** as a pointer to **Base**. As soon as the array iteration part enters the stage, however, such substitutability breaks down because an array of **Derived** isn't the same as an array of **Base**. To illustrate: Mice and elephants are both mammals, but that doesn't mean a convoy of a thousand elephants would be as long as one of a thousand mice.

Size does matter. When substituting a pointer to **Derived** to a pointer to **Base**, the compiler knows exactly how to adjust the pointer (if necessary) because it has enough information about both classes. However, when doing pointer arithmetic on a pointer **p** to **Base**, the compiler computes **p[n]** as ***(p + n * sizeof(Base))**, thus assuming that the objects lying in memory are all **Base** objects—and not objects of some derived type that might have a different size. Imagine, now, just how easy it is to tromp all over of an array of **Derived** if you convert the pointer marking its start to **Base*** (with compiler's silent approval) and then perform pointer arithmetic on that pointer (while the compiler doesn't blink an eye either)!

Such accidents are an unfortunate interaction between substitutability, which dictates that pointers to derived classes should be usable as pointers to their bases, and C's legacy pointer arithmetic, which assumes pointers are monomorphic and uses solely static information to compute strides.

To store arrays of polymorphic objects, you need an array (or, better still, a real container; see Item 77) of pointers to the base class (e.g., plain pointers or, better still, **shared_ptr**s; see Item 79). Then each pointer in the array refers to a polymorphic object, likely an object allocated on the free store. Or, if you want to expose an interface to a container of polymorphic objects, you need to encapsulate the entire array and offer a polymorphic interface for iteration.

Incidentally, a good reason to prefer references to pointers in interfaces is to make it clear that you're talking about one object, as opposed to possibly an array of them.

References

[C++TR104] • [Dewhurst03] §33, §89 • [Meyers96] §3 • [Sutter00] §36

Bibliography

Note: For browsing convenience, this bibliography is also available online at:

http://www.gotw.ca/publications/c++cs/bibliography.htm

The bold references (e.g., **[Abrahams96]**) are hyperlinks in the online bibliography.

[Abelson96]	H. Abelson and G. J. Sussman. *Structure and Interpretation of Computer Programs (2nd Edition)* (MIT Press, 1996).
[Abrahams96]	D. Abrahams. "Exception Safety in STLport" (STLport website, 1996).
[Abrahams01a]	D. Abrahams. "Exception Safety in Generic Components," in M. Jazayeri, R. Loos, D. Musser (eds.), *Generic Programming: International Seminar on Generic Programming, Dagstuhl Castle, Germany, April/May 1998, Selected Papers*, Lecture Notes in Computer Science 1766 (Springer, 2001).
[Abrahams01b]	D. Abrahams. "Error and Exception Handling" ([Boost] website, 2001).
[Alexandrescu00a]	A. Alexandrescu. "Traits: The else-if-then of Types" (*C++ Report*, 12(4), April 2000).
[Alexandrescu00b]	A. Alexandrescu. "Traits on Steroids" (*C++ Report*, 12(6), June 2000).
[Alexandrescu00c]	A. Alexandrescu and P. Marginean. "Change the Way You Write Exception-Safe Code—Forever" (*C/C++ Users Journal*, 18(12), December 2000).
[Alexandrescu01]	A. Alexandrescu. *Modern C++ Design* (Addison-Wesley, 2001).

[Alexandrescu01a]   A. Alexandrescu. "A Policy-Based basic_string Implementation" (*C/C++ Users Journal*, 19(6), June 2001).

[Alexandrescu02a]   A. Alexandrescu. "Multithreading and the C++ Type System" (InformIT website, February 2002).

[Alexandrescu02b]   A. Alexandrescu. "Discriminated Unions (I)," "… (II)," and "… (III)" (*C/C++ Users Journal*, 20(4,6,8), April/June/August 2002).

[Alexandrescu03a]   A. Alexandrescu. "Move Constructors" (*C/C++ Users Journal*, 21(2), February 2003).

[Alexandrescu03b]   A. Alexandrescu. "Assertions" (*C/C++ Users Journal*, 21(4), April 2003).

[Alexandrescu03c]   A. Alexandrescu and P. Marginean. "Enforcements" (*C/C++ Users Journal*, 21(6), June 2003).

[Alexandrescu03d]   A. Alexandrescu and D. Held. "Smart Pointers Reloaded" (*C/C++ Users Journal*, 21(10), October 2003).

[Alexandrescu04]   A. Alexandrescu. "Lock-Free Data Structures" (*C/C++ Users Journal*, 22(10), October 2004).

[Allison98]   C. Allison. *C & C++ Code Capsules* (Prentice Hall, 1998).

[Austern99]   M. H. Austern. *Generic Programming and the STL* (Addison-Wesley, 1999).

[Barton94]   J. Barton and L. Nackman. *Scientific and Engineering C++* (Addison-Wesley, 1994).

[Bentley00]   J. Bentley. *Programming Pearls (2nd Edition)* (Addison-Wesley, 2000).

[BetterSCM]   Better SCM Initiative website.

[Boost]   C++ Boost.

[BoostLRG]   "Boost Library Requirements and Guidelines" (Boost website).

[Brooks95]   F. Brooks. *The Mythical Man-Month* (Addison-Wesley, 1975; reprinted with corrections in 1995).

[Butenhof97]   D. Butenhof. *Programming with POSIX Threads* (Addison-Wesley, 1997).

[Cargill92]	T. Cargill. *C++ Programming Style* (Addison-Wesley, 1992).
[C90]	ISO/IEC 9899:1990(E), *Programming Languages — C* (ISO C90 and ANSI C89 Standard).
[C99]	ISO/IEC 9899:1999(E), *Programming Languages — C* (revised ISO and ANSI C99 Standard).
[C++98]	ISO/IEC 14882:1998(E), *Programming Languages—C++* (ISO and ANSI C++ Standard).
[C++03]	ISO/IEC 14882:2003(E), *Programming Languages—C++* (updated ISO and ANSI C++ Standard including the contents of [C++98] plus errata corrections).
[C++TR104]	ISO/IEC JTC1/SC22/WG21/N1711. *(Draft) Technical Report on Standard Library Extensions* (ISO C++ committee working document, November 2004). This is a near-final draft of the extensions to the C++ standard library due to be published in 2005, including **shared_ptr**.
[Cline99]	M. Cline, G. Lomow, and M. Girou. *C++ FAQs (2nd Edition)* (Addison-Wesley, 1999).
[Constantine95]	L. Constantine. *Constantine on Peopleware* (Yourdon Press, 1995).
[Coplien92]	J. Coplien. *Advanced C++ Programming Styles and Idioms* (Addison-Wesley, 1992).
[Cormen01]	T. Cormen, C. Leiserson, R. Rivest, C. Stein. *Introduction to Algorithms (2nd Edition)* (MIT Press, 2001).
[CVS]	CVS home page.
[Cowan01]	C. Cowan, M. Barringer, S. Beattie, and G. Kroah-Hartman. "FormatGuard: Automatic Protection From printf Format String Vulnerabilities" (*Proceedings of the 2001 USENIX Security Symposium*, August 2001, Washington, D.C.).
[Dewhurst03]	S. Dewhurst. *C++ Gotchas* (Addison-Wesley, 2003).
[Dinkumware-Safe]	Dinkum Unabridged Library documentation (Dinkumware Ltd. website).
[Ellis90]	M. Ellis and B. Stroustrup. *The Annotated C++ Reference Manual* (Addison-Wesley, 1990).

[Gamma95]	E. Gamma, R. Helm, R. Johnson, and J. Vlissides. *Design Patterns: Elements of Reusable Object-Oriented Software* (Addison-Wesley, 1995).
[GnuMake]	Gnu make (Gnu website).
[GotW]	H. Sutter. *Guru of the Week* column.
[Henney00]	K. Henney. "C++ Patterns: Executing Around Sequences" (EuroPLoP 2000 proceedings).
[Henney01]	K. Henney. "C++ Patterns: Reference Accounting" (EuroPLoP 2001 proceedings).
[Henney02a]	K. Henney. "Stringing Things Along" (*Application Development Advisor*, July-August 2002).
[Henney02b]	K. Henney. "The Next Best String" (*Application Development Advisor*, October 2002).
[Henricson97]	M. Henricson and E. Nyquist. *Industrial Strength C++* (Prentice Hall,1997).
[Horstmann95]	C. S. Horstmann. "Safe STL" (1995).
[Josuttis99]	N. Josuttis. *The C++ Standard Library* (Addison-Wesley, 1999).
[Keffer95]	T. Keffer. *Rogue Wave C++ Design, Implementation, and Style Guide* (Rogue Wave Software, 1995).
[Kernighan99]	B. Kernighan and R. Pike. *The Practice of Programming* (Addison-Wesley, 1999).
[Knuth89]	D. Knuth. "The Errors of TeX" (*Software—Practice & Experience*, 19(7), July 1989.
[Knuth97a]	D. Knuth. *The Art of Computer Programming, Volume 1: Fundamental Algorithms (3rd Edition)* (Addison-Wesley, 1997).
[Knuth97b]	D. Knuth. *The Art of Computer Programming, Volume 2: Seminumerical Algorithms (3rd Edition)* (Addison-Wesley, 1997).
[Knuth98]	D. Knuth. *The Art of Computer Programming, Volume 3: Sorting and Searching (2nd Edition)* (Addison-Wesley, 1998).
[Koenig97]	A. Koenig and B. Moo. *Ruminations on C++* (Addison-Wesley, 1997).

[Lakos96]   J. Lakos. *Large-Scale C++ Software Design* (Addison-Wesley, 1996).

[Liskov88]   B. Liskov. "Data Abstraction and Hierarchy" (*SIGPLAN Notices*, 23(5), May 1988).

[Martin96a] R. C. Martin. "The Dependency Inversion Principle" (*C++ Report*, 8(5), May 1996).

[Martin96b] R. C. Martin. "Granularity" (*C++ Report*, 8(9), October 1996).

[Martin96c] R. C. Martin. "The Open-Closed Principle" (*C++ Report*, 8(1), January 1996).

[Martin98]   R. C. Martin, D. Riehle, F. Buschmann (eds.). *Pattern Languages of Program Design 3* (Addison-Wesley, 1998).

[Martin00]   R. C. Martin, "Abstract Classes and Pure Virtual Functions" in R. C. Martin (ed.), *More C++ Gems* (Cambridge University Press, 2000).

[McConnell93]   S. McConnell. *Code Complete* (Microsoft Press, 1993).

[Metrowerks]   Metrowerks.

[Meyer00]   B. Meyer. *Object-Oriented Software Construction (2nd Edition)* (Prentice Hall, 2000).

[Meyers96]   S. Meyers. *More Effective C++* (Addison-Wesley, 1996).

[Meyers97]   S. Meyers. *Effective C++ (2nd Edition)* (Addison-Wesley, 1997).

[Meyers00]   S. Meyers. "How Non-Member Functions Improve Encapsulation" (*C/C++ Users Journal*, 18(2), February 2000).

[Meyers01]   S. Meyers. *Effective STL* (Addison-Wesley, 2001).

[Meyers04]   S. Meyers and A. Alexandrescu. "C++ and the Perils of Double-Checked Locking, Part 1" and "...Part 2" (*Dr. Dobb's Journal*, 29(7,8), July and August 2004).

[Milewski01]   B. Milewski. *C++ In Action* (Addison-Wesley, 2001).

[Miller56]   G. A. Miller. "The Magical Number Seven, Plus or Minus Two: Some Limits on Our Capacity for Processing Information" (*The Psychological Review*, 1956, vol. 63).

[MozillaCRFAQ] "Frequently Asked Questions About mozilla.org's Code Review Process" (Mozilla website).

[Murray93]   R. Murray. *C++ Strategies and Tactics* (Addison-Wesley, 1993).

[Musser01]   D. R. Musser, G. J. Derge, and A. Saini. *STL Tutorial and Reference Guide, 2nd Edition* (Addison-Wesley, 2001).

[Parnas02]   D. Parnas. "The Secret History of Information Hiding" (*Software Pioneers: Contributions To Software Engineering*, Springer-Verlag, New York, 2002).

[Peters99]   T. Peters. "The Zen of Python" (comp.lang.python, June 1999).

[Piwowarski82]   P. Piwowarski. "A Nesting Level Complexity Measure" (*ACM SIGPLAN Notices*, 9/1982).

[Saks99]   D. Saks. "Thinking Deeply," "Thinking Deeper," and "Thinking Even Deeper" (*C/C++ Users Journal*, 17(4,5,6), April, May, and June 1999).

[Schmidt01]   D. Schmidt, M. Stal, H. Rohnert, F. Buschmann. *Pattern-Oriented Software Architecture, Volume 2: Patterns for Concurrent and Networked Objects* (Wiley, 2001).

[SeamonkeyCR]   "Seamonkey Code Reviewer's Guide" (Mozilla website).

[Sedgewick98]   R. Sedgewick. *Algorithms in C++, Parts 1-4: Fundamentals, Data Structure, Sorting, Searching (3rd Edition)* (Addison-Wesley, 1998).

[STLport-Debug] B. Fomitchev. "STLport: Debug Mode" (STLport website).

[Stroustrup94]   B. Stroustrup. *The Design and Evolution of C++* (Addison-Wesley, 1994).

[Stroustrup00]   B. Stroustrup. *The C++ Programming Language (Special 3rd Edition)* (Addison-Wesley, 2000).

[Sutter99]   H. Sutter. "ACID Programming" (*Guru of the Week #61*).

[Sutter00]   H. Sutter. *Exceptional C++* (Addison-Wesley, 2000).

[Sutter02]   H. Sutter. *More Exceptional C++* (Addison-Wesley, 2002).

[Sutter03]   H. Sutter. "Generalizing Observer" (*C/C++ Users Journal*, 21(9), September 2003).

[Sutter04]   H. Sutter. *Exceptional C++ Style* (Addison-Wesley, 2004).

[Sutter04a]   H. Sutter. "Function Types" (*C/C++ Users Journal*, 22(7), July 2004).

[Sutter04b]   H. Sutter. "When and How To Use Exceptions" (*C/C++ Users Journal*, 22(8), August 2004).

[Sutter04c]   H. Sutter. "'Just Enough' Thread Safety" (*C/C++ Users Journal*, 22(9), September 2004).

[Sutter04d]   H. Sutter. "How to Provide (or Avoid) Points of Customization in Templates" (*C/C++ Users Journal*, 22(11), November 2004).

[SuttHysl01]   H. Sutter and J. Hyslop. "Hungarian wartHogs" (*C/C++ Users Journal*, 19(11), November 2001).

[SuttHysl02]   H. Sutter and J. Hyslop. "A Midsummer Night's Madness" (*C/C++ Users Journal*, 20(8), August 2002).

[SuttHysl03]   H. Sutter and J. Hyslop. "Sharing Causes Contention" (*C/C++ Users Journal*, 21(4), April 2003).

[SuttHysl04a]   H. Sutter and J. Hyslop. "Getting Abstractions" (*C/C++ Users Journal*, 22(6), June 2004).

[SuttHysl04b]   H. Sutter and J. Hyslop. "Collecting Shared Objects" (*C/C++ Users Journal*, 22(8), August 2004).

[Taligent94]   *Taligent's Guide to Designing Programs* (Addison-Wesley, 1994).

[Tsai01]   T. Tsai and N. Singh. "Libsafe 2.0: Detection of Format String Vulnerability Exploits" (Avaya Labs, March 2001).

[Vandevoorde03]   D. Vandevoorde and N. Josuttis. *C++ Templates* (Addison-Wesley, 2003).

[Webber03]   A. B. Webber. *Modern Programming Languages: A Practical Introduction* (Franklin, Beedle & Associates, 2003).

Summary of Summaries

Organizational and Policy Issues

0. Don't sweat the small stuff. (Or: Know what not to standardize.)

   Say only what needs saying: Don't enforce personal tastes or obsolete practices.

1. Compile cleanly at high warning levels.

   Take warnings to heart: Use your compiler's highest warning level. Require clean (warning-free) builds. Understand all warnings. Eliminate warnings by changing your code, not by reducing the warning level.

2. Use an automated build system.

   Push the (singular) button: Use a fully automatic ("one-action") build system that builds the whole project without user intervention.

3. Use a version control system.

   The palest of ink is better than the best memory (Chinese proverb): Use a version control system (VCS). Never keep files checked out for long periods. Check in frequently after your updated unit tests pass. Ensure that checked-in code does not break the build.

4. Invest in code reviews.

   Re-view code: More eyes will help make more quality. Show your code, and read others'. You'll all learn and benefit.

Design Style

5. Give one entity one cohesive responsibility.

   Focus on one thing at a time: Prefer to give each entity (variable, class, function, namespace, module, library) one well-defined responsibility. As an entity grows, its scope of responsibility naturally increases, but its responsibility should not diverge.

6. Correctness, simplicity, and clarity come first.

   KISS (Keep It Simple Software): Correct is better than fast. Simple is better than complex. Clear is better than cute. Safe is better than insecure (see Items 83 and 99).

7. Know when and how to code for scalability.

   Beware of explosive data growth: Without optimizing prematurely, keep an eye on asymptotic complexity. Algorithms that work on user data should take a predictable, and preferably no worse than linear, time

195

with the amount of data processed. When optimization is provably necessary and important, and especially if it's because data volumes are growing, focus on improving big-Oh complexity rather than on micro-optimizations like saving that one extra addition.

8. Don't optimize prematurely.

    Spur not a willing horse (Latin proverb): Premature optimization is as addictive as it is unproductive. The first rule of optimization is: Don't do it. The second rule of optimization (for experts only) is: Don't do it yet. Measure twice, optimize once.

9. Don't pessimize prematurely.

    Easy on yourself, easy on the code: All other things being equal, notably code complexity and readability, certain efficient design patterns and coding idioms should just flow naturally from your fingertips and are no harder to write than the pessimized alternatives. This is not premature optimization; it is avoiding gratuitous pessimization.

10. Minimize global and shared data.

    Sharing causes contention: Avoid shared data, especially global data. Shared data increases coupling, which reduces maintainability and often performance.

11. Hide information.

    Don't tell: Don't expose internal information from an entity that provides an abstraction.

12. Know when and how to code for concurrency.

    Th$_{sa}$rea$_{fe}$d$_{ly}$: If your application uses multiple threads or processes, know how to minimize sharing objects where possible (see Item 10) and share the right ones safely.

13. Ensure resources are owned by objects. Use explicit RAII and smart pointers.

    Don't saw by hand when you have power tools: C++'s "resource acquisition is initialization" (RAII) idiom is the power tool for correct resource handling. RAII allows the compiler to provide strong and automated guarantees that in other languages require fragile hand-coded idioms. When allocating a raw resource, immediately pass it to an owning object. Never allocate more than one resource in a single statement.

Coding Style

14. Prefer compile- and link-time errors to run-time errors.

    Don't put off 'til run time what you can do at build time: Prefer to write code that uses the compiler to check for invariants during compilation, instead of checking them at run time. Run-time checks are control- and data-dependent, which means you'll seldom know whether they are exhaustive. In contrast, compile-time checking is not control- or data-dependent and typically offers higher degrees of confidence.

15. Use **const** proactively.

    ***const** is your friend: Immutable values are easier to understand, track, and reason about, so prefer constants over variables wherever it is sensible and make **const** your default choice when you define a value: It's safe, it's checked at compile time (see Item 14), and it's integrated with C++'s type system. Don't cast away **const** except to call a const-incorrect function (see Item 94).*

16. Avoid macros.

    TO_PUT_IT_BLUNTLY*: Macros are the bluntest instrument of C and C++'s abstraction facilities, ravenous wolves in functions' clothing, hard to tame, marching to their own beat all over your scopes. Avoid them.*

17. Avoid magic numbers.

    *Programming isn't magic, so don't incant it: Avoid spelling literal constants like **42** or **3.14159** in code. They are not self-explanatory and complicate maintenance by adding a hard-to-detect form of duplication. Use symbolic names and expressions instead, such as **width * aspectRatio**.*

18. Declare variables as locally as possible.

    Avoid scope bloat, as with requirements so too with variables: Variables introduce state, and you should have to deal with as little state as possible, with lifetimes as short as possible. This is a specific case of Item 10 that deserves its own treatment.

19. Always initialize variables.

    Start with a clean slate: Uninitialized variables are a common source of bugs in C and C++ programs. Avoid such bugs by being disciplined about cleaning memory before you use it; initialize variables upon definition.

20. Avoid long functions. Avoid deep nesting.

    Short is better than long, flat is better than deep: Excessively long functions and nested code blocks are often caused by failing to give one function one cohesive responsibility (see Item 5), and both are usually solved by better refactoring.

21. Avoid initialization dependencies across compilation units.

    Keep (initialization) order: Namespace-level objects in different compilation units should never depend on each other for initialization, because their initialization order is undefined. Doing otherwise causes headaches ranging from mysterious crashes when you make small changes in your project to severe non-portability even to new releases of the same compiler.

22. Minimize definitional dependencies. Avoid cyclic dependencies.

    *Don't be over-dependent: Don't **#include** a definition when a forward declaration will do.*

    Don't be co-dependent: Cyclic dependencies occur when two modules depend directly or indirectly on one another. A module is a cohesive unit of release (see page 103); modules that are interdependent are not really individual modules, but super-glued together into what's really a larger module, a larger unit of release. Thus, cyclic dependencies work against modularity and are a bane of large projects. Avoid them.

23. Make header files self-sufficient.

    Behave responsibly: Ensure that each header you write is compilable standalone, by having it include any headers its contents depend upon.

24. Always write internal **#include** guards. Never write external **#include** guards.

    *Wear head(er) protection: Prevent unintended multiple inclusions by using **#include** guards with unique names for all of your header files.*

Functions and Operators

25. Take parameters appropriately by value, (smart) pointer, or reference.

    Parameterize well: Distinguish among input, output, and input/output parameters, and between value and reference parameters. Take them appropriately.

26. Preserve natural semantics for overloaded operators.

    Programmers hate surprises: Overload operators only for good reason, and preserve natural semantics; if that's difficult, you might be misusing operator overloading.

27. Prefer the canonical forms of arithmetic and assignment operators.

    If you a+b, also a+=b: When defining binary arithmetic operators, provide their assignment versions as well, and write to minimize duplication and maximize efficiency.

28. Prefer the canonical form of ++ and --. Prefer calling the prefix forms.

    *If you ++c, also c++: The increment and decrement operators are tricky because each has pre- and postfix forms, with slightly different semantics. Define **operator++** and **operator--** such that they mimic the behavior of their built-in counterparts. Prefer to call the prefix versions if you don't need the original value.*

29. Consider overloading to avoid implicit type conversions.

    Do not multiply objects beyond necessity (Occam's Razor): Implicit type conversions provide syntactic convenience (but see Item 40). But when the work of creating temporary objects is unnecessary and optimization is appropriate (see Item 8), you can provide overloaded functions with signatures that match common argument types exactly and won't cause conversions.

30. Avoid overloading &&, ||, or , (comma) .

    *Wisdom means knowing when to refrain: The built-in **&&**, **||**, and **,** (comma) enjoy special treatment from the compiler. If you overload them, they become ordinary functions with very different semantics (you will violate Items 26 and 31), and this is a sure way to introduce subtle bugs and fragilities. Don't overload these operators naïvely.*

31. Don't write code that depends on the order of evaluation of function arguments.

    Keep (evaluation) order: The order in which arguments of a function are evaluated is unspecified, so don't rely on a specific ordering.

Class Design and Inheritance

32. Be clear what kind of class you're writing.

    Know thyself: There are different kinds of classes. Know which kind you are writing.

33. Prefer minimal classes to monolithic classes.

    Divide and conquer: Small classes are easier to write, get right, test, and use. They are also more likely to be usable in a variety of situations. Prefer such small classes that embody simple concepts instead of kitchen-sink classes that try to implement many and/or complex concepts (see Items 5 and 6).

34. Prefer composition to inheritance.

    Avoid inheritance taxes: Inheritance is the second-tightest coupling relationship in C++, second only to friendship. Tight coupling is undesirable and should be avoided where possible. Therefore, prefer composition to inheritance unless you know that the latter truly benefits your design.

35. Avoid inheriting from classes that were not designed to be base classes.

    Some people don't want to have kids: Classes meant to be used standalone obey a different blueprint than base classes (see Item 32). Using a standalone class as a base is a serious design error and should be avoided. To add behavior, prefer to add nonmember functions instead of member functions (see Item 44). To add state, prefer composition instead of inheritance (see Item 34). Avoid inheriting from concrete base classes.

36. Prefer providing abstract interfaces.

    Love abstract art: Abstract interfaces help you focus on getting an abstraction right without muddling it with implementation or state management details. Prefer to design hierarchies that implement abstract interfaces that model abstract concepts.

37. Public inheritance is substitutability. Inherit, not to reuse, but to be reused.

    Know what: Public inheritance allows a pointer or reference to the base class to actually refer to an object of some derived class, without destroying code correctness and without needing to change existing code.

    Know why: Don't inherit publicly to reuse code (that exists in the base class); inherit publicly in order to be reused (by existing code that already uses base objects polymorphically).

38. Practice safe overriding.

    Override responsibly: When overriding a virtual function, preserve substitutability; in particular, observe the function's pre- and post-conditions in the base class. Don't change default arguments of virtual functions. Prefer explicitly redeclaring overrides as **virtual**. *Beware of hiding overloads in the base class.*

39. Consider making virtual functions nonpublic, and public functions nonvirtual.

    In base classes with a high cost of change (particularly ones in libraries and frameworks): Prefer to make public functions nonvirtual. Prefer to make virtual functions private, or protected if derived classes need to be able to call the base versions. (Note that this advice does not apply to destructors; see Item 50.)

40. Avoid providing implicit conversions.

    *Not all change is progress: Implicit conversions can often do more damage than good. Think twice before providing implicit conversions to and from the types you define, and prefer to rely on explicit conversions (*explicit *constructors and named conversion functions).*

41. Make data members private, except in behaviorless aggregates (C-style **struct**s).

    They're none of your caller's business: Keep data members private. Only in the case of simple C-style **struct** *types that aggregate a bunch of values but don't pretend to encapsulate or provide behavior, make all data members public. Avoid mixes of public and nonpublic data, which almost always signal a muddled design.*

42. Don't give away your internals.

    Don't volunteer too much: Avoid returning handles to internal data managed by your class, so clients won't uncontrollably modify state that your object thinks it owns.

43. Pimpl judiciously.

    Overcome the language's separation anxiety: C++ makes private members inaccessible, but not invisible. Where the benefits warrant it, consider making private members truly invisible using the Pimpl idiom to implement compiler firewalls and increase information hiding. (See Items 11 and 41.)

44. Prefer writing nonmember nonfriend functions.

    Avoid membership fees: Where possible, prefer making functions nonmember nonfriends.

45. Always provide **new** and **delete** together.

    *They're a package deal: Every class-specific overload **void* operator new(parms)** must be accompanied by a corresponding overload **void operator delete(void*, parms)**, where **parms** is a list of extra parameter types (of which the first is always **std::size_t**). The same goes for the array forms **new[]** and **delete[]**.*

46. If you provide any class-specific **new**, provide all of the standard forms (plain, in-place, and **nothrow**).

    *Don't hide good **new**s: If a class defines any overload of **operator new**, it should provide overloads of all three of plain, in-place, and non-throwing **operator new**. If you don't, they'll be hidden and unavailable to users of your class.*

Construction, Destruction, and Copying

47. Define and initialize member variables in the same order.

    Agree with your compiler: Member variables are always initialized in the order they are declared in the class definition; the order in which you write them in the constructor initialization list is ignored. Make sure the constructor code doesn't confusingly specify a different order.

48. Prefer initialization to assignment in constructors.

    Set once, use everywhere: In constructors, using initialization instead of assignment to set member variables prevents needless run-time work and takes the same amount of typing.

49. Avoid calling virtual functions in constructors and destructors.

    Virtual functions only "virtually" always behave virtually: Inside constructors and destructors, they don't. Worse, any direct or indirect call to an unimplemented pure virtual function from a constructor or destructor results in undefined behavior. If your design wants virtual dispatch into a derived class from a base class constructor or destructor, you need other techniques such as post-constructors.

50. Make base class destructors public and virtual, or protected and nonvirtual.

    *To delete, or not to delete; that is the question: If deletion through a pointer to a base **Base** should be allowed, then **Base**'s destructor must be public and virtual. Otherwise, it should be protected and nonvirtual.*

51. Destructors, deallocation, and **swap** never fail.

*Everything they attempt shall succeed: Never allow an error to be reported from a destructor, a resource deallocation function (e.g., **operator delete**), or a swap function. Specifically, types whose destructors may throw an exception are flatly forbidden from use with the C++ standard library.*

52. Copy and destroy consistently.

What you create, also clean up: If you define any of the copy constructor, copy assignment operator, or destructor, you might need to define one or both of the others.

53. Explicitly enable or disable copying.

Copy consciously: Knowingly choose among using the compiler-generated copy constructor and assignment operator, writing your own versions, or explicitly disabling both if copying should not be allowed.

54. Avoid slicing. Consider **Clone** instead of copying in base classes.

*Sliced bread is good; sliced objects aren't: Object slicing is automatic, invisible, and likely to bring wonderful polymorphic designs to a screeching halt. In base classes, consider disabling the copy constructor and copy assignment operator, and instead supplying a virtual **Clone** member function if clients need to make polymorphic (complete, deep) copies.*

55. Prefer the canonical form of assignment.

*Your assignment: When implementing **operator=**, prefer the canonical form—nonvirtual and with a specific signature.*

56. Whenever it makes sense, provide a no-fail **swap** (and provide it correctly).

***swap** is both a lightweight and a workhorse: Consider providing a **swap** function to efficiently and infallibly swap the internals of this object with another's. Such a function can be handy for implementing a number of idioms, from smoothly moving objects around to implementing assignment easily to providing a guaranteed commit function that enables strongly error-safe calling code. (See also Item 51.)*

Namespaces and Modules

57. Keep a type and its nonmember function interface in the same namespace.

*Nonmembers are functions too: Nonmember functions that are designed to be part of the interface of a class **X** (notably operators and helper functions) must be defined in the same namespace as the **X** in order to be called correctly.*

58. Keep types and functions in separate namespaces unless they're specifically intended to work together.

Help prevent name lookup accidents: Isolate types from unintentional argument-dependent lookup (ADL, also known as Koenig lookup), and encourage intentional ADL, by putting them in their own namespaces (along with their directly related nonmember functions; see Item 57). Avoid putting a type into the same namespace as a templated function or operator.

59. Don't write namespace **using**s in a header file or before an **#include**.

*Namespace **using**s are for your convenience, not for you to inflict on others: Never write a **using** declaration or a **using** directive before an **#include** directive.*

*Corollary: In header files, don't write namespace-level **using** directives or **using** declarations; instead, explicitly namespace-qualify all names. (The second rule follows from the first, because headers can never know what other header **#include**s might appear after them.)*

60. Avoid allocating and deallocating memory in different modules.

*Put things back where you found them: Allocating memory in one module and deallocating it in a different module makes your program fragile by creating a subtle long-distance dependency between those modules. They must be compiled with the same compiler version and same flags (notably debug vs. **NDEBUG**) and the same standard library implementation, and in practice the module allocating the memory had better still be loaded when the deallocation happens.*

61. Don't define entities with linkage in a header file.

Repetition causes bloat: Entities with linkage, including namespace-level variables or functions, have memory allocated for them. Defining such entities in header files results in either link-time errors or memory waste. Put all entities with linkage in implementation files.

62. Don't allow exceptions to propagate across module boundaries.

Don't throw stones into your neighbor's garden: There is no ubiquitous binary standard for C++ exception handling. Don't allow exceptions to propagate between two pieces of code unless you control the compiler and compiler options used to build both sides; otherwise, the modules might not support compatible implementations for exception propagation. Typically, this boils down to: Don't let exceptions propagate across module/subsystem boundaries.

63. Use sufficiently portable types in a module's interface.

Take extra care when living on the edge (of a module): Don't allow a type to appear in a module's external interface unless you can ensure that all clients understand the type correctly. Use the highest level of abstraction that clients can understand.

Templates and Genericity

64. Blend static and dynamic polymorphism judiciously.

So much more than a mere sum of parts: Static and dynamic polymorphism are complementary. Understand their tradeoffs, use each for what it's best at, and mix them to get the best of both worlds.

65. Customize intentionally and explicitly.

Intentional is better than accidental, and explicit is better than implicit: When writing a template, provide points of customization knowingly and correctly, and document them clearly. When using a template, know how the template intends for you to customize it for use with your type, and customize it appropriately.

66. Don't specialize function templates.

*Specialization is good only when it can be done correctly: When extending someone else's function template (including **std::swap**), avoid trying to write a specialization; instead, write an overload of the function template, and put it in the namespace of the type(s) the overload is designed to be used for. (See Item 57.) When you write your own function template, avoid encouraging direct specialization of the function template itself.*

67. Don't write unintentionally nongeneric code.

    Commit to abstractions, not to details: Use the most generic and abstract means to implement a piece of functionality.

Error Handling and Exceptions

68. Assert liberally to document internal assumptions and invariants.

    *Be assertive! Use **assert** or an equivalent liberally to document assumptions internal to a module (i.e., where the caller and callee are maintained by the same person or team) that must always be true and otherwise represent programming errors (e.g., violations of a function's postconditions detected by the caller of the function). (See also Item 70.) Ensure that assertions don't perform side effects.*

69. Establish a rational error handling policy, and follow it strictly.

    Consciously specify, and conscientiously apply, what so many projects leave to ad-hoc (mis)judgment: Develop a practical, consistent, and rational error handling policy early in design, and then stick to it. Ensure that it includes:

    - *Identification: What conditions are errors.*
    - *Severity: How important or urgent each error is.*
    - *Detection: Which code is responsible for detecting the error.*
    - *Propagation: What mechanisms are used to report and propagate error notifications in each module.*
    - *Handling: What code is responsible for doing something about the error.*
    - *Reporting: How the error will be logged or users notified.*

    Change error handling mechanisms only on module boundaries.

70. Distinguish between errors and non-errors.

    A breach of contract is an error: A function is a unit of work. Thus, failures should be viewed as errors or otherwise based on their impact on functions. Within a function f, a failure is an error if and only if it violates one of f's preconditions or prevents f from meeting any of its callees' preconditions, achieving any of f's own postconditions, or reestablishing any invariant that f shares responsibility for maintaining.

    In particular, here we exclude internal programming errors (i.e., where the caller and callee are the responsibility of the same person or team, such as inside a module), which are a separate category normally dealt with using assertions (see Item 68).

71. Design and write error-safe code.

    Promise, but don't punish: In each function, give the strongest safety guarantee that won't penalize callers who don't need it. Always give at least the basic guarantee.

    Ensure that errors always leave your program in a valid state. This is the basic guarantee. Beware of invariant-destroying errors (including but not limited to leaks), which are just plain bugs.

    Prefer to additionally guarantee that the final state is either the original state (if there was an error the operation was rolled back) or the intended target state (if there was no error the operation was committed). This is the strong guarantee.

Prefer to additionally guarantee that the operation can never fail at all. Although this is not possible for most functions, it is required for functions like destructors and deallocation functions. This is the no-fail guarantee.

72. Prefer to use exceptions to report errors.

   *When harmed, take exception: Prefer using exceptions over error codes to report errors. Use status codes (e.g., return codes, **errno**) for errors when exceptions cannot be used (see Item 62), and for conditions that are not errors. Use other methods, such as graceful or ungraceful termination, when recovery is impossible or not required.*

73. Throw by value, catch by reference.

   *Learn to **catch** properly: Throw exceptions by value (not pointer) and catch them by reference (usually to **const**). This is the combination that meshes best with exception semantics. When rethrowing the same exception, prefer just **throw;** to **throw e;**.*

74. Report, handle, and translate errors appropriately.

   Know when to say when: Report errors at the point they are detected and identified as errors. Handle or translate each error at the nearest level that can do it correctly.

75. Avoid exception specifications.

   Take exception to these specifications: Don't write exception specifications on your functions unless you're forced to (because other code you can't change has already introduced them; see Exceptions).

STL: Containers

76. Use **vector** by default. Otherwise, choose an appropriate container.

   Using the "right container" is great: If you have a good reason to use a specific container type, use that container type knowing that you did the right thing.

   *So is using **vector**: Otherwise, write **vector** and keep going without breaking stride, also knowing you did the right thing.*

77. Use **vector** and **string** instead of arrays.

   *Why juggle Ming vases? Avoid implementing array abstractions with C-style arrays, pointer arithmetic, and memory management primitives. Using **vector** or **string** not only makes your life easier, but also helps you write safer and more scalable software.*

78. Use **vector** (and **string::c_str**) to exchange data with non-C++ APIs.

   ***vector** isn't lost in translation: **vector** and **string::c_str** are your gateway to communicate with non-C++ APIs. But don't assume iterators are pointers; to get the address of the element referred to by a **vector<T>::iterator iter**, use **&*iter**.*

79. Store only values and smart pointers in containers.

   Store objects of value in containers: Containers assume they contain value-like types, including value types (held directly), smart pointers, and iterators.

80. Prefer **push_back** to other ways of expanding a sequence.

    *push_back all you can: If you don't need to care about the insert position, prefer using **push_back** to add an element to a sequence. Other means can be both vastly slower and less clear.*

81. Prefer range operations to single-element operations.

    *Don't use oars when the wind is fair (based on a Latin proverb): When adding elements to sequence containers, prefer to use range operations (e.g., the form of **insert** that takes a pair of iterators) instead of a series of calls to the single-element form of the operation. Calling the range operation is generally easier to write, easier to read, and more efficient than an explicit loop. (See also Item 84.)*

82. Use the accepted idioms to really shrink capacity and really erase elements.

    Use a diet that works: To really shed excess capacity from a container, use the "swap trick." To really erase elements from a container, use the erase-remove idiom.

STL: Algorithms

83. Use a checked STL implementation.

    Safety first (see Item 6): Use a checked STL implementation, even if it's only available for one of your compiler platforms, and even if it's only used during pre-release testing.

84. Prefer algorithm calls to handwritten loops.

    Use function objects judiciously: For very simple loops, handwritten loops can be the simplest and most efficient solution. But writing algorithm calls instead of handwritten loops can be more expressive and maintainable, less error-prone, and as efficient.

    *When calling algorithms, consider writing your own custom function object that encapsulates the logic you need. Avoid cobbling together parameter-binders and simple function objects (e.g., **bind2nd**, **plus**), which usually degrade clarity. Consider trying the [Boost] Lambda library, which automates the task of writing function objects.*

85. Use the right STL search algorithm.

    *Search "just enough"—the right search may be STL (slower than light), but it'll still be pretty fast: This Item applies to searching for a particular value in a range, or for the location where it would be if it were in the range. To search an unsorted range, use **find/find_if** or **count/count_if**. To search a sorted range, use **lower_bound**, **upper_bound**, **equal_range**, or (rarely) **binary_search**. (Despite its common name, **binary_search** is usually not the right choice.)*

86. Use the right STL sort algorithm.

    Sort "just enough:" Understand what each of the sorting algorithms does, and use the cheapest algorithm that does what you need.

87. Make predicates pure functions.

    *Predicate purity: A predicate is a function object that returns a yes/no answer, typically as a **bool** value. A function is pure in the mathematical sense if its result depends only on its arguments (note that this use of "pure" has nothing to do with pure virtual functions).*

    *Don't allow predicates to hold or access state that affects the result of their **operator()**, including both member and global state. Prefer to make **operator()** a **const** member function for predicates (see Item 15).*

88. Prefer function objects over functions as algorithm and comparer arguments.

    Objects plug in better than functions: Prefer passing function objects, not functions, to algorithms. Comparers for associative containers must be function objects. Function objects are adaptable and, counterintuitively, they typically produce faster code than functions.

89. Write function objects correctly.

    *Be cheap, be adaptable: Design function objects to be values that are cheap to copy. Where possible, make them adaptable by inheriting from **unary_-** or **binary_function**.*

Type Safety

90. Avoid type switching; prefer polymorphism.

    Switch off: Avoid switching on the type of an object to customize behavior. Use templates and virtual functions to let types (not their calling code) decide their behavior.

91. Rely on types, not on representations.

    Don't try to X-ray objects (see Item 96): Don't make assumptions about how objects are exactly represented in memory. Instead, let types decide how their objects are written to and read from memory.

92. Avoid using **reinterpret_cast**.

    *Lies have short legs (German and Romanian proverb): Don't try to use **reinterpret_cast** to force the compiler to reinterpret the bits of an object of one type as being the bits of an object of a different type. That's the opposite of maintaining type safety, and **reinterpret_cast** isn't even guaranteed to do that or anything else in particular.*

93. Avoid using **static_cast** on pointers.

    *Pointers to dynamic objects don't **static_cast**: Safe alternatives range from using **dynamic_cast** to refactoring to redesigning.*

94. Avoid casting away **const**.

    *Some fibs are punishable: Casting away **const** sometimes results in undefined behavior, and it is a staple of poor programming style even when legal.*

95. Don't use C-style casts.

    Age doesn't always imply wisdom: C-style casts have different (and often dangerous) semantics depending on context, all disguised behind a single syntax. Replacing C-style casts with C++-style casts helps guard against unexpected errors.

96. Don't **memcpy** or **memcmp** non-PODs.

    *Don't try to X-ray objects (see Item 91): Don't use **memcpy** and **memcmp** to copy or compare anything more structured than raw memory.*

97. Don't use unions to reinterpret representation.

    *A deceit is still a lie: Unions can be abused into obtaining a "cast without a cast" by writing one member and reading another. This is more insidious and even less predictable than **reinterpret_cast** (see Item 92).*

98. Don't use varargs (ellipsis).

    Ellipses cause collapses: The ellipsis is a dangerous carryover from C. Avoid varargs, and use higher-level C++ constructs and libraries instead.

99. Don't use invalid objects. Don't use unsafe functions.

    Don't use expired medicines: Both invalid objects and historical but unsafe functions wreak havoc on your program's health.

100. Don't treat arrays polymorphically.

    Arrays are ill-adjusted: Treating arrays polymorphically is a gross type error that your compiler will probably remain silent about. Don't fall into the trap.

Index

#include
  and using, 108
  vs. forward declaration, 40
#include guards, 27, 33
  internal vs. external, 43
#undef
  as soon as possible, 33
&&
  preferable to nested ifs, 38
?:, 36
[]. *See* operators, []
++C, 50

A

Abelson, Harold, 13
Abrahams, Dave, xv
abstraction, 20
  and dependency
    management, 11
  and get/set, 20, 72, 73
  and interfaces, 62
abstractions
  build higher-level from
    lower-level, 12
  depending upon instead of
    details, 41
  vs. details, 128
accumulate, 125
Acyclic Visitor, 41
ADL, 104, 105, 106, 107, 122
  and template customization,
    122
  disabling unwanted, 124

aggregates, 20
Albaugh, Tyrrell, xv
algorithmic complexity, 14
  and STL, 14
  exponential, 15
  linear-looking that is really
    quadratic, 15, 156
algorithms
  and design patterns, 162
  are loops, 159
  binary_search, 165
  count, 165
  count_if, 165
  equal_range, 165
  find, 165
  find_if, 165
  lower_bound, 165
  nth_element, 166
  partial_sort, 166
  partial_sort_copy, 166
  partition, 166
  searching, 165
  sort, 166
  sorting, 166
  stable_partition, 166
  stable_sort, 166
  upper_bound, 165
  vs. loops, 38, 162
alignment, 176
Allison, Chuck, xv
allocation, 111
  never allocate more than
    once per statement, 25
allocator

example use of, 5
ambiguities, 77
ambiguities,
  avoiding declaration, 13
amortized constant time, 155
append, 135
arithmetic operators. *See*
  operators, arithmetic
arrays
  fixed-size, 15
  inferior to containers, 152
assert, 33, 130, 135
  example of, 5, 98, 175
  macro needed for, 33
  only for internal
    programming errors, 132,
    134
  prefer instead of logic_error,
    131
assertions. *See* assert
assignment
  copy. *See* copy assignment
  self, 99, 138
assignment operators. *See*
  operators, assignment
asymptotic complexity. *See*
  algorithmic complexity
at
  vs. [], 136
atomic operations, 21
auto_ptr, 94, 154

209

The C++ In-Depth Series

Bjarne Stroustrup, Series Editor

Modern C++ Design
**Generic Programming and Design
Patterns Applied**
By Andrei Alexandrescu
0201704315
Paperback
352 pages
© 2001

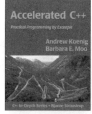

Accelerated C++
Practical Programming by Example
By Andrew Koenig and
Barbara E. Moo
020170353X
Paperback
352 pages
© 2000

Essential C++
By Stanley B. Lippman
0201485184
Paperback
304 pages
© 2000

C++ Network Programming, Volume 1
**Mastering Complexity with ACE and
Patterns**
By Douglas C. Schmidt and
Stephen D. Huston
0201604647
Paperback
336 pages
© 2002

The Boost Graph Library
User Guide and Reference Manual
By Jeremy G. Siek, Lie-Quan Lee, and
Andrew Lumsdaine
0201729148
Paperback
352 pages
© 2002

Exceptional C++
**47 Engineering Puzzles, Programming
Problems, and Solutions**
By Herb Sutter
0201615622
Paperback
240 pages
© 2000

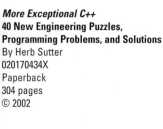

More Exceptional C++
**40 New Engineering Puzzles,
Programming Problems, and Solutions**
By Herb Sutter
020170434X
Paperback
304 pages
© 2002

C++ Network Programming, Volume 2
**Systematic Reuse with ACE and
Frameworks**
By Douglas C. Schmidt and
Stephen D. Huston
0201795256
Paperback
384 pages
© 2003

Applied C++
**Practical Techniques for
Building Better Software**
By Philip Romanik and Amy Muntz
0321108949
Paperback
352 pages
© 2003

Exceptional C++ Style
**40 New Engineering Puzzles, Programming
Problems, and Solutions**
By Herb Sutter
0201760428
Paperback
352 pages
© 2005

Also Available

The C++ Programming Language, Special Edition
By Bjarne Stroustrup
0201700735
Hardcover | 1,040 pages | © 2000

Written by the creator of C++, this is the most widely read and most trusted book on C++.